A Feeling of Belonging

AMERICAN HISTORY AND CULTURE

GENERAL EDITORS: Neil Foley, Kevin Gaines,
Martha Hodes, and Scott Sandage

A Feeling of Belonging

Asian American Women's Public Culture, 1930–1960

Shirley Jennifer Lim

NEW YORK UNIVERSITY PRESS

New York and London

NEW YORK UNIVERSITY PRESS
New York and London
www.nyupress.org

Library of Congress Cataloging-in-Publication Data
Lim, Shirley Jennifer, 1968–
A feeling of belonging : Asian American women's public culture, 1930–
1960 / Shirley Jennifer Lim.
p. cm. — (American history and culture)—
Includes bibliographical references and index.
ISBN–13: 978–0–8147–5193–0 (cloth : alk. paper)
ISBN–10: 0–8147–5193–8 (cloth : alk. paper)
ISBN–13: 978–0–8147–5194–7 (pbk. : alk. paper)
ISBN–10: 0–8147–5194–6 (pbk. : alk. paper)
1. Asian American women—Social life and customs—20th century.
2. Asian Americans—Cultural assimilation—History—20th century.
3. Young women—United States—Social life and customs—20th century.
4. Single women—United States—Social life and customs—20th century.
5. Leisure—United States—History—20th century.   6. Popular
culture—United States—History—20th century.   7. United States—
Social life and customs—1918–1945.   8. United States—Social life and
customs—1945–1970.   I. Title.   II. Series.
E184.A75L56   2005
305.48'895073'0904—dc22   2005020727

Manufactured in the United States of America
c 10 9 8 7 6 5 4 3 2 1
p 10 9 8 7 6 5 4 3 2 1

Contents

Preface

To paraphrase Alice Walker citing Toni Morrison, I wished to create a book that I should have been able to read in school, but had not found.[1] Since there were no models for what I murkily envisioned, I considered "acceptable" topics, ranging from the social history of Chinese American women in Los Angeles to a labor/organizational history of Asian Americans and entertainment. After uncovering previously unexamined historical sources such as actress Anna May Wong's Chinese American Paramount Studio films and the papers of the Chi Alpha Delta sorority, my topic finally resonated with me and evolved into an analysis of Asian American women's reworking of American cultural practices during an age of racial segregation and immigration exclusion. As an Indonesian American woman, which signifies that I come from a numerically small American racial minority group, I did not grow up with Asian-ethnic community practices and was fascinated when I discovered their historical prominence in the mid-twentieth century.

My own life history influenced how I understand the importance of cultural practices for female racial minorities. Having lived outside the United States for most of my childhood, I became acutely aware that despite my being born in the United States, people were not willing to grant me my birthright of cultural American citizenship. Rather, I had to earn it. The way I proved my Americanness on the playgrounds of Scotland and Libya despite my Asian face was to speak the latest American slang and show that my lunch box contained Kool-Aid and Toll House cookies, to wear Wrangler jeans. By showing my Americanness through my cultural knowledge, I gained prestige on those playgrounds. My successful displays of being American resulted in my entire class at the Oil Companies' School in Tripoli, Libya, voting me the coveted title of seventh-grade Valentine's Day Dance Queen. As the daughter of people who had come of age under Dutch colonialism and subsequent Indonesian independence, I was haunted by the political implications of cultural practices: namely, that culture had the ability to grant power, prestige, rights, and privileges to those who could master its symbolism, yet that such cultural fluency did not always signify capitulation to the dominant order.

Given these experiences, as a scholar I am attuned to the perils and promises of Asian American women's self-representations of gender and race through the remaking of mainstream culture. Although it is a serious work of American history, this book risks condemnation or trivialization, for it focuses on a marginalized group in American society, Asian American women, as they perform "inauthentic" activities. In selecting this topic, I hope to validate creative and risk-taking subjects of scholarly inquiry.

This work comes from one of the deepest impulses I know, that of survival. In times of trouble that come from facing life as a racial minority woman, clothes, books, movies, magazines, gossip, and get-togethers have all jostled me out of paralysis and prompted me to lumber out of bed in the morning and face the world. For anyone who has endured the same, this book is for you.

It gives me great pleasure to acknowledge all the individuals and institutions that have made this work possible. Especially vital have been the Chi Alpha Delta Collection, University Archives, UCLA; the Japanese American National Museum; the Margaret Herrick Library at the Academy of Motion Pictures Arts and Sciences; and the UCLA Newspaper and Periodicals Collections. Also of great help have been the New York Public Library, the Chicago Historical Society, the Bancroft Library at UC Berkeley, the San Francisco Public Library, the Los Angeles Public Library, and the Chinese Historical Society of Southern California. I also thank the following for their support of this project: the Asian American Studies Center at UCLA, the Nuala McGann Drescher Foundation, the Institute of American Cultures, and the United University Professions.

Many thanks to the women who made my research possible: Lulu Kwan, Bessie Loo, Beulah Quo, Linda Yuen, Frances Kitagawa.

This work benefited greatly from the comments and questions of Valerie Matsumoto, Matthew Christensen, Sharon Traweek, King-kok Cheung, Shirley Hune, Gail Nomura, Jennifer Lee, Min Zhou, Amanda Frisken, Peggy Pascoe, Vicki L. Ruiz, Kathleen Wilson, Valerie Smith, Ellen Carol DuBois, Kerwin Klein, Gordon Chang, Jaime Cardenas, Michelle Moravec, Arleen G. de Vera, Edith Chen, Dorinne Kondo, and the Asian

American Women's Writing Group of New York City: Lok Siu, Sanda Lwin, Mary Lui, Sandhya Shukla, Evelyn Chi'en, Susette Min, Cynthia Tolentino, Shuang Shen, Mae Ngai, Grace Hong, Juliana Chang, and Lisa Yun. Special thanks to my series editor Scott Sandage, to Eric Zinner and Emily Park, and to my anonymous readers at NYU Press.

For intellectual sustenance I would like to recognize Nancy Tomes, Susan Englander, John Durham, Katherine King, Sondra Hale, Jasamin Rostam-Kolayi, Gisele Fong, Dean Toji, Muriel McClendon, Iona Man-Cheong, Marci Lobel, Thomas Klubock, Janet Clarke, Young-sun Hong, Karen Leong, Lloys Frates, Mary Dillard, Daphne Brooks, and Judy Wu. For making this endeavor worthwhile, thank you to all my graduate and undergraduate students at SUNY Stony Brook and UCLA. Last but not least, my eternal gratitude goes to my family for encouraging me to follow my heart.

A Feeling of Belonging is dedicated to the memory of my grandmothers, Gertruda Dermawan and Winifred Sunataraja, and to Joy Adams Slingerland.

Introduction

Lightbulbs flash. Pop! This way Miss Wong, over here. She smiles, turns, then smiles at the camera from a different angle. Her straw coolie hat is set at a rakish angle. Fashion writers note the details of her cream suit that is cut in the current Western style with Chinese fastenings, her rectangular clutch handbag made in Paris, customized with her Chinese name, Frosted Yellow Willow, in Chinese characters down the right side. She has won the Mayfair Mannequin award for her style. Reporters ask her about her upcoming film role as a Chinese American surgeon. In melodious tones modulated by her theater-trained British accent, she replies that she is pleased to play professional roles. As she will be on the March 1938 cover of *Look* magazine, people all over the United States, including young Chinese American women, read about her.

A Feeling of Belonging: Asian American Women's Public Culture, 1930–1960, is a historical exploration of the significance of Asian American women's engagement with cultural venues such as beauty pageants, sororities, movies, parades, and magazines. During an age of restricted citizenship rights under immigration exclusion and racial segregation, the adoption of such cultural practices by racial minority women cannot be interpreted merely as assimilation but must be seen as a set of transformative social acts that constituted Asian American culture. From the writing of the three-fifths slave clause into the U.S. Constitution to immigration policy in the twentieth century, race is at the core of the American nation-state. How a racial minority group such as Asian Americans represents and portrays race is of the utmost significance since race permeates every aspect of modern life. This book explores the historical significance of Asian American women's experiences, such as those of Anna May Wong's, through the lenses of performance, modernity, and cultural citizenship.

This work aims to shed light on American society by probing the meanings of racially marked subjects, Asian American women, who have been rendered invisible in mainstream histories by racial paradigms that privilege the black–white binary and by gender paradigms that privilege white women. The all-too-frequent equation of race with blackness erases other categories of racial difference, just as equating women with European Americans denies the racial hierarchy that attends to gender. In response to that double invisibility, Asian American women have long joined other women of color in challenging the prevalence of European American domination of public culture and standards of femininity. Key to understanding this process is to recognize the mechanisms by which race critically shifts gender politics.[1] The intersection of race and gender is evident in, for example, Chinese American actress Anna May Wong's struggle for roles as Chinese women against European American actresses in yellowface such as Myrna Loy, Katherine Hepburn, and Luise Rainer. At the University of California, Los Angeles (UCLA), the members of the first Asian American sorority in the country, Chi Alpha Delta, fought for equal access to scholarship money and housing that had been denied to them on racial grounds. To many, Asian American beauty queens such as Elizabeth Pa—Miss Football at the University of Hawaii—and Frances Tenchavez—the Los Angeles Filipino American community's Fourth of July queen—signaled rupture in European American standards of beauty. Since mainstream magazines lacked representations of Asian American women, *Scene* magazine articles such as "Woman President," "Beauty, Basically Speaking," and "Nancy Ito, Star Athlete" showed Asian American women as physically attractive athletic leaders. Dehumanized and stereotyped in dominant culture, Asian American women performed beauty and modernity in order to prove humanity and thus claim a place in the American nation-state.

As this is one of the first book-length scholarly studies of Asian American women's cultural history, I did not know precisely where Asian American women would appear in the historical record. Instead of a study of how mainstream society viewed Asian American women, I was committed to the ethnic studies, women's studies, and social history projects of centering the story on Asian American women by making racial minority community sources a priority. Sorority participation, beauty pageants, magazine reading, films, parades are the sites where I found Asian American women's activities. To examine these "unofficial" histories, I had to expand what constituted legitimate historical inquiry to include evidence from clothing, hairstyles, manners, and food as revealed by photographs, films, sorority records, ethnic newspapers, and magazines.[2] *A Feeling of Belonging* champions the cultural studies project of attention to quotidian practices—from the art of managing dripping barbequed spare ribs while chatting with judges at the Nisei Week queen contests, to reading magazine articles on how to customize gun cartridges in order to turn them into purses—as culturally rich spaces.[3] Indeed, the scholarly prohibitions against these types of studies are so strong that currently there are surprisingly few book-length academic historical studies on European American women's popular culture, let alone on Asian American women's cultural practices. As elite white male culture acquires status as "high" and "worthy," the practices of those deemed other, especially female, become marginalized. I situate this work as part of a larger feminist-inspired movement in the academy to analyze phenomena—fashion, beauty pageants, movies, magazines, sorority activities—that have been dismissed or left to trade books.[4] Political power does not reside solely within official institutions of the state; rather, as Nancy Armstrong stated, one must recognize the "political history of the whole domain over which our culture grants women authority: the use of leisure time, the ordinary care of the body, courtship practices, the operations of desire, the forms of pleasure, gender differences, and family relations."[5] Thus, official organized political activity is not the only arena for serious scholarly inquiry. In this book, I appraise seemingly suspect arenas of femininity both for their reinscription of power relations and for their contestatory edge.

Arranged chronologically and thematically, this study traces the performance of Asian American public culture through gendered narratives of modernity and national belonging from roughly 1930 to 1960. Although power and politics are continually articulated through culture, this book insists on the historical perspective for race and its cultural meanings are not universal throughout time and location but are mutable, contingent, and particular in time and space. Chinese American actress Anna May Wong was not the only Asian American woman who continually grappled with how to present racial difference during the turbulent middle decades of the twentieth century. Others faced similar dilemmas in public venues such as beauty pageants, magazines and ethnic presses, parades, and performances. The sheer volume of these practices and their significance is the subject of this book.

The five chapters presented here investigate Asian American women's history through particular sites in the production of public culture. In each, I place Asian American women's interventions at the center of the story and scrutinize the development of their cultural practices as well as their subversions, disruptions, and partially successful mimicries. Chapter 1, "A Feeling of Belonging" delineates how the members of the sorority Chi Alpha Delta attempted to carve out a space of belonging within the world of the university during racial segregation. Chapter 2, "'I Protest': Anna May Wong and the Performance of Modernity," investigates the historical circumstances that allowed Wong to portray a Chinese American surgeon and to grace the cover of a national magazine, *Look*. Wong and Chi Alpha Delta appear in each of the subsequent chapters. Chapter 3, "Shortcut to Glamour," focuses on Asian American youth popular and consumer cultures. Chapter 4, "Contested Beauty," elucidates beauty culture during the Cold War era. Finally, Chapter 5, "Riding the Crest of an Oriental Wave," examines Asian American women during both the resurgence of interest in Asia and the opening up of immigration and naturalization to people of Asian descent.

Historical Legacies of Being Asian American

Linda Yuen waves from her float at the 1957 Eisenhower inaugural parade. Dressed in a cheongsam, her hair is coiffed in a contemporary American style and she sports fashionable American makeup. She is the first Chinese American queen at a presidential inaugural parade and, as far as she can tell, is the only such racial minority queen present.

The American liberal creed promulgated a narrative of liberty and equality for all. That seemingly inclusive narrative masked the inequalities of who could actually be a citizen, a status that, at the nation's founding, was limited to all free white men of property.[6] Thus, from the beginning, race, class, and gender were incorporated into the American body politic. As unpropertied white men were granted the franchise in the nineteenth century, the citizenship color line was inscribed through military campaigns that dispossessed Native Americans, the 1848 Treaty of Guadalupe Hidalgo that dictated the terms of Mexican citizenship, as well as imperialism in the Philippines and Puerto Rico. Women did not gain the vote until the Nineteenth Amendment (1920) to the U.S. Constitution was passed. The historical contradictions posed by race and gender to American democratic equality reveal the imperatives for Asian Americans claiming belonging to the nation-state through cultural acts such as Linda Yuen resplendent as the American Chinatown Queen at Dwight D. Eisenhower's 1957 presidential inaugural.

After citizenship was granted to enslaved Africans at the end of the Civil War, the dynamic shifted to that of immigration. After the Fourteenth Amendment during Reconstruction granted citizenship to African American men, the American racial imaginary replaced the enslaved with the male Asian alien-laborer as the citizen-subject's antithesis.[7] The discursive manipulation of the categories of (Asian) "immigrant" and "citizen" (and material control over their respective bodies) has been foundational in the production of U.S. citizenship, by defining these categories as mutually exclusive.[8] The conceptual U.S. citizen-subject comes into being, in other words, through the expulsion of Asianness in the figure of the Asian immigrant. Thus, with the end of slavery, the dominant citizenship paradigm of free versus enslaved changed to that of immigrant versus American citizen.[9]

Race and gender hierarchy intersected with the conceptual immigrant to create new categories of immigration exclusion. The very first American law to restrict immigration, the Page Law (1875), targeted Chinese women.[10] Although the law was originally written to exclude the entire Chinese working class, anxiety around the bodies of women of Asian descent ensured that the law was enforced exclusively against Chinese female migration. Chinese immigrant women responded to the exclusion laws through their performance of class-inflected respectability during the immigration review process at the Angel Island detention center. For example, working-class Chinese women who aimed to migrate to the United States deliberately dressed in fine clothing and displayed a "respectable" manner in order to convince U.S. immigration officials that they should be admitted.[11]

The ability to display appropriate visual traits also allowed Japanese American and Filipina American women to migrate to the United States. When Chinese immigration exclusion was in effect, the Japanese migrated to fill plantation and other cheap labor needs in Hawaii and the West Coast. As Japan's government had much greater international standing, the Gentlemen's Agreement (1907) allowed for the migration of Japanese women as picture brides. Men who wished to marry a Japanese woman had to prove certain savings and income levels. Hence the Japanese were able to establish families and sex ratio equality far earlier than other Asian immigrant groups. What is interesting is that men selected their future wives on the basis of a photograph. If her image and any accompanying information were found to be suitable, the woman would be sent passage and could then migrate to the United States. Visuality and performance also constituted the experiences of Filipina American women, for many first entered the United States after the Spanish-American War in order to perform in World Fairs colonial "Philippine Village" exhibitions. Thus Filipina Americans had to contend with American colonial occupation and the ensuing racial fantasies concocted around their bodies.

Given this gendered legacy, Asian American women acted as central figures in their communities' public claims for inclusion in the American polity. Sometimes this was a deliberate strategy, sometimes not. Linda Yuen's participation in the Eisenhower inaugural parade represented hopes for the political recognition of Washington, D.C.'s Taiwanese American community during the Cold War era. Twenty years earlier, the Mei Wah (American) Girls drum corps marched in parades throughout Los Angeles, sporting permanent-waved hair and *au courant* lipstick shades while wearing cheongsam tops and marching-band pants. Performing at the opening of Los Angeles' Union Station and other citywide events, the Mei Wah Girls attempted to make visible the historical Asian American presence as well as counteract the residual public image of Chinese female prostitution.

Although people of Asian descent have been in the United States in significant numbers since the mid-nineteenth century, due to demographics and migration patterns the Asian American women in this book comprised the first sizable group of American-born Asians. This cohort owed its genesis to the convergence of three historical factors.[12] First, in the twentieth century, Asian American sex ratios became more even, families reproduced, and the first substantial group of American-born Asians came of age. Second, this generation gained American citizenship through their birth, which set them apart from their parents' immigrant generation. Third, American immigration exclusion from 1924 to 1965 meant that any population increase would come from the American-born. Thus Asian American communities deployed cultural practices in order to respond to the historical legacy of immigration and citizenship exclusion, construction as forever-foreign men, and present-day racial segregation and community-specific issues such as Japanese American internment and Filipino American decolonization. The fresh-faced, smartly dressed, and smiling Asian American woman represented by Linda Yuen and the Mei Wah Girls became a prevalent community response to the mainstream's image of the shuffling, sepia-dour, foreign male coolie, as well as to the mute Chinese-garbed prostitute.

Feminist studies of gender and nationalism corroborate that modern nationalism depends on differentially marking men and women's bodies.[13] The continued inability of American laws and customs as well as public attitudes to hail Asian Americans as Americans highlights how the "language of nation" is racialized.[14] Thus the nation-state's masked construction of "universal" citizenship as male, white, and propertied depends on racial, sexual, and economic difference.[15] Women in particular are produced by and within cultural narratives, typically of a past whose negotiations with the present of a new nation centrally require the reconfiguring of gender relations.[16] What is being reconfigured in the middle of the twentieth century is the representation of Asian American women as exemplars of a race that was becoming increasingly feminized.

Making Sense of Culture

Okay, this year let's try "Sakura"! After heated debate, the young members of Chi Alpha Delta decide to perform "Sakura," the hit song from the film *Teahouse of the August Moon* (1957), for the UCLA annual Spring Sing competition. Since most members, Japanese American and other Asian-ethnic American alike, have never worn kimonos, they enlist the help of kimono specialists so they can authenticate their performance. Last year they sang an American song, dressed in American clothing, and did not place. Maybe this year?

A Feeling of Belonging analyzes the performance of cultural citizenship and investigates meanings of modernity in order to elucidate Asian American women's social practices, such as the founding of Chi Alpha Delta as a means to combat institutionalized campus racism in the 1920s. As the members of the first Asian American sorority in the nation, the women of Chi Alpha Delta strove to create a feeling of belonging in a university that denied them access to white sororities as well as scholarship money and a place to live on campus. Claiming a feeling of belonging is key to cultural citizenship. According to the Latino Studies working group, anthropologist Renato Rosaldo coined the term *cultural citizenship* to signify the demands of disadvantaged subjects for full citizenship in spite of cultural differences from mainstream society.[17] As William Flores and Rita Benmayor argued, those distanced from power will make alternative uses of mainstream forms of culture and, in doing so, make it their own. In other words, although Chi Alpha Delta used the mainstream form of a sorority to gain living space and scholarships at UCLA, they disrupted sorority elitism by admitting all women who wanted to join. Thus, as practitioners of cultural citizenship, the women of Chi Alpha Delta not only demanded full rights of belonging to the university but also transformed an exclusive European American sorority form into a more inclusive entity marked by their Asian American culture. The rubric of cultural citizenship would explain Chi Alpha Delta's decision to wear kimonos while performing "Sakura" at Spring Sing as a strategic one that increased the sorority's prestige in the world of the university, since it allowed them to place fourth in the competition, the best they had ever done. Although the women of Chi Alpha Delta would not have recognized the term *cultural citizenship,* the concept as we understand it today beautifully illustrates the political dimensions of their struggles.

As Chi Alpha Delta's debate over what costume to wear to Spring Sing reveals, the concept of performance can be a helpful analytical tool. As studies of minstrel shows, the slave marketplace, early cinema, and World Fairs have demonstrated, American ideas around race were enacted, created, and contested through performance. Numerous scholars, artists, activists, and observers of everyday life have found no psychological core in humans, no true, fixed identity. In everyday life, race, sexuality, gender, and nationality are not fixed identities rooted in "natural" bodies but are understood as dynamic and dramatic modes, as the sum of one's cultural practices. Since the Japanese American and Asian-ethnic members of Chi Alpha Delta did not know how to wear kimonos, they hired kimono experts to help them wear them properly, which beautifully illustrates the concept of performance. Chi Alpha Delta's clothing dilemmas and Anna May Wong's Edith Head–designed Hollywood costumes show that cultural practices are bound up with style. Style not only manifests race, class, and gender subtexts but also histories and power dynamics.[18] Yet, race is more than theatricality—it is also a coercive attribution. Remember, only those Chinese immigrant women who successfully performed what U.S. immigration officials felt to be an upper-class merchant's wife's behaviors could enter the United States, whether or not they actually occupied that class position.

The increasing significance of regimes of visuality throughout the twentieth century lends support to the importance of performance, cultural citizenship, and modernity. The burden and proof of race have heavily resided in the visual. From the beginning, race has been central to photography and film.[19] For racial minorities, how to present race has been a key issue in intervening in racialized discourses. As a tactic to combat primitive stereotypes, W. E. B. Du Bois exhibited a photographic series of scenes of African American life at the 1900 Paris Exposition. Similarly, African American filmmaker Oscar Micheaux wrote, produced, and directed race movies as responses to D. W. Griffith's *Birth of a Nation* (1915). The infamous *Time* magazine article produced in the immediate aftermath of Pearl Harbor on how to tell your Chinese friend from the Japanese enemy relied on dubious visual "cultural" cues such as the Chinese shuffle and the propensity of the Japanese to wear round glasses.[20] In the aftermath of World War II, Chicago-area Japanese Americans founded *Scene* magazine to counter those harmful stereotypes.

For those who do not bear the dominant markers of national belonging —in the case of the U.S. nonwhite, female—such narratives of belonging and citizenship are frequently renegotiated through acts of modernity. Modernity is a complex historical and cultural situation defined against the past, the traditional, and the "Other," with shifting values attached to each category. As numerous scholars have elaborated, modernity constructs the nation as the preeminent political unit through a series of oppositions that become masked or homogenized: male and female, citizen and alien, civilized and primitive.[21] As the nonmodern, nonassimilable aliens, American women of Asian descent had particular stakes in performing the modern. Chinese American actress Anna May Wong's British-tinged upper-class accent and costumes that hybridized Western and Asian fashions belied any facile dichotomy that categorized cultural practices from Asia as "traditional" and ones from the United States as "modern."

Analysis of colonial societies provides ways to think about racial minorities' adoption of hegemonic practices such as beauty pageants, sororities, magazines, and movies as more than assimilation or identity creation. Appropriate displays of gender and femininity have been key to racial minority and postcolonial societies enacting modernity and progress. For example, Trudy and Glo's *Philippines Star Press* newspaper column, "Salinas Tid-Bits," discussed women's clothing choices, dating practices, and social lives as emblems of Filipino American modernity that could prove the efficacy of the Philippines decolonization. Although on the surface these behaviors may seem to indicate assimilation to American society, the situation was far more complex. Paradoxically, the need to adopt hegemonic cultural practices gives colonized and racial minority subjects the means to disrupt hegemonic power.[22] Hence, given asymmetrical power relations, Asian American adoption of cultural practices such as beauty pageants or mainstream fashions can create the grounds for signaling exclusion from rights and privileges. They also create a new basis for inclusion and break down the dichotomy between exclusion and inclusion. Translations of cultural forms are not mere mimicry, to use Homi Bhabha's evocative formulation, but are new hybrid entities in their own right. Through hybridity, the women's uses of mainstream cultural forms are transformed into distinctly Asian American female practices.

Although the performance of cultural citizenship and modernity entailed gaining greater national acceptance by participating in mainstream cultural practices, it frequently led to conflicts and tensions along both racial lines, with dominant white society, and gender and class lines within Asian American communities. These clashes help define the limits of belonging at all of the various overlapping arenas of affiliation, from Asian-ethnic community to the American nation-state. The tragedy of the internment of Japanese Americans highlights how prewar efforts to prove cultural citizenship—Nisei Week festival queens, Organdie dances—failed to confirm legal status in the eyes of the American population. In other cases, the demands of the larger Asian American community on the young women expected to represent it clashed with the imperatives of the women themselves. *A Feeling of Belonging* examines the contradictory desires created by the imperatives of cultural citizenship—the need to prove and claim Americanness—versus the benefits of racial and group identity such as political mobilization and emotional support. By using women symbolically to represent race and community, Asian Americans attempted to ameliorate those contradictions. During the Cold War era, for example, the leading Chinese American civil rights organization, the Chinese American Citizens Alliance, held a queen contest as the centerpiece of its annual meeting. Young Chinese American women were called upon to demonstrate the community's progressive neo-liberalism by parading in bathing suits in front of the thousands that made up the largest gathering of Chinese Americans to date. Although some did participate, others steadfastly refused, despite intensive cajoling. However, controversies and ruptures over the cultural figures and practices both within the community and in mainstream society demonstrate the difficulties of resolving race politics through gender and point to the disjunctures in being "not quite, not white."

1

"A Feeling of Belonging"
Chi Alpha Delta, 1928–1941

Spring 1941. The sun sparkles and the flowers glow against the terracotta-colored brick buildings at the University of California, Los Angeles. Imagine, if you will, that you are a new member of the sorority Chi Alpha Delta. You have just been initiated into membership with your eager pledge class and have just discovered that your sorority has the campus's highest grade point average.[1] For your first Spring Formal dance, your sorors suggest smooth dates, rejecting all drips, and propose a shopping trip to pick out snazzy shoes in which to groove the night away. You have just been reprimanded for whispering too loudly in College Library, debating which beautician could best help you achieve Judy Garland–esque permanent waves. But next year you will not be on campus. You are not just any young co-ed at UCLA. You are Japanese American. During spring 1942, instead of hurrying across Royce Quad, exchanging greetings with classmates, you will be stripped of all of your legal rights as an American citizen and summarily incarcerated as a "prisoner without trial" for three years in an internment camp.[2]

Predominantly second-generation Japanese Americans, members of Chi Alpha Delta spoke English at home and with each other, permanent-waved their hair, wore poodle skirts with saddle shoes, and nicknamed themselves the "Chis." Like women in European American sororities, they staged barnyard frolics, ski weekends, and beach outings and, at their banquets, savored fried chicken, green beans, and three-layer cake. Yet, to set the mood for their annual outdoor Faculty Tea, the women of Chi Alpha Delta dressed in kimonos and arranged their hair in "Japanese" styles. For public performances, they displayed Japanese ethnic pride and/or "exoticism," but in their everyday lives they would be as American as their flared skirts and pearl-buttoned sweaters.

A Feeling of Belonging's story of modernity, gender, and public culture begins with the story of Chi Alpha Delta because Japanese American women represented the first generation of American-born women of Asian descent to attain numerical and cultural significance. Moreover, the 1930s second generation known as the Nisei was unique in American history. In a nation-state that validated racial segregation with the Supreme Court decision *Plessy* v. *Ferguson* (1896), the Nisei faced obstacles to claiming their place in America that no other ethnic or racial group had ever faced.[3] The 1924 Immigration Act that limited European migration and excluded Asians in actuality targeted Japanese immigration. In addition, California's alien land laws, which forbade immigrants from owning land, were passed directly against the Japanese. In sum, 1920s American racial hostilities targeted the Japanese as the ultimate non-American aliens. The burden, then, was on the sisters of Chi Alpha Delta and their American-born cohort to prove their American citizenship.

Although activities such as deciding whether to wear poodle skirts or kimonos may appear trivial, against the backdrop of the racial hatreds that made possible Japanese American incarceration during World War II, the stakes were enormous. The social reality of pre–World War II American racial apartheid overshadowed all cultural decisions that young Japanese American women like the Chis faced. As the visible, both in terms of race and in terms of markers such as clothing, was understood as indicating political and national allegiance, public culture was contested terrain. Acts of cultural citizenship ranging from forming a sorority to planning a fox-trot competition at Chi Whoopee demonstrated belonging to American society. Although the members of Chi Alpha Delta did not use the term *cultural citizenship* to describe their activities, the concept is useful because it shows the cumulative political meaning in quotidian events. Cultural citizenship is defined as everyday practices through which racial minorities and other marginalized groups claim a place in society, which leads to claiming rights.[4] Such acts that "claim space in society" are counternarratives to the mainstream construction of racial minorities as unassimilable peoples occupying a liminal space outside the imagined nation-state. Although performing ethnic cultural heritage (kimonos) and modern American culture (poodle skirts and permanent waves) should be seen as mutually constitutive identificatory processes instead of oppositional ones, mainstream society frequently conflated homage to Japanese ancestry with loyalty to Japan. For reasons ranging from Japan's pre–World War II military campaigns in

Asia to the bombing of Pearl Harbor, any alleged allegiance to Japan was suspect.

A very rich and complete array of Chi Alpha Delta documents, ranging from minutes of meetings to scrapbooks and oral history interviews, has preserved this story of daily decisions that make up cultural citizenship.[5] The prewar records are particularly valuable since few Japanese American institutional records survived World War II internment.[6] In addition, since it is exceedingly rare to have access to local sorority records, there has been very little scholarly literature on the history of roughly 3 million women who joined sororities.[7] In fact, there is only one in-depth work that focuses on sorority women's history: journalist Paula Giddings's *In Search of Sisterhood.*[8] Giddings examines the institutional history of African American sorority Delta Sigma Theta's national governing board. Instead of national leadership and expansion, local Chi Alpha Delta records reveal the day-to-day struggles over race, class, femininity, and culture.

This chapter, "A Feeling of Belonging," explores the development of public culture in three interrelated ways. First, I examine the founding of the sorority as an act of claiming a space of belonging in the world of the university. A ringing declaration of cultural citizenship, the creation of an Asian American sorority demonstrates the significance of establishing race-safe spaces in a racially segregated society. Second, I explore the parameters of Chi Alpha Delta's democratic practices that differentiated them from exclusionary European American sororities. Third, sororities provided numerous opportunities for pleasure, and the women in Chi Alpha Delta used "fun" to play with, explore, and create cultural citizenship practices. In an era of racial segregation, the sorority allowed the women to claim advantages such as glamour, dating, and parties, as well as to create democratic and hybrid cultural forms.[9] Though part of an intrinsically heteronormative conservative organization, the women of Chi Alpha Delta nonetheless made visible and called attention to hidden racialized structures within the supposedly democratic nation-state.

"A Feeling of Belonging": *The Rationale for Chi Alpha Delta*

In 1928, Helen Tomio Mizuhara and Alyce Asahi founded Chi Alpha Delta at the University of California, Southern Branch, as a haven against racism. In the early years at the university, since Japanese American women faced institutional discrimination and lacked support networks, they wanted an organization to alleviate those problems. In addition, sororities provided material benefits such as student dwellings close to the university. Moreover, many Japanese Americans on campus, in Los Angeles and across the nation, considered sororities prestigious for the social status they accrued to their members. However, Japanese American women were not allowed into European American sororities. Hence Mizuhara and Asahi created an organization of their own.

Fourteen charter members formed the first Japanese American (and Asian American) sorority in the United States. Sponsored by the dean of women, Helen Laughlin, Chi Alpha Delta received official recognition from the university known today as the University of California, Los Angeles, on April 5, 1929. The Los Angeles Japanese American newspaper, the *Rafu Shimpo*, subsequently reported: "Following the footsteps of the men students, the co-eds of UCLA have organized into a society which is known as the A. O. Society. It is an organization which is open to all of the Japanese women students at the University of California in Los Angeles. The only requirement is the paying of club dues."[10] Like their male counterparts, the Nisei Bruin Club, Japanese American women decided to form a racially exclusive organization.

As oral history interviews reveal, racial discrimination and segregation instigated the founding of Chi Alpha Delta. According to one of the charter members, Shizue Morey Yoshina, since the numbers of Japanese American women who attended the university were few, those women believed they needed a same-sex, same-race organization in order to feel at home at the university. Yoshina described American society in the 1920s as racially polarized: "You have no idea, at the present time, what sort of a wall there was between the whites and anybody else. And it was pretty bad. And all this persisted until World War II. That was a long time coming. So in the meantime we fought our own battle."[11] As a Nisei, a second-generation Japanese American, Yoshina recognized the multitude of laws that restricted citizenship according to race. The 1924 immigration act codified two significant ones.[12] First, it curtailed migration from Asia, including Japan. Second, it forbade the immigrant generation, the Issei (the Nisei's parents), from becoming naturalized American citizens. In addition to national laws, Southern California regulations segregated many popular recreational venues, such as swimming pools and movie theaters.[13] In a classic act of cultural citizenship, Yoshina and other Japanese American women fought their own battle against racism by banding together so that they could benefit by strength in numbers.

CHI ALPHA DELTA

ΧΑΔ

Top row: Chuman, Saito, Fujioka. Second row: Imoto, Kawashima, Sugihara. Third row: Watanabe, Suzuki, Endo. Fourth row: Fujikawa, Hasama, Morey, Nozawa. Bottom row: Okura, Sumida, Uchiyama, Yuzawa.

Chi Alpha Delta was originally founded in 1928 as a club for Japanese girls. In 1929 through the efforts of Dean Laughlin the club became an active social sorority. It started with a membership of fourteen and has expanded to a group of fifty active members including alumni. Chi Alpha Delta is the only Japanese social sorority in the United States. Six of its members have gone to Japan and have started the Beta chapter of alumnae there. In April the girls gave a faculty tea at the home of Mrs. Robson. It was their first attempt at entertaining the faculty and was so successful that they are planning more faculty teas for the near future.

FACULTY: Mrs. Ruth Boynton, Mrs. Bernice Nelson. SENIORS: Yemi Chuman, Aiko Saito. JUNIORS: Alice Fujioka, Sunab Imoto, Mabel Kawashima, Hideko Sugihara, Yoshi Watanabe. SOPHOMORES: Margaret Suzuki. PLEDGES: Mary Endo, Fujie Fujikawa, Michiye Hasama, Rose Morey, Kazuko Nozawa, Dorothy Misao Okura, Emmy Sumida, Emily Uchiyama, Chieko Yuzawa.

The Chi Alpha Delta's in full party dress ready for tea-time.

UCLA 1937

— 363 —

Chi Alpha Delta Year Book Page, 1937. *(Used by permission of the University Archives, UCLA)*.

15

Yoshina described the motivations for founding the sorority as being both racially and economically based:

> [We] used to get together, see each other in the library. We noticed that all the scholarships, competition for this award and that award all went through the Greek letter organizations. [We had a] Japanese women's club. But we saw that all the goodies went to the Greek people, and none of us was ever asked to join one of them and we decided to make our own. The reason why we got going was because we just wanted to be able to compete with them.[14]

Japanese American women were excluded from European American sororities, which had a monopoly on scholarship funds. Yoshina and other charter members wanted equal access to that money. Since the Japanese women's club at UCLA did not have the same institutional power that a university-sanctioned organization such as a sorority had, Japanese American women realized they could compete for educational funds by starting their own Greek-letter association. Thus cultural citizenship in the guise of sorority participation ensured access to "rights" such as scholarship funding.

Japanese American women's desire to form a sorority was completely in keeping with the collegiate culture of the times. In the early twentieth century, fraternal organizations proved to be the central social clubs at universities.[15] As soon as UCLA was founded in 1919, ten sororities and one fraternity established chapters.[16] As a former teacher's college, the California State Normal School, UCLA was predominantly female until it gained in prestige in the mid-1930s; hence the greater number of sororities. All eleven of the fraternal organizations were locally founded groups that had grown out of social clubs formed at the California State Normal School. The proliferation of sororities was so rapid that by 1929, the year Chi Alpha Delta was recognized as a campus organization and UCLA moved to Westwood, all thirty-eight existing national sororities had chapters at the university. The availability of relatively inexpensive older homes for rent near the old Vermont Avenue campus assisted the sororities' founding. At UCLA, sororities enjoyed strong membership throughout the prewar years. In 1941, the campus's chapters claimed 822 members, roughly a quarter of the female student population.[17] Judging by their yearbook photograph, that same year Chi Alpha Delta had at least twenty-seven active members.[18] Nationally, the number of college and university women who joined sororities is staggering. Between 1851 and 1993, over 2.8 million women joined one of the twenty-six existing National Panhellenic sororities.[19]

At UCLA and across the nation, sororities were the leading social organizations on campus. For example, *The Claw,* a UCLA campus magazine that was published for over four decades, glamorized sorority women.[20] The periodical frequently profiled rush recruitment by dedicating five or six pages of a fall issue to formal photographs of the newly pledged members smiling triumphantly in their new sorority houses' parlors.[21] A regular column entitled "Glass Houses" discussed dating habits and the social whirl *ad nauseam.* These types of magazines were not just information sources but arbiters of social standing on campus. They were designed to instill envy in those not in the "in" crowd and to normalize unequal power relations.

As could be expected given the racialized nature of sorority hierarchy, women of color almost never appeared in *The Claw.* Chi Alpha Delta was represented only once, and only in name. For the December 1934 issue, *The Claw's* cover depicted Christmas-present boxes, with each of the campus's Greek letter organizations appearing on a different box; the picture included a box embossed with the Greek letters Chi, Alpha, and Delta.[22] However, that was the only time they ever appeared in the magazine. The fact that it was not a racialized photographic representation of the members probably allowed its inclusion. Given that numerous members of Chi Alpha Delta were Buddhist, inclusion as a symbolic Christmas gift speaks volumes to the Christian assumptions of the Greek system.

In fact, one of the only times an embodied woman of color appeared in *The Claw* was in a derogatory cartoon. This 1931 image deserves close scrutiny, for it demonstrates how the race, class, and sexual hierarchies embedded within the Greek system became apparent at the cultural level. In the cartoon, an African American woman carrying a load of laundry approaches a streetcar and says to the conductor: "Just a minute, mister, 'till I get my clothes on."[23] While the "mammy" wants the conductor to wait until she gets her load of laundry onto the streetcar, if one did not see the cartoon, one might assume that she was nude. Since she is African American and is drawn with an "Aunt Jemima" figure, she is presumed to be the exact opposite of socially desirable white femininity. Hence the punch line: working-class African American women are not sexually desirable even when naked. Thus the asexual mammy who unintentionally provides the material that others can deride stands as the necessary foil to

1931 Cartoon. *(University Archives, UCLA)*.

the blonde sorority woman, who is desirable precisely because she is neither black nor poor nor overweight. The use of this type of racialized caricature showed that universities shared broader American societal mores exemplified by *Amos 'n' Andy* cartoons and mammy stereotypes. Such racial images act as "controlling images" that delineate people's roles in society and reinforce unequal social hierarchies.[24]

By representing white sorority life as glamorous, mainstream media reinforced cultural racial hierarchies. In fact, in 1939, the glamour of the UCLA sorority woman was so great that *Look,* a national pictorial that had a reputation equivalent to today's *People* and *Time* magazines, profiled the UCLA woman in a four-page photo spread.[25] In a manner similar to the magazine's portrayal of movie-star lifestyles, the 1939 article entitled "Country Club College," focused almost exclusively on sorority women, depicted the young women surrounded by movie stars and basking in sunshine, leading the lives of Hollywood starlets. The pictorial essay showed them playing various sports, relaxing around campus, and wearing sophisticated dress and hair fashions. It displayed photographs of sorority rush, and the accompanying text stated that only the most beautiful and popular girls became sorority members, with the most worthy of them selected by the best sorority. Since educational pursuits were not profiled, a reader might expect university life to be chiefly made up of social activities. Throughout the United States, white UCLA sorority women exemplified the ultimate co-eds.

Racial barriers compelled Japanese American women at UCLA to found an all–Japanese American sorority as a race-safe space in which they could claim their rights as university citizens. Joining an existing sorority was not an option because many had racial and religious membership restrictions, also known as discriminatory or segregation clauses. In sorority and fraternity policies, the criteria for membership of being European American and Christian sometimes would be explicit, sometimes implicit. In fact, at UCLA it was not until 1966 that all male and female fraternal organizations signed the nondiscriminatory pledge, an oath that stated they would not restrict membership according to race, religion, or national origin.[26] Reminiscing about the 1920s, Yoshina revealed that she and other Japanese American women did not even consider joining an existing sorority, for they knew they would not be asked to become members: "Well, shucks, we were outsiders all that time. Awful lot of racism, prejudice, no one ever thought of including any Asians in their group, you know. They were strictly white."[27] "Flapper" Flora Belle Jan reported similar anti-Asian discrimination at Fresno State College: "Of course being a Chinese girl, I'm not eligible to membership in a [European American] sorority."[28] It was impossible for a racial or religious minority woman to join an all-white Christian sorority unless somehow she could pass for Christian and white.

Exclusion from the mainstream sororal social-prestige system mirrored the challenges racial and religious minority women faced in realizing their career aspirations. Since higher education is one of the chief means for working-class, religious minority, and racial minority students to rise in status, participation in such a prestige system has special salience for women who fit those categories.[29] Though UCLA began as a teacher's college, that feminized profession was considered too American to be practiced by "foreign" Japanese American women. In other words, Japanese American women could teach only other Japanese Americans, not European Americans. Reported Frances Kitagawa, president of the sorority from 1935 to 1936: "Dean [Helen] Laughlin, who was also a Chi advisor, didn't want me to continue in education or to get my teaching credentials. She wanted me to change my major. She said to me, 'Where are you going to teach? They're not going to hire you. Are you going to teach in Japan or

Hawaii?'"[30] The dean mentioned Hawaii because, as the Japanese constituted the Territory of Hawaii's largest laboring group, Hawaii had a sizable Japanese American student population. In spite of the dean of women's warning, Kitagawa enjoyed a distinguished thirty-four-year teaching career in California. Though Laughlin's support ensured Chi Alpha Delta's continuance, she did not counsel her advisees to break down racialized occupational barriers. Kitagawa's experience was dismayingly common. Few Japanese Americans went into education and teaching, both because they were discouraged from direct competition with European Americans and because there were no job opportunities.[31]

In addition to job segregation, the barriers faced by the women of Chi Alpha Delta when trying to secure on-campus housing underscored their particular need for a sorority. In 1932, UCLA built its first dormitory, Mira Hershey Hall, as an all-women's residence hall. However, the university barred Japanese American women from living there. Mabel Ota, president of the sorority from 1938 to 1939, condemned the racially restricted housing: "Since I was from out of town, I wanted to stay in the dormitories. But they didn't allow any Japanese. I ended up staying at the Japanese YWCA in Boyle Heights and commuted back and forth every day."[32] Although there did not seem to be any written clauses that explicitly excluded non–European Americans from living in Hershey Hall before World War II, given American society's unspoken racial codes, upon applying to live in the dormitory, racial and religious minorities such as Ota would be told that no rooms were available.

Housing issues highlighted the hurdles facing Chi Alpha Delta. For all students, UCLA's relocation to Westwood in 1929 created a housing crisis. Westwood was a locale surrounded by neighborhoods with restrictive housing covenants and expensive real estate: Beverly and Holmby Hills to the east, Bel-Air to the north, and Brentwood to the west. In conjunction with city officials and leaders, developers priced Westwood's real estate artificially high to keep the area out of the income range of not only students but also racial and ethnic minorities and working-class European Americans. Claiming that the land had been donated by the state for classroom use, the university refused to let fraternities and sororities build on the 383-acre campus. The Janss Investment Company, which owned significant portions of the empty land in Westwood surrounding the campus, offered to sell twenty-eight housing lots on Hilgard Avenue to Greek organizations, priced from $7,500 to $9,500, well below the standard asking price of $8,000 to $12,000.[33]

Twenty-one European American sororities bought land from the Janss Investment Company in the 1920s.[34] House purchases were not confined to UCLA; nationwide, the 1920s were the boom years in acquiring local chapter houses.[35] A sorority's visibility, strength, and prestige depended on having a successful local chapter house. Usually each chapter would obtain loans from its national organization and pay off the housing costs through assessing dues and fees on its local members.

Over the years, the Chi members contributed a regular part of their dues to a fund so they could obtain a house near UCLA. In 1938, they assembled a group of Japanese investors, and, supported by the alumnae, initiated the proceedings to purchase a house. As the sorority minutes of the day stated, student and soror Hideko Sugihara reported on "the UCLA Religious Conference Building property which is being offered for sale to the Japanese Students."[36] However, due to restrictive housing covenants and racial prejudice, the Janss family denied members of Chi Alpha Delta the opportunity to buy a house. Though presumably the university was willing to sell the land to the Chis, the aforementioned Janss family had the final say in the matter. Two of the family members were favorably inclined, but one refused to sell to "Orientals," and thus Chi Alpha Delta could not purchase the land.[37] California's alien land laws forbade the Issei (who by law could not naturalize) and other noncitizens from owning land, and these were not repealed until 1956.[38] Not surprisingly, the American-born generations also had difficulty obtaining property. Practices ranging from red-lining home mortgages to restrictive housing covenants ensured the whiteness of "exclusive" neighborhoods.[39] Thus, like many other racial minorities, the women of Chi Alpha Delta were not allowed to exercise the full privileges of their legal American citizenship.

Not owning a house had severe repercussions, for it meant that the members of Chi Alpha Delta would continually search for locations in which to hold their meetings; they did not enjoy campus visibility; and they commuted to the university. Without a house, Chi Alpha Delta's members remained scattered in locations ranging from West Los Angeles, three miles south and west of campus, to Mabel Ota's domicile in the Boyle Heights YWCA, twenty-five miles to the east. After the restrictive housing covenants were abolished in the postwar era, Los Angeles housing prices skyrocketed, so it became impossible for Chi Alpha Delta to raise enough money to buy a house.[40]

UCLA's housing segregation was the norm, not the exception. California's most prestigious universities barred Asian American students from campus accommodations. At another Los Angeles institution, the University of Southern California, students of Chinese descent were routinely rejected from student housing.[41] At Stanford University, Chinese American students were expelled from dormitories and hence founded the Chinese Students' Alliance residence.[42] Similarly, at the University of California–Berkeley, Saiki Muneno recollected that discriminatory housing practices compelled Japanese American leaders to raise money to build Euclid House for the Japanese American students.[43] At the University of California, Los Angeles, Japanese Americans' applications were particularly vulnerable to rejection because, for the most part, their last names identified them as being of Asian descent. Mabel Ota's narrative shows why housing discrimination and racial segregation encouraged her to join Chi Alpha Delta. Presaging one definition of cultural citizenship almost word for word, Ota stated, "So you can see why the girls felt a need to band together. We were really excluded. The sorority gave the girls the feeling of belonging."[44]

Not a (White) Sorority

Religious and racial minority sororities were one of the only places on college campuses where their members could devise their own rules and regulations and could self-govern free from the scrutiny and interference of either white women or men from their own racial minority group. In 1908, two decades before Chi Alpha Delta's founding at UCLA, a group of women organized the first African American sorority, Alpha Kappa Alpha, at Howard University for those reasons.[45] Likewise, the second African American sorority, Delta Sigma Theta (Delta), was chartered in 1913, also at Howard University.[46] Delta-oath author Mary Church Terrell recruited those young Delta members into suffrage marches and antilynching campaigns.[47] Delta alumnae include luminaries such as Congresswoman Barbara Jordan and opera star Leontyne Price. Mary McLeod Bethune, founder of the National Council of Negro Women, spoke at the sorority's national conventions and shaped its agenda in the 1930s and 1940s. National groups and alumnae groups provided young women with role models and networks of association that would prove valuable both for their moral support and for professional mentoring.

What is striking is that the mere presence of Chi Alpha Delta, a conservative, heteronormative organization that did not intend radical change, showed the racialized structures of sororities, universities, and American society and offered democratic alternatives to their elitism. Being a non-white organization, Chi Alpha Delta's existence demonstrated the degree to which European American sororities were marked as white, and how being nonwhite hampered the members' ability to exercise their rights. Indeed, mimicry or the *seeming* copying of dominant social practices by those outside power was not mere copying but a significant politicized way of breaking the hegemony of the power elite.[48] What is particularly important is that though the members mimicked the sorority in form, in practice they consciously chose to depart from the exclusionary, elitist, and individualistic norms of elite European American ones. Since racial segregation excluded them from mainstream rush recruitment and the National Panhellenic, Chi Alpha Delta formed alternative practices and structures.

The women of Chi Alpha Delta practiced cultural citizenship's critical "feeling of belonging" invoked by Mabel Ota by disrupting the most sacred tenet of sorority elitism: exclusive membership. From founding to 1960, Chi Alpha Delta's membership policies radically differed from European American sororities because they extended "open" membership. According to Lilly Fujioka Tsukahira, the Chis accepted all women.[49] Unlike most WASP sororities and upper-tier Jewish American ones such as Alpha Epsilon Phi and Sigma Delta Tau, Chi Alpha Delta prided itself on not rejecting potential members. "Exclusive" European American sororities, by contrast, required letters of introduction from alumnae in order for young women to be invited to the series of recruitment events known as "rush." Many judged women according to criteria such as family background, income, manners, and fashion. Thus many women were not invited to rush events, and even greater numbers were not asked to join. During the "social" events, which were nerve-wracking tests of manners, the sisters and alumnae rush advisers would rigorously rate the women according to family background, social graces, and physical attractiveness. One misstep —say, needing to blow one's nose, fishing around for a handkerchief, then proceeding to sneeze on a cocktail napkin—was grounds for immediate elimination. Usually the final event would be a formal dinner where the prospective soror would have to wear an exquisite evening gown and display impeccable table manners while engaging in witty conversation. Only the women with the highest rankings would be issued Panhellenic-supervised bids inviting them to join the house. The sororities had their own pecking order, with the most desirable inviting the highest-status women, thus reinforcing elite societal structures. In addition, alumnae legacies were given preferential treatment.

Not surprisingly, the mainly non-Greek UCLA campus did not idolize "exclusive" sororities. Conscious of the animosities between sorority and nonsorority women, Chi adviser Dean Helen Laughlin helped found Phrateres, a group with social activities and rituals open to all women.[50] Features and letters to the editor in campus publications such as the *Daily Bruin* and *The Claw* indicated that many had misgivings about the selection process for sorority rush. As one letter to the chancellor from a father of a first-year student indicates, sororities were considered by many to be cruel in their rejection of potential members:

> There is just one matter on which I have heard a lot of adverse criticism from alumni, who have sent their daughters to the university, that is, the manner in which the women students are rushed. From the accounts that I have heard and the hardships and heartburns that not only the students but also their mothers go through, it seems that the present system is wrong. It is very artificial and is causing people to send their daughters elsewhere.[51]

Competition for membership in the exclusive and prestigious European American sororities was so fierce that many women who wished to join a sorority could not pledge their organization of choice. Chinese American Flora Belle Jan reported that at Fresno State College "the Sorority girls talk over the possible candidates to membership in their sorority. . . . They judge people entirely by the clothes they wear and the amount of money they spend, and they get awfully stung this way sometimes."[52] Since Chi Alpha Delta opened membership to all women of Japanese descent, they did not cause similar heartache. It was the European American sororities that came under criticism for elitist membership policies.

Although National Panhellenic determined which sororities belonged on American college campuses, at UCLA undergraduate male students influenced the local social standings of each European American sorority house. In articles such as the one entitled "Who Went Where," *The Claw*'s male editorial staff would rate the attractiveness of new sorority pledges. As if that were not sufficient objectification, a feature entitled "Our Stock Exchange" awarded the "exclusive" sororities points according to how "well" they had done in rush.[53] The article's authors granted the young female pledges of each house points that had "worth" according to a numer-

The Claw, December 1934. *(University Archives, UCLA).*

ical scale from zero to one thousand, as if they were commodities or shares of companies. At UCLA, the pledges' heights, weights, and ages were included in *The Claw's* rating table. Though many people then and today would find judging women solely according to physical criteria repugnant, the coverage was meant to be complimentary. Thus the men and women on campus could look at the average of each house and know which were perceived to have the most attractive women and hence know the pecking order of the sorority houses. And by inference, if a man dated a woman from a house with lots of points, his own worth would increase! In the 1930s, rating-dating systems were widespread across college campuses.[54] However, the fraternity houses were not rated by points, indicating the gendered nature of the system.

Since Chi Alpha Delta was not an exclusive group that restricted membership, and since they did not participate in Panhellenic-guided UCLA rush, they could avoid the male-created ranking system put forth in the *Claw* campus magazine. In addition, members differentiated themselves from the snobbery and cliquishness of mainstream exclusive sororities. By referring to a sympathetic member of prestigious Kappa Kappa Gamma as an "oddball" sorority girl, Chi Alpha Delta member Frances Kitagawa equated sororities with exclusive and elite white ones, not with organizations like Chi Alpha Delta.[55] Kitagawa found "mainstream" (not oddball) sorority members to be those who snubbed the Chi Alpha Deltas.

Since the national and local Panhellenic council that governed European American sorority policies, most importantly sorority rush, barred Jewish American and racial minority organizations, Chi Alpha Delta had to form its own networks and rituals.[56] In addition, since Panhellenic created rules to ensure that no sorority would have an unfair advantage during recruitment drives, it would not have served Chi Alpha Delta's purpose to join because it targeted a different constituency.[57] Like other sororities, Chi Alpha Delta recruited new members during the first two weeks in the fall and, at times, during the spring. However, in keeping with its open membership policy, to form its rush lists it sent out invitations to all women of Japanese descent who entered UCLA.

During the prewar years, second-generation Japanese American women dominated the membership rolls. Japanese American women comprised the first sizable group of American-born Asians, as well as the first significant cohort of Asian American women. In 1930, sixty-eight thousand, or 49 percent, of Japanese Americans were American-born, whereas it was not until 1940 that the forty thousand American-born Chinese made up 52 percent of their ethnic population.[58] This aligned with student demographics for prior to World War II; most of the Asian Pacific American students at UCLA were Japanese American. In 1941, there were approximately twenty-five hundred college students of Japanese descent in the United States. In contrast, as Rose Hum Lee's study on the Chinese in America shows, in 1944, only 823 Chinese students attended colleges and universities in the United States.[59]

Given the importance of the Japanese American community in Southern California, it is not surprising that Japanese American women at UCLA founded the first Asian American sorority in the nation. Racial segregation prompted the formation of Nisei youth groups all over Southern California. In the 1930s, since mainstream clubs affiliated with schools, communities, and national organizations were not open to Japanese

American membership, Nisei clubs were established. In the 1930s, the presence of sixty-six Nisei clubs in Los Angeles reflected a need for alternative spaces. Showcasing the region as a Nisei stronghold, local Japanese American newspapers reported that by 1940, four hundred Nisei clubs existed in Southern California.[60] Thus the Chi Alpha Delta sorors' drive to organize into an official entity was completely in keeping with their Japanese American peers.

To make membership a greater possibility for more women during the Great Depression, the Chi Alpha Delta sorors kept fees and dues low. Founding member Yoshina reported having to work during college: "It's not like I could get a job because of prejudice and we depended on our folks for help . . . my dad had a company, one of three department stores in Japantown. I guess my family was not hurting too much, but we didn't have a lot of extra money, we had to work in the store every weekend, and whenever there were sales. . . ."[61] Before the war, women like Yoshina tended to work in family businesses and in ethnic enclaves because employment was not available elsewhere. Affordability was key during the depression era; on at least one occasion, they could not raise enough funds for a motion-picture evening and hence canceled the event.

If open membership and other inclusive policies illustrated one major way that the Chi Alpha Deltas practiced an alternative vision of sorority membership, creating a local organization demonstrated the other. Jewish American sororities' failed attempts to join National Panhellenic illuminated not only the very WASP whiteness of sororities but the reasons why Chi Alpha Delta remained a local organization and formed an alternative structure. Starting in 1917, for over three decades, prestigious Alpha Epsilon Phi's petition to join National Panhellenic was systematically blocked at the national and local levels. In one incident, Mary B. Davidson, the University of California–Berkeley associate dean of women, told an Alpha Epsilon Phi national officer (who reported the conversation back to the sorority's national governing board) that she did not want Jewish sororities admitted to Panhellenic because "if they granted the privilege to us [Alpha Epsilon Phi] they would have to grant the same privilege to the Japanese, Chinese, and Negro sororities if they wanted it."[62] Davidson feared that admitting Alpha Epsilon Phi would mean having to include sororities such as Chi Alpha Delta into UCLA's Panhellenic Congress. Admittance would strengthen Chi Alpha Delta by increasing its size and could potentially facilitate its national growth. In addition, as National

Panhellenic oversaw all European American sororities' membership policies, acceptance into the organization was a sign that a sorority had "arrived." Thus the Jewish sororities at UCLA were not part of local Panhellenic until 1941, a decade before their admission to National Panhellenic. African American and Asian American sororities never belonged to Panhellenic, for by the time fraternal organizations desegregated, the Black and the Asian Greek Councils oversaw their respective organizations.

Like their Japanese American counterparts, Chinese American women in the San Francisco Bay Area discovered similar racial barriers. In a heartfelt editorial, Alice Fong Yu, president of the Square and Circle Club, reported that European American women there imposed racial segregation. Upon the club's 1937 application for admission to the local Federation of Women's Clubs (the equivalent of Panhellenic), the European American women amended their constitution to bar "non-Caucasians."[63] Humorously, Fong Yu observed: "Some of the much heated clubwomen, doing considerable chestheaving, said that though they would be willing to work for 'colored women,' they wished—oh, so ardently—to reserve the right to choose their own club friends, and so on, ad nauseam."[64] Like missionary and colonial women, the San Francisco club women could "lift up" their darker sisters but did not consider them to be their equals.

Though the Chi Alpha Delta women shared with African American and Jewish American sororities the need to band together in race- and gender-specific organizations, they had strategic organizational differences. The biggest was that African American sororities such as Delta Sigma Theta and Alpha Kappa Alpha and Jewish American sororities such as Alpha Epsilon Phi and Sigma Delta Tau were extensive organizations with chapters across the nation. As did the mainstream European American sororities, local Jewish American and African American chapters enjoyed the benefits of financial support and rush expertise from their strong national organization. However, they would also be subject to the potentially restrictive imposition of the national organization's rules about who could join— that is, daughters of alumnae—as well as nationally determined rituals. As part of national organizations, Deltas and AEPhis visited sorors at chapters across the country and gathered yearly to attend their respective annual national conventions. Hence they formed networks with female activists and career women across the nation. Since Chi Alpha Delta was UCLA-specific, the nature of affiliation and participation was local.

Nationally organized sororities have greater chances of establishing and maintaining chapters than do local-only sororities because they have access to national funds, guidance, and sponsorship. Given their local membership, Chi Alpha Delta formed an alumnae organization as an alternative to a national. A group of graduates founded the chapter on May 2, 1933, in Los Angeles. In their constitution, they stated that their purpose was to "support and aid the active chapter of the sorority, to participate in Japanese community welfare work, and to foster cultural interest among the members."[65] The alumnae group functioned as a national sorority board without the financial burden, for none of the dues paid by the actives were earmarked for the alumnae as they would have been for a national. The alumnae guided the perpetually rotating new membership and new officers and served as repositories of historical memory. During the depression, they supplied financial support to the active chapter members by donating funds to pay for rush party refreshments and by holding fundraisers whose proceeds supported undergraduate UCLA scholarships, so important to the original goals of the organization.

In addition, the alumnae chapter met the challenges of life beyond undergraduate college years by building mutual support networks. They held an annual dinner, wrote a monthly newsletter, and, in 1979, organized an elaborate party for the sorority's fiftieth anniversary. Six alumnae who migrated to Japan formed the "Beta" or second alumnae chapter in 1937.[66] Very little is known about this Beta Chapter, but lack of correspondence after the 1930s implies that it did not survive beyond World War II. In addition to regular meetings, they elected their own officers and executive board, compiled their own scrapbooks, celebrated engagements, and held bridge parties and luncheons. Thus the alumnae chapter provided a critical amount of stability, structure, and longevity to Chi Alpha Delta.

However, I do not want to overstate Chi Alpha Delta's ability to be an alternative organization. A sorority, though modified in its practices, is nonetheless a sorority, and Chi Alpha Delta still suffered from de facto exclusivity. Despite the sorors' claim that membership was equally open to all, from the sorority photographs it is clear that the majority of those interested in joining the sorority came from the middle and upper classes. Since college education, especially for women, was expensive, time-consuming, and elite, middle-and upper-class students mainly pursued it. As one woman said, the members of Chi Alpha Delta were considered to be "top drawer," meaning that they were women with status in their communities. Soror Alice Suzuki's father was an insurance salesman. Frances Kitagawa explained that her father owned a building in town, and with the stock market crash, he lost everything but one piece of land, which he farmed, a form of work he had never done before. Her parents bought her a car, albeit an "old Ford," to get to and from school. Due to ethnic-enclave employment, racial minorities' middle and upper classes were not as economically devastated by the Great Depression as were their European American equivalents.[67] And during the depression, class status, income, and occupation did not necessarily align, for people who had enjoyed substantial economic privilege before the crash faced reduced purchasing power and/or professional status but retained their previous class expectations and training.

In some ways Chi Alpha Delta practiced collegiate cultural citizenship too well; Asian American women who did not fit class and cultural parameters felt excluded. Despite all the measures to be inclusive, not all Japanese American women agreed that joining a sorority was a good idea. Explains Yoshina, "There were some people, Japanese girls, who had a prejudice against the idea of a sorority and didn't want to join us, [they] join[ed] another women's club."[68] Not only would the idea of a sorority be unappealing to some women, but not all could afford the time or dues (even minimal ones) necessary for sorority membership, especially during the depression. Though members such as Yoshina and Fujioka claim nonexclusivity, their respective ownership of a family department store and a car indicate that some Chi Alpha Delta members had means beyond mere economic survival.

Despite an initial constitution that stated it was a sorority for women of Japanese descent, unsuccessful attempts were made to recruit other ethnicities.[69] In the 1930s, Lilly Fujioka Tsukahira recalls, the sorority tried to pledge a Korean American woman, but her parents wouldn't let her join because of animosities between Japanese and Koreans due to Japanese imperialism in Korea.[70] Though technically open to all, cultural practices such as wearing kimonos for faculty teas or promoting philanthropic activities within the Japanese American community acted to exclude other races and ethnicities.

"Girls Just Wanna Have Fun": Chi Alpha Delta and Cultural Citizenship

> If each one of us during this coming year were to go out of our way to make one or two meaningful contacts with Americans on the basis of sympathetic understanding and mutual appreciation, we could accom-

plish much toward hastening the day when we American citizens of Japanese ancestry shall be recognized as such.

—Masao Satow, *The Courier*, New Year's Day 1934

As the Issei, the immigrant generation, had failed to prevent the passage of the Immigration Act of 1924 that targeted the Japanese, the second generation shouldered the burden of civil rights in the United States.[71] As exemplified by newspapers, correspondence, club activities, and cultural events, how to best reconcile their American citizenship with their racial legacy obsessed the Nisei. Armed with the desire to claim a place in the American nation, the women of Chi Alpha Delta used sorority membership to shape the parameters of their twentieth-century American cultural citizenship. Although the women who joined Chi Alpha Delta did not necessarily intend their membership to be political in the traditional sense of the word, when faced with segregated cultural venues such as youth organizations, movie theaters, and swimming pools, many became inadvertent agitators for racial equality. Stemming from marginalized populations, acts of cultural citizenship encompassed practices ranging from learning how to host a "proper" sorority tea to exhibiting ethnic pride by dressing in kimonos in an attempt to include Japanese heritage as part of the American historical legacy. Yet attempts to foster "meaningful contacts with Americans on the basis of sympathetic understanding and mutual appreciation" by dressing in kimonos for a faculty tea were fraught with possible orientalist interpretations. As the tragedy of the World War II internment of Japanese Americans shows, the general American public refused to acknowledge that the first and second generations of Japanese Americans were genuine American citizens and instead believed them to be unassimilable aliens.

In the pre–World War II era, the women of Chi Alpha Delta were the most significant nonwhite group to flourish on UCLA's campus. In terms of performing cultural citizenship for a UCLA audience, Chi Alpha Delta bore the brunt of racialized sorority representation. Before 1941, Chi Alpha Delta was the only nonwhite sorority to appear continually in the yearbook and in other campus publications. Until World War II prompted Los Angeles' African American population growth and economic improvement, black fraternities and sororities did not have prominence or persistence in the UCLA yearbook or on the list of undergraduate clubs.[72] No African American sorority published pictures of the active members in the yearbook until after World War II.[73] Though there does not seem to be any evidence of Native American or Chicana sororities, members of Chi Alpha Delta mentioned that they knew of one Jewish sorority that had formed at UCLA in the late 1920s. When establishing their chapter at UCLA, the Chis understood that they were the only nonwhite Greek organization on the new campus.[74]

Chi Alpha Delta's longevity in comparison to the male Asian American groups spoke to women's special need for persisting, officially recognized all-female groups. While men at the time had sports, student government, and other organizations in which to develop a sense of self and group affiliation, for women, sororities were the main organization. At UCLA the Nisei Bruin Club, a club of young second-generation Japanese American men, was loosely and informally organized and had neither the same status as an official fraternity nor a yearbook page, nor a listing in the Frosh Bible. In fact, though a picture of the all-male Nisei Bruin Club appeared in the 1930s Chi Alpha Delta photo collection, the informational paragraph for the club in the 1956 yearbook stated that it was a coeducational club that had been founded in 1949.[75] Similar patterns of nonpersistence occurred in other male Asian American groups.[76] In 1925 only, the Filipino Bruin Club tantalizingly submitted a UCLA yearbook picture of six of its members.[77] At UCLA, there was no discernable Chinese students club in the pre–World War II era. At the University of California–Berkeley, the Chinese American sorority Sigma Omicron Pi was founded in 1930 and exists today.[78] At both institutions, male Asian American fraternities did not organize until the late 1950s. Thus, on their respective campuses, Asian American sororities bore the burden and privilege of being the visible Asian American organizations.

Within the parameters of sororal affiliation, practices such as fashion and dating elucidate the imperatives of cultural citizenship. The wide array of social activities provided the women of Chi Alpha Delta appealing ways to explore and play with the formation of racialized middle-class femininity. For the purposes of pinpointing the significance of the practices, this segment is organized into cultural citizenship as (1) performing modern mainstream American culture, (2) hybridity, and (3) demonstrating ethnic pride to those outside of the Japanese American community. Although these trajectories are separated for clarity's sake, they are not mutually exclusive; all involve some degree of hybridity between ethnic and American cultures. Within that overall rubric, they are grouped according to the dominant cultural tendency.

Performing Modern Mainstream American Culture

Cultural citizenship through performing modern mainstream culture had special salience for the members of Chi Alpha Delta. As the growth of leisure time and gendered consumer culture exploded in the middle of the twentieth century, cultural practices were changing for all Americans.[79] The reconceptualization of time due to industrial production and the creation of leisure time allowed for new practices such as dance halls and saloons to arise. Furthermore, the advent of mass culture in the twentieth century through motion pictures, consolidation of advertising, radio, gramophone, cosmetics, and department stores altered the landscape of American life.[80] These changes had particular effects on women of color. As historian Vicki Ruiz has found, Chicana women deployed cultural coalescence—pick, borrow, retain—to create distinctive cultural forms.[81]

The women of Chi Alpha Delta had the opportunity to intervene in the newly emerging cultural practices wrought by all of these changes. For Japanese American women, three historical factors collided that made modern American culture particularly enticing. First, participating in mainstream leisure allowed racial minorities possible avenues of mitigating or overcoming racism and segregation.[82] Second, as daughters of immigrants, the members did not benefit from mothers who could guide them through the process of being young collegiate women, and as many historians have shown, daughters of immigrants have had to shoulder the complex burden of cultural representation.[83] Third, given that the right to become an American citizen through naturalization was denied exclusively to Asian immigrants, it is no wonder that their daughters sought to distance themselves culturally from immigrant non-American status. Furthermore, Japanese American leaders looked to the Nisei generation to "defuse anti-Japanese tension."[84]

To prove their fitness as American citizens, the women of Chi Alpha Delta were eager to display their active citizenship to the UCLA campus. The 1941 yearbook photo accompanying the headshots showed some Chi Alpha Delta members sitting in a group, reading and laughing over the daily campus newspaper. The caption stated: "Well informed on most campus affairs, the Chi Alpha Delts keep up with the march of events by perusing the Daily Bruin."[85] Thus, to the rest of the campus, the women showed their mainstream participation in university life. As Isamu Masuda, winner of the 1938 Japanese American Citizens' League's oratorical contest explained, such examples of active citizenship would prove that "we are beneficial to America's social and economic welfare."[86]

The women of Chi Alpha Delta demonstrated cultural citizenship in other visible ways. For example, when they honored four new pledges, the Chis planned a "chicken dinner served in novel southern style." Likewise, in 1930 they organized a fundraiser carnival called Chi Whoopee, with the money benefiting the newly formed organization. During the first part of the evening, they promoted a carnival with booths. In the second part, wearing organdie gowns that distinguished them from all other Japanese American women, they staged fox-trot and waltz contests with music by the Wanderers. Some members also performed a tap dance.[87] Apparently the event drew "one of the biggest crowds to attend an event," speaking to the popularity of the offerings and the Chi Alpha Deltas.

The alumnae organization also participated in events that marked their participation in mainstream modern American culture. Events included wienie bakes, bridge, tennis, badminton, linen showers, and stork showers. On December 18, 1938, for example, for dinner they served each other rolls, meatloaf, potato chips, pickles, cake, and macaroni salad. Nisei daughters, in fact, introduced their immigrant parents to American-style meals.[88] Yet, belying the notion that sororities were merely founded for "fun," members discussed whether or not it was appropriate to announce marital engagements and celebrate them during meetings.

Rush recruitment events were some of the most effective ways that the women of Chi Alpha Delta learned appropriate American social practices. Since their immigrant mothers were not necessarily well versed in American social norms, the sorors of Chi Alpha Delta turned to collegiate culture and each other for initiation. For sorority women of all races and religions, the recruitment process helped them gain crucial skills in middle- and upper-class hosting. Women who were wives of prominent businessmen or politicians would find this knowledge particularly helpful. It would also be useful for women in professional settings, where they would have to interact with clients and bosses. These skills had particular salience for women who would not have learned them at home because of working-class and/or immigrant backgrounds. In addition, since prestigious European American clubs such as the Junior League were not open to racial and religious minority membership, same-race and religious clubs at colleges and universities were important socializers into middle- and upper-class activities that served to demarcate those who knew class-appropriate behaviors and those who did not, and hence who was a "true" member of the class.

As an open membership group, Chi Alpha Deltas' need to attract new members put some of the charm burden on them, whereas "exclusive" sororities placed the onus of social fitness on prospective members. The members of Chi Alpha Delta held "rush teas" to attract new sorors. They served refreshments such as pastries and cake and greeted unfamiliar women while making them feel at home with friendly conversation. The women who were rushing would have to meet the sorors and express their personalities through conversation while accepting refreshments and dressing appropriately for each event.

In case the sorors or prospective members needed guidance in what to wear, they had ample venues to observe appropriate fashions. The greater Los Angeles Japanese American community showed analogous preoccupation with correct contemporary clothing. For example, the annual Nisei Week festival typically held a fashion parade that showcased Nisei designers. Supported by the leading Japanese American civil rights group, the Japanese American Citizen's League, Nisei Week is the Los Angeles Japanese American community's annual celebration named in honor of the American-born generations.[89] As the Nisei Week queen personified the community's ideal young Japanese American woman, members of Chi Alpha Delta often ran for the title. For example, one such candidate, Masa Fujioka, boasted the following credentials: "a member of Hollywood Queen Esthers, Chi Alpha Delta, and Keisen Gakuyukai."[90] Thus members of Chi Alpha Delta who participated in the queen contest could take their knowledge of fashion and appearance to the sorority and vice versa.

In honor of the first Nisei Week in 1934, the front page of the *Rafu Shimpo* exhibited three dresses modeled in the fashion show. Note the Hollywood romance plotline of one of the following captions: "When the boy friend whisks you away from the beach party to ballroom, this informal evening gown in pink celanese organdie gives the serene, warm atmosphere of autumn days. The salmon pink shade blends majestically with suntan complexion so stylish at this time of the year."[91] Wearing this creation, a Nisei woman could be a star in her own American production in ways that *Look* magazine would never have allowed. It is interesting to note that the fashion designers and the women of Chi Alpha Delta concurred that organdie was the most suitable material for informal evening dance (Chi Whoopee) dresses.

Another newspaper article signaled that Nisei women echoed Chi Alpha Deltas' interest in appropriate fashion. As the headline, "Styles on Parade at Smart Show," advertising the Nisei Week fashion parade, claimed, a "smart" woman—in both the intelligent and chic senses of the word—paid attention to fashion. The organizers expected hundreds of Nisei to attend the show that had "[e]verything that's correct for morning, noon, and night . . . climaxed by a beautiful mock wedding." The use of the word *correct* emphasized anxiety about propriety. The show featured not just morning and evening wear but fashions for "Late Morning Wear," "Spectators [of sporting events]," and "Informal Evening." Though the fashion show attendees would not realistically have different items of clothing for each occasion, the parade did instill the knowledge that time of day and type of event proscribed certain clothing choices. This type of event-specific knowledge would assist both prospective and active members of Chi Alpha Delta in picking the perfect outfit for occasions ranging from a rush dinner to a formal fundraising dance.

The Chi Alpha Deltas were not unusual in their function as an organization that could initiate members into the dress and manners of bourgeois behavior. Another group invested in American cultural citizenship practices, Jewish Americans, found sorority behaviors of the utmost importance. Inaugurated in 1938, Joan Loewy Cohen's "Greek P's and Q's" column covered topics such as who poured the tea at formal functions, guest corsages, appropriate skirt length, and creating refreshments in the sorority colors.[92] Through such mastery of upper-class skills through sorority events, members of ethnic sororities could display their social fitness to each other, to WASP women such as faculty advisers, and to the larger campus community. Upper-class behavioral conventions draw from European American culture, so having the skills to display those behaviors allowed women considered to be immigrant non-Americans to transcend that status.

Like rush events, fashion signaled modern middle-class femininity that was a break from the cultural iconography of their parents' generation. In Chi Alpha Delta rush photographs, the young aspiring sorority members exhibit perfect mainstream American cultural citizenship by wearing gloves and hats and the latest in hair, clothing, and shoes.[93] For the rush events, they dressed in their fashionable best.[94] One distinction that becomes clear from photographs rather than from written documents is the relative class position of the women in Chi Alpha Delta. In one 1931 rush photograph taken in front of Bruin House, two of the young ladies wore

Chi Alpha Delta Rush. *(University Archives, UCLA).*

fur coats, and their dresses and hairstyles displayed the height of American fashion.[95] Taken during the early years of the Great Depression, this photograph demonstrates the women's elite status.[96] The coats were not just remnants of better days. Their dresses, hats, gloves, and shoes, all of which looked new, signaled that someone close to them had money. The clothes were signs of mainstream American, not Japanese, culture, and second-generation, not immigrant, identity.

Within the sororities, dress codes carried notions of propriety, purity, and status that echoed female dress codes in other rituals, such as marriage. As these were not the practices of their immigrant mothers, they would originate from mainstream American society. In Chi Alpha Delta, as in most sororities, to differentiate the noninitiated from the members, there would be color distinctions reminiscent of bridal conventions. For example, in March 1936 the sorors asked the pledges to dress only in white gowns, to denote their pure, virginal, uninitiated status and to subsume their individuality to the group.[97] The active members wore black or darker colors to show their senior status.

An act as seemingly innocuous as dating shows how racial segregation and being the daughters of immigrants affected the women of Chi Alpha Delta. Operating on the assumption of heterosexuality, sororities provided members with organized socials with "approved" male groups.[98] Sorority control over the courtship and marriage process ensured nuptials that would maintain class, ethnic, and community distinctions. In an article published in a UCLA campus publication, sociologist John Finley Scott argued that the institution of sororities "can ward off the wrong kind of men. It can facilitate moving-up for middle status girls. It can solve the Brahmin problem—the difficulty of proper marriage that afflicts high status girls."[99] Scott points out that sororities "are different from fraternities because marriage is a more important determinant of social position for women than for men in American society and because standards of conduct associated with marriage correspondingly bear stronger sanctions for women than for men."[100] Yet being Japanese American added layers of complexity.

For women of color, including the women of Chi Alpha Delta, the term *approved* had special salience that underscored the racialized nature of dating practices. In the South and in the West, antimiscegenation laws forbade white–people of color marriages. In the American West, laws were explicitly written to prohibit the legal recognition of Asian-white marriages.[101] Thus a sorority like Chi Alpha Delta provided Japanese American women with the means to date within the parameters of a racially stratified society. In addition, community and family pressured these women to marry within their ethnicity. Since family networks provided them with only a small pool of eligible young men, a sorority (and those four hundred other Nisei clubs) extended their networks.

Since many recreational facilities were segregated before the war and did not admit people of color, the location of events shows the geography of racial segregation. Many of the Chi Alpha Delta socials were held at the International Institute on Boyle Avenue in Boyle Heights. Then a Jewish American and Japanese American enclave, and today predominantly a Latino area, Boyle Heights, about twenty miles east of UCLA, was an ethnically "diverse" part of Los Angeles. Events were also held at the downtown "Y" or in a church social hall.

The automobile encouraged regional and statewide group "dating" parties and further allows us to trace the recreational geography of segregation. By the 1920s, Los Angeles was the most automobile-oriented city in the world, and Japanese American students used the automobile to mitigate recreation segregation and to increase their ability to claim spaces of their own.[102] Frances Kitagawa extended her pool of dating candidates by seeing a Pasadena "fella" who lived thirty miles away from the campus. The Chi Alpha Deltas acted as regional hostesses, for they held a Barnyard

Frolic and invited all the Japanese organizations in the Southern California to attend, as well as sending complimentary tickets to the newspapers *Rafu Shimpo* and *Kashu Mainichi*. The UCLA versus UC–Berkeley football games were important events, and when the UC–Berkeley contingent drove down to Los Angeles, the Chis hosted the Berkeley Japanese American students for the football game and arranged social activities for them.

To participate in contemporary American dating practices while circumventing ugly questions of miscegenation, Chi Alpha Delta women invited to their mixers educated Asian American men who could be potential husbands. Chi Alpha Delta offered group events to facilitate meeting men outside one's immediate circle and family connections. Because the University of Southern California (USC) had a more established graduate school than UCLA, the young Japanese American women would frequently date young men from USC's Nisei Trojan Club. Unlike many who attended UCLA, the Chi Alpha Deltas did not consider USC to be UCLA's bitter foe in the war for LA's university crown but rather believed its students of Asian descent to be allies. In fact, Frances Kitagawa could not recollect "going out" with more than one or two UCLA men and remembered numerous events with men from USC.

Dating has been a way that American-born women broke with their immigrant parents' customs. As historian Valerie Matsumoto has argued, "In contrast to the Issei women, they [the Nisei] expected their marital relations to be based on romantic attraction and individual choices—the hallmarks of mainstream ideals—as well as duty."[103] Hence a sorority like Chi Alpha Delta would equip its members with the tools to make individual dating choices by providing the "lessons" on suitable locations for dates, what to wear on any particular occasion, as well as the means to meet future dates. These lessons were especially useful because the women's Issei mothers had had arranged marriages and usually could not impart dating expertise. Older sorors were mentors who guided their mentees through the dating process and arranged blind dates for those without boyfriends. For example, Frances Kitagawa recollected how she did not have a companion for her first formal initiation and dance and that her soror Doris found her the aforementioned "Pasadena fella, a real nice guy." Kitagawa professed that at the beginning, she did not know any eligible dates.[104]

Like their African American club-women counterparts, the women of Chi Alpha Delta were simultaneously conservative on class and gender issues and radical on race. For example, in adopting middle-class European

American values such as sexual purity, temperance, and piety, the women's convention of the black Baptist church challenged racism.[105] Like African American club women, the women of Chi Alpha Delta promoted distinctly middle-class cultural behaviors generated from middle- and upper-class European Americans precisely so that they would be distinguishable from working-class and immigrant women. Though both African American women and Japanese American women had to fight racism in order to assert middle-class femininity, the key difference between the groups is that while both African American and Japanese American women wished to claim respectability, Japanese American women additionally needed to affirm American cultural citizenship.

Hybridity

Though at times Chi Alpha Delta sorors showed "all-American" cultural behaviors, to a great degree their behaviors were hybrid entities that exhibited both American and ethnic specific traits. These cultural acts call attention to the instability of hegemonic categories and practices by making visible the ways in which law, racialization, and gendering work to prohibit Asian Americans from gaining full cultural and legal citizenship. Indeed, hybridity is key to cultural citizenship because it not only inscribes alternative histories onto mainstream ones, it shifts mainstream histories. Thus hybrid cultural forms show not only ethnic pride but avenues through which the women of Chi Alpha Delta resisted second-class citizen status.

In form and name, most Chi Alpha Delta social events hybridized European American collegiate culture. This hybridity is key to cultural citizenship because it demonstrates how cultural practices are not assimilation but events that rework racial categories. One prime example is that of Chi Whoopee. This event was, in all likelihood, inspired by the 1930 Busby Berkeley musical film *Whoopee!* Based on a 1927 Broadway show, the film featured the comic ties between Jewish Americans and Native Americans, and its star, Jewish American Eddie Cantor, performed in blackface. In fact, it has been argued that, unlike other films such as *Old San Francisco* (1927), *Whoopee!* supported Americanizing ethnic self-assertion.[106] Thus one can see its appeal as a program theme for the women of Chi Alpha Delta. One could argue that at Chi Whoopee, since they wore organdie dresses, participated in hop and waltz contests, and requested "The Kiss

Waltz," they appeared all-American. Yet, during early part of the evening, they also held a Japanese play performance. In addition, before the dance they savored dinner at a Chinese restaurant, Sam Hoo Low. (As both Jewish Americans and Japanese Americans have noted, many elite European American restaurants did not welcome customers marked racially and ethnically, but Chinese establishments were both hospitable and relatively inexpensive.) Other markers of hybridity show up in the Chis activities. For example, they staged an annual choral with a Hawaiian theme that marked the historical traces of Japanese plantation labor in Hawaii.[107] In addition, they hosted a Kabuki theater party with sukiyaki for dinner.

The women of Chi Alpha Delta manifested fascinating displays of hybridity. For example, for the all-American Thanksgiving holiday, they raised money to donate to the Buddhist *shoien* temple. The sorors marked the American custom of giving thanks once a year and transformed it into the Japanese American context. They reracialized a practice that originated from European Americans in the Northeast, intent on giving Christian thanks for surviving so that they could continue to claim lands belonging to indigenous peoples, and they resignified it as marking their debts to Buddhist culture.

Such religious hybridity was part of Japanese American community life. Particular religious affiliations were not important for admittance into Chi Alpha Delta (or other Nisei clubs) as they were for joining predominantly Protestant European American ones. For example, within the mainstream Greek system, secret rituals, such as those performed when pledges become members, creeds, and songs, all have traceable Christian overtones.[108] Several Chi Alpha Delta members, such as Frances Wakamatsu Kitagawa and Mary Paik, did community service with Christian organizations such as the YWCA and the University Religious Council.[109] However, though many of the sorors were Christian, significant portions of the Japanese American community as well as of Chi Alpha Delta membership were Buddhist. For the Japanese Americans, these religious distinctions were not completely polarized but were hybridized. The Buddhist temple in Los Angeles syncretically had taken on a number of Christian features in nomenclature—temples were frequently called churches—and celebrations and services were held on Sundays. Since many members of Chi Alpha Delta were Buddhist, some of the sorority's activities would take place in Buddhist temple community rooms.[110]

What is remarkable about the women of Chi Alpha Delta is that in the pre–World War II years, they dated interethnically. Breaking with the

Girls Just Wanna Have Fun. *(University Archives, UCLA).*

practices not only of other Japanese Americans but of mainstream society, they planned excursions with men outside their ethnic group: Chinese American male graduate students at USC. In fact, Frances Kitagawa remembered dancing with a young man who later became an important general in Chiang Kai-shek's Chinese Nationalist Army![111] Given that China and Japan were at war, dating in the American context did not have the same political resonance. However, though they dated Chinese American men, in the 1930s few married them, for the ethos of racial solidarity mandated intraethnic marriages.[112] In the post–World War II era, increasing numbers of Japanese American women married non-Japanese Americans, predominantly members of other Asian-ethnic groups and whites.

Another way that the women of Chi Alpha Delta transformed European American dating practices into their own was by eschewing individual dates in favor of group social events. The Chi Alpha Deltas' group socializing underscored their community orientation by providing an alternative to individualistic dating practices. During the twentieth century, courtship shifted from Victorian, female-controlled calling centered in the family parlor to male-initiated dating outside the home.[113] For mainstream American youth (European American with middle-class cultural markers), the interwar rating-dating system marked success by the number of one-on-one dates. Matching capitalistic and liberal imperatives of the time, one wanted numerous individual dates rather than going steady or socializing in groups. In contrast, the women of Chi Alpha Delta held inclusive group activities that included trips to the YWCA-owned Eliza Cottage in Hermosa Beach and ski trips. They hosted skating parties with the Bruin Club as well as co-ed card parties. Similarly, historian Judy Yung has found that in the 1930s, Chinese Americans seldom went on individual dates but went on group outings such as hikes, hayrides, dances, and athletic programs.[114] Thus, contrary to elite European American practices, community participation and socializing were emphasized over individuality and popularity. Group events (Frances Kitagawa's "Pasadena fella" being an exception rather than the rule) sidestepped questions of popularity and heterosexual pairing off by providing democratic recreational opportunities for all.

Ethnic Pride

Ethnic-pride cultural activities also made visible the ways in which the law, racialization, and gendering worked to prohibit Asian Americans from gaining full cultural and legal citizenship. On the one hand, displaying ethnic pride by, for instance, dressing in kimonos for public events signaled the Japanese American communities' desire to expand the definition of American to include Asian cultural references. On the other hand, in an age restricted by immigration, naturalization, and segregation, displaying ethnic pride was fraught with danger. During a xenophobic era, many Americans mistook displays of ethnic pride as markers of foreign allegiance. Thus, although meanings of cultural symbols such as kimonos were mutable, those meanings were circumscribed by historical events.

The members of Chi Alpha Delta attempted to shift the parameters of American cultural citizenship to include Japanese culture. They would play on both orientalist audience expectations and ethnic pride by appearing "Japanese" in official functions. Starting in 1937, for the faculty teas with European American advisers the active members would dress in kimonos and serve Japanese tea. This act of ethnic pride was so symbolically significant that photographs of the tea represented Chi Alpha Delta in that year's yearbook.

This desire for the larger American public to recognize their Japanese ancestry also happened at Nisei Week. Even though Nisei Week showcased "smart" fashion shows that demonstrated the correct fashions for every conceivable event, the queen and her court wore kimonos when acting as representatives of Little Tokyo. Clad in kimonos, the queen and her court would present invitations to Los Angeles merchants and the mayor's office. What is particularly interesting is that the young women themselves generally did not know how to wear the kimono, and experts were hired to teach the young women how properly to attire themselves and how to walk while wearing one. Thus young Japanese American women had to be taught how to bear the markers of supposed cultural authenticity.[115]

An action as seemingly trivial as choosing to dress in kimonos to serve tea to UCLA faculty members or to publicize Nisei Week can be interpreted as a sign of orientalness, a sign of exoticism, a sign of honoring ancestral culture, a means of educating the general public, a means of the women educating themselves, a way to claim class and cultural status, a way to play into the vogue for japonaiserie, a sign of femininity, and a way for these women to distinguish themselves from all other Asian ethnicities. Yet choosing to wear kimonos should not be seen as antithetical to performing American cultural citizenship but instead as an attempt to display both Japanese and American traits: kimonos with Max Factor red lipstick and permanent-waved hair.

Yet Japanese Americans were not ignorant of the dangers involved in displaying ethnic pride. An editorial in the local newspaper *Rafu Shimpo* explained its viewpoint on the importance of Japanese versus American dress. Significantly, this editorial was placed next to the biographies and pictures of 1941's ten Nisei Week queen finalists, all of whom wore American clothing. The controversy arose that year because of a picnic that had been held at Elysian Park in Los Angeles. There was nothing wrong with the picnic itself; rather, as the editorial explained, "[a] photograph of two young nisei girls, clad in Japanese kimonos, was published in the *L.A. Examiner*. The caption said a 'patriotic' speech was made at the picnic."[116] The word *patriotic* was not clearly defined as being American patriotism. Thus, suspecting that Americans might see the kimonos as proof of allegiance to Japan, "the editors of the *Rafu Shimpo* went out to determine what the average American reaction to the photo & caption was."[117] After the investigation, the editors found that "[t]he[ir] worst fears were confirmed. . . . The typical belief was held that Japanese picnickers had gathered to reaffirm their patriotism to Japan."[118] Especially given the linkage of kimonos and Japan, such a representation would signal to mainstream American communities that Japanese Americans were Japanese, not Americans. Hybrid cultural citizenship was understood differently depending on mainstream or ethnic community context.

In the context of 1941, the eve of American participation in World War II, such supposedly Japanese patriotism was suspect. In addition, Japanese imperial military ventures in Asia alarmed many, especially as the United States sided with China. The Japanese American editorial writer worried, "But at a time when the nisei are seeking to emphasize the points in common they have with their fellow Americans, the kimono only sets off their differences."[119] Displaying eerie prescience of the consequences of the larger society's inability to distinguish between Japanese Americans and Japanese, the editorial warned, "We hope that the practice of parading our kimono-clad girls will be eased off gracefully, before some unfortunate public incident rudely shocks some of us out of our complacency." Thus the editorial concluded, "Kimonos don't fit the times. Your smartly-tailored dresses do."[120] Though smartly tailored dresses would not have saved Japanese Americans from internment, such statements show awareness of the high stakes of cultural appearance in the political arena.

Culture was a key arena and testing ground for race, loyalty, and citizenship. Given their fears of appearing foreign, the organizers of the 1941 Nisei Week festival foregrounded the community's American allegiances. According to the 1941 *Nisei Week Festival Booklet,* the decorations emphasized U.S. patriotism. For all events, the American flag was prominently displayed. The queen's float, which was driven through the streets of Los Angeles, was decorated with a statue of liberty and a sign proclaiming "America is our home."[121] Such displays of American patriotism demonstrated that many Japanese Americans believed that appropriate cultural representation was vital. However, the internment of Japanese Americans in 1942 showed that these cultural displays of Americanism failed to establish them as patriotic citizens.[122]

Conclusion

Despite the Chi Alpha Delta's efforts to appear American through their sorority activities, December 7, 1941, forever changed the lives of Japanese

Americans. As has been extensively documented, Japanese American internment during World War II made a travesty of American civil rights. Internment signaled that the U.S. government and society did not treat Japanese Americans as full citizens with the rights of legal due process.

Despite cultural practices that showed Americanized identity such as dress, food, use of the English language, and participation in American leisure pursuits, Japanese American claims to Americanness were brushed aside. Without due process, the U.S. military incarcerated more than 110,000 people of Japanese descent, including approximately 2,500 college students. All in all, internment forced 244 Japanese American students to leave UCLA, including Chi Alpha Delta president Aki Hirashiki Yamazaki, who was sixteen credits and one term short of earning her bachelor of arts degree.[123] The general American public refused to acknowledge that the first and second generations of Japanese Americans were genuine American citizens and instead believed them to be unassimilable aliens.

Although internment forced the sorority to disband, Chi Alpha Delta enjoyed a rapid postwar reestablishment and growth in membership. After the war, public Japanese dress "performances" would not be repeated until the late 1950s with the resurgence of ethnic pride. Though the Chi Alpha Deltas were at the forefront of creating American cultural citizenship through education and fashion, such claims still have not been incorporated into American society. Their story continues in chapter 3.

The next chapter scrutinizes the production of Asian American public culture in a different 1930s forum: Hollywood and the most successful Asian American motion picture star of all time, the Chinese American actress Anna May Wong. Like the Chi Alpha Deltas, Wong had to operate within the parameters of a European American power structure. Wong's success, like the social lives of the sorority women, depended on her ability to portray race and gender in particular ways.

2

"I Protest"

*Anna May Wong and
the Performance of Modernity*

In the 1939 movie *King of Chinatown,* one first glimpses Chinese American actress Anna May Wong putting down her surgical implements, taking off her cap and mask after a successful emergency room operation.[1] *King of Chinatown* underscores the professional competence of Wong's character, Dr. Mary Ling, for immediately after the surgery the Bay Area hospital director offers her the position of resident surgeon. In melodious tones tinged with an upper-class British accent, Wong firmly but politely declines the prestigious appointment because she wishes to raise money to bring medical supplies to China to combat the Japanese invasion. Flashing her trademark smile, Wong gracefully strides across the room, Edith Head–designed skirt and blouse highlighting her all-American modern professionalism.

King of Chinatown not only pioneered Chinese American women's film roles; it also examined European American preconceptions about Chinese food and culture. After the surgery, Wong returns home, where her father has supper waiting for her and her guests—a European American nurse and the nurse's boyfriend. While walking toward the dinner table, the nurse's boyfriend rubs his hands together and says, "Lead me to that chop suey!" Mr. Ling replies, "Not many in China know of your great American dish, chop suey! Rice is our national dish." They then dine on "real" Chinese food. While at the dinner table, the nurse's boyfriend chokes on the Chinese beverage offered as a toast, and this time Wong crisply informs him that drinking the unfamiliar alcohol requires "an acquired taste." Based on a real-life Chinese American woman, Dr. Margaret Chung, Wong's role represents a modern American woman who is proud of her Chinese heritage.[2]

Anna May Wong (1905–1961) was the major Asian American actress of the twentieth century. In the late 1930s she starred in three Paramount Studio films, *King of Chinatown, Daughter of Shanghai,* and *Island of Lost Men*—that cast her in breakthrough roles as American professional women.[3] Adding to her national fame, during these years Wong graced the cover of *Look*. Roughly the equivalent of today's *People* magazine, the March 1938 issue comprised a two-page pictorial subtitled "The World's Most Beautiful Chinese Girl," including the famous photograph of Wong flanked by German actresses Marlene Dietrich and Leni Riefenstahl. Although the sensationalized cover depicted Wong brandishing a dagger over her bosom, the inside of the magazine showed a more complex range of her work and life. Such fame and publicity was the result of decades-long struggles to gain leverage in her movie career. It would not be until 1958 that another Asian American motion-picture actress, France Nuyen, adorned the cover of a nationally circulating popular American magazine.[4] With the cover of *Look* magazine as well as numerous articles and features on her that appeared throughout her career, Wong secured the attention not only of her Chinese American community but also of the general American public.

This chapter investigates the historical circumstances that allowed Anna May Wong to portray a Chinese American surgeon and to grace the cover of a national magazine. Since the mid-1970s, the dominant thrust amid the scant scholarship on Wong has focused on her as an exploited actress who only played "foreign" or "negative" stereotypical roles. Instead of investigating good and bad stereotypes in Wong's film roles, I will trace both her press coverage and her cinematic performances of gender and race within the discourses of American modernity.[5]

In the atmosphere of scientific racism that prevailed into the early twentieth century, proving modernity was key to cultural citizenship. According to one of scientific racism's many strands, there was a hierarchy of races and racial traits that could be charted on a linear continuum: savage, barbaric, civilized, and enlightened. This was not just an aesthetic exercise but one that had real political consequences. Indeed, placing indigenous peoples such as those from Africa or the Philippines on the bottom of the hierarchy justified slavery and colonialism. For Asians in particular, scientific racism grafted onto older strains of orientalism, rendering Asians the objects of study and fascination. U.S. colonialism in the Philippines, the Pacific Islands, and Shanghai concessions ensured continuing American material interests in Asia. As cultural citizenship is racial minorities' claiming of full belonging into the nation-state, Anna May Wong's Chinese American films and iconography intervened in all the above in U.S. culture.[6]

Visual regimes of race and gender intersected in the early twentieth century to produce the space for an Anna May Wong. The importance of Wong's Chinese American film roles and the cover of *Look* magazine was threefold. First, through her portrayal of beauty and modern fashion, as exemplified in her films and press, Wong proved that Asians are human. Proving humanity was the essential step in establishing civilized status within scientific racism. Once established, that civilized status laid the foundation for legal rights, civil rights, and thus cultural citizenship's feeling of belonging to the American nation-state. Although it is debatable whether acquiring "civilized" traits such as European manners, gestures, speech patterns, and upper-class social status are acts of resistance per se (and in a world overdetermined by capitalism, what constitutes "true" resistance?), nonetheless they signal the possibility of access to tools of power.[7]

Anna May Wong was under double scrutiny, for under modern regimes, as gender hyperaccentuates race, women have symbolically represented culture and nation. Thus a leading litmus test for the social fitness of immigrants and third world nations has been the cultural status of their women. Parallel to scientific racism, this paradigm posits a linear model of development that situates first world (white) imperial women as the modern referent and measures all others accordingly, with the greater differences signifying "backwardness" and thus greater distance from modernity. In addition, in an age of cinematic structuring of visuality, women have had a special relationship to visuality as objects of the gaze. In the power of looking relations, men look at women, women look at women, and women see themselves being looked at. Thus women bearing markers of race/ethnicity were under double visual scrutiny.[8]

Second, Anna May Wong's Chinese American films and iconography intervened in reworking the definition of the American nation as white and placed Chinese Americans in the realm of the citizen-subject. The controlling image for Asian Americans was and still is that of perpetual foreigner-alien, and that originated with the Chinese.[9] Representations of China and Chinese people played key roles in the formation of American identity as white.[10] Thus, placing Asians as belonging within the American nation-state was indeed radical. After all, numerous legal and structural elements singled out Asian Americans and rendered them not just second-class citizens but unwanted ones, consigned to outside the nation-state.

Anna May Wong and her portrayals of professional Chinese Americans deserve a separate chapter because it was the Chinese who served as the primary undesired American immigrant group, and the exclusion of all other immigrant groups, Asian and otherwise, resulted from that precedent. For example, the 1882 Chinese Exclusion Act was the first American immigration act to bar a group by name.[11] Moreover, American immigration acts and laws have demonized Chinese American women in particular. The 1875 Page Law, which theoretically restricted the immigration of Chinese American male and female workers and felons, in reality curtailed the immigration only of Chinese American women. Although the 1922 Cable Act stripped all American women of their citizenship if they married Asian immigrant men (aliens ineligible for citizenship), because of skewed sex-ratio demographics and marriage patterns, it applied chiefly to Chinese American women. Given how the American national imaginary had previously placed people of Asian descent in general and Chinese American women in particular outside the nation-state, Wong's Chinese American cinema roles and *Look* cover made key ideological moves by claiming American cultural citizenship.

Third, Anna May Wong's adoption of hybrid Chinese and American iconography reworked modernity.[12] Wong's star persona on- and off-screen established a tension between a modern Western image and a "primitive" or "decadent" Chinese or Asian identity.[13] Imperialism places the "other" in primitive time, the West in modern time; thus backward peoples need the imperial help of "modern" societies.[14] To counter that formulation and to break up the temporal linearity of scientific racism's civilization continuum, Wong deployed hybridity, which is the blending of both Asian and Western cultural traits. Wong used hybridity to disrupt the binary between the civilized (West) and primitive (China) by interweaving China and the West within—and this is key—modern time. Hybridity situated in twentieth-century time rendered Wong central to the project of reworking race within modernity and continued importance in representing the visual.[15]

Movies and fashion lend themselves especially well to the study of the cultural production of modernity and gendered racial difference because their embodiment is visual and performative.[16] In other words, much of how we understand race in the twentieth century has to do with appearance. Photographs and films provide rich sources of visual and oral evidence and act as historical records of Wong's work.[17] The first part of this chapter examines the stardom Wong achieved during her European sojourn, which she secured through capitalizing on imperial Europe's fascination with the "other." This segment traces how Wong's acquisition of European manners, gestures, and speech patterns allowed her to negotiate the space of modernity in the United States. The second portion of this chapter examines Wong's Hollywood Paramount Studio "B" Chinese American movies. Since they are not widely available and have never received in-depth scholarly attention, analyzing the movies' Chinese American upper-class narratives adds a new dimension to understanding the possibilities of and limits to the performance of American cultural citizenship in the late 1930s. The third segment of the chapter focuses on Wong's hybrid reworking of modernity through fashion and the 1938 *Look* magazine cover.

Anna May Wong Establishes Her Career

Anna May Wong was born at 351 Flower Street near Los Angeles' Chinatown on January 3, 1905, as the second daughter of two American-born people of Chinese descent. Her father was a laundryman, so Wong's work as a successful actress enabled her to transcend her working-class roots. Cutting classes at Los Angeles High School in order to frequent the back lots of Hollywood movie studios, Wong began her career as an extra in the Alla Nazimova's classic *The Red Lantern* (1919).[18] She landed her first starring role in *Toll of the Sea* (1922), the earliest full-length two-tone Technicolor movie. That led to national prominence: she played the Mongol slave in the *Thief of Baghdad* (1924).[19]

Examining Anna May Wong's career is particularly fruitful because of race's centrality to motion pictures' construction of the modern American nation-state. Wong's emergence is especially noteworthy not solely because of her talent but because the racial stakes were so high. As numerous fine studies have shown, U.S. cinema was critical in not only shaping but also creating America as a modern nation. Cinema emerged at a key moment of racialized anxiety around the American nation-state. At the turn of the century, the United States had to cope not only with Asian immigration exclusion but with healing the nation after the Civil War; incorporating former Mexican lands; the place of African Americans under racial segregation legalized by the U.S. Supreme Court decision *Plessy* v. *Ferguson* (1896); the extermination or displacement onto reservations of indigenous Native Americans; and empire and conquest in the Philippines,

"Flapper" Anna May Wong.

Pacific Islands, and the Caribbean. The most infamous example of racial anxiety about the American nation-state being reworked cinematically occurred in D. W. Griffith's epic *Birth of a Nation* (1915), which reconceptualized race relations by conjuring up the specter of the black male rapist in order to justify segregation and black disfranchisement. To further complicate matters, whiteness itself was an unstable category that historically, through minstrelsy, and contemporaneously, through the motion pictures and other cultural venues, was being consolidated against all the other racialized groups. By showing that all humans have not been treated equally, race has been the central contradiction to the American ideals of democracy and freedom. American movies shaped the historical imaginary to recreate and deal with those contradictions so that the U.S. nation-state could reinvent itself and its racial origins.[20]

Anna May Wong's cinematic career emerged at a particularly significant historical juncture.[21] Early twentieth-century U.S. orientalisms created a tremendous demand for films with Asian themes and locales. Coined by scholar Edward Said, the term *orientalism* refers to Europe's long-standing fascination with the Orient, through which it used the Orient as a mirror for its own desires and ambitions. Building on that European orientalism, U.S. orientalism geographically shifted its focus from the Middle East to the eastern Pacific. The narrative of American imperialism conjoined the trope of orientalism with that of the American frontier, the deep historical national narrative marking America's difference from Europe. According to the frontier myth, American national formation was unique because class-based conflict could be mitigated by the promise of opportunity and "empty" lands in the West. As the U.S. nation-state borders reached the Pacific Ocean, historian Frederick Jackson Turner famously lamented that the United States had lost its frontier and thus its basis for class harmony. Colonizing Asia and imaginatively extending the American West into the Pacific reinstated the myth of the frontier as safety valve. The Spanish-American war of 1898, which resulted in the United States gaining colonies in the Pacific and the Philippines as well as the Caribbean, reinvigorated the promise of class mobility within the American nation-state. That came at the cost of race. In fact, in the initial 1898 battles in the Philippines, 87 percent of American generals had honed their skills in the wars against Native Americans.[22] Like that in Europe, American orientalism was fascinated with China in particular, as evidenced by the treaty ports and Shanghai concessions, thus strengthening U.S. orientalism and Anna May Wong's cinematic career.[23]

Despite shining as an extra and gaining starring parts, to Anna May Wong's chagrin, in the 1920s European American women dominated the main "positive" Hollywood Chinese roles, relegating her to the "tragic" or "evil" orientalist ones. A prime example is *Toll of the Sea* (1922), whose screenplay was created by the noted writer Frances Marion. Even though Wong was incredibly charming in *Toll of the Sea,* the film reworked one of the most orientalist of all tropes, that of Madame Butterfly. Madame Butterfly, predicated on the fixed signifier of Eastern/female and Western/male, stands in for the dynamics of Western imperialism in Asia. Wong's character, Lotus Flower, has a baby with an American ship's captain (Allen), under the illusion that they are married and he will bring her to America. However, Allen becomes engaged to a white European American woman; he takes Wong's (and his) baby away to America, and, at the end of the film, she, still in China, commits suicide. The colonial metaphors and tropes—substitute baby for laboring bodies or raw goods that the colonizers ship to the metropole and elsewhere—are rife.[24]

Anna May Wong's clothing in *Toll of the Sea* situated her as nonmodern and thus (both her and China) as a colonial subject. Throughout the movie Wong wears silk Chinese garments. However, when Captain Allen announces his first return to the United States, Wong's character, believing he will take her with him, strives to be brought to America through knowledge of appropriate fashion. Copying from her grandmother's book, Wong's character emerges in full nineteenth-century long skirts, believing her clothes are contemporary chic. The 1922 audience would have howled with laughter, knowing her character appeared fifty years out of date. To underscore that point, when Allen returns to China a second time, his European American wife, Elsie, wears modern short skirts made from softer, lighter materials. Thus her clothing suggests the undercurrent behind Wong giving up her child to Elsie and Allen; she does not know what is modern, she cannot raise a child in a modern era, and thus her son is better off with the modern white couple, to be raised in America. One could extend the metaphor to colonial relations. Colonial subjects do not understand modernity; they cannot rule themselves or their own people. Marion's plot device—that Wong confides in Elsie that the child is Allen's because women around the world unite, which sets up Allen and Elsie taking the child from Wong—rings hollow. Under regimes of slavery and colonialism, white women have gained status at the expense of women of color.[25]

Modernity factored into orientalism and was heightened by the need to manage the "yellow peril" and "Asian menace," which manifested itself in movies of the 1920s such as *Old San Francisco* and the *Fu Manchu* films. Through a strong Americanization movement, World War I set the tone for the ensuing decade's xenophobia. Thus *Old San Francisco,* in which Anna May Wong played a nameless Chinese girl, secured the American West for the European Americans and excised the Mexican American and Asian American contributions by situating them as nonmodern.[26] Genre movies such as the *Fu Manchu* series that highlighted sinister Orientals as being decadent, savage, and nonmodern worked in tandem with legal cases such as *Ozawa* and *Thind,* which situated Asians as nonwhites within the American racial landscape. Both U.S. Supreme Court decisions invoked the "common" understanding of race to rule that Asians were nonwhites, and that common understanding of race had derived in part from movies such as the *Fu Manchu* series.[27] Within this 1920s racial framework, Wong's options as an actress were limited. "Yellowface," the playing of Asian roles by white actors made up to look Asian, was prevalent throughout the twentieth century. Hollywood orientalism and yellowface in particular could conjure up and ameliorate racial anxieties if and only if actual Asian American bodies were banned.[28] Thus it was impossible for Hollywood actually to embody the Chinese or the Asian as Chinese American or Asian American; instead, it relied on yellowface.

Up to here, my narrative about Anna May Wong's career agrees with that of the current scholarship. However, here is where I depart from past historiography, because I believe that her European sojourn and her 1930s Chinese American films and iconography made significant interventions that allowed a space, albeit a small one, for Asian Americans to claim modernity. Like other racial minority performing artists such as Paul Robeson, Marian Anderson, and Sessue Hayakawa, in 1928, Wong traveled to Europe because limited Hollywood roles discouraged her.[29] Wong's sojourn in Europe paralleled that of contemporary African American performer Josephine Baker.[30] Born in 1906 in St. Louis, in the mid-1920s Baker, like Wong, went to France and Germany to further her stalled American career. Under the ethos of modernity, the racial and primitive "other" was the foil against which Europe proved its civilization.[31] At first glance, Wong and Baker presented the image of the exotic American to European audiences as ethnically "other" and sexually primitive. These are the most enduring tropes of European fascination with the "New World," ones that both Baker and Wong played on and exploited, and to which Europe continues to respond. They arrived in a Europe primed for them by interests in jazz, chinoiserie, and negritude. Pablo Picasso and Henri Matisse, for example, were just two of the European painters borrowing from African and Asian aesthetics. As Wong's and Baker's American national citizenship was frequently subsumed to essentialized racial categories, they functioned as ambiguous representatives of empire. Working in London, Berlin, and Paris during the height of imperialism, Wong and Baker represented the desired female colonial body (playing women from Singapore and Haiti) as well as the forbidden, dark sexual "other" (both depicted Arab women).[32] As they became established in their careers in the 1930s, both women became legendary for wearing sophisticated designer gowns that contradicted their sexual and "primitive" dance performances.[33]

While in Europe, Anna May Wong acquired the credentials that would allow her to enter modernity. There she gained upper-class social skills and acting polish that, upon her return to the United States, would win her a broader repertoire of starring theater and film roles. After theater critics decried her American twang, Wong invested in elocution lessons in order to master an upper-class British accent. Later, to lend distinction to her work, she invoked traces of that accent in her American movie parts. In addition, she learned French and German, utilizing her German in films such as *Pavement Butterfly* and to sing in the Viennese opera *Springtime*.[34] Working in theater, Wong garnered top billing over her co-star Laurence Olivier in *A Circle of Chalk* and headlined *On the Spot* in the United States.[35] For private acting lessons, Wong sought out theater legends such as Kate Rork and Mabel Terry Lewis.[36] Living the life of an upper-class socialite, she met the prince of Wales, and her elegance and beauty stopped Parliament when she sauntered into the visitors gallery.[37] While in Europe, numerous periodicals featured Wong, culminating in the covers of the society magazines *Tatler* and *Sketch*.[38]

Anna May Wong's 1931 return to the United States marked a turning point in her status in the American entertainment industry. The newfound privilege conferred by her European training enabled her to headline a Broadway theater production and to reenter Hollywood with more power, especially since "talkie" movies meant that her voice would be an integral part of her work. Not only did her training win her Hollywood roles, but for the next few years she would continue to travel between Europe and Hollywood, for she remained in great demand in English movies. Her British-inflected upper-class tones projected vocal authority while playing characters such as that of a surgeon in *King of Chinatown*. Her stylish mode of dress set fashion trends around the world and ensured that while on screen and stage, all eyes would be focused on her. And that newfound power aided her efforts to control her image and roles.

Many Chinese Americans remembered Anna May Wong's European sojourn as key to her later American success. *Charlie Chan* series actor Keye Luke, who at one point was cast as Wong's love interest in *Hold for Shanghai*, a movie that was to star Fred Astaire and Ginger Rogers but was never made, remembered how Wong gained fame in England and on the Continent. Los Angeles casting agent and actress Bessie Loo reminisced: "Anna May Wong was a prominent Chinese actress, but never got ahead in the U.S. before she became famous in England."[39] Loo remarked that Wong's height and appearance aided her fame.

Upon her return to the United States, Anna May Wong played upon her "Oriental" cachet and newfound fame to incorporate the modern into her acting roles. Emblematic of her long career as cultural ambassador be-tween her Chinese heritage and Western nationality, in 1930, Wong protested what she felt to be an incorrect interpretation of Asian women's proper gait. In the Broadway play *On the Spot*, directed by Lee Ephraim and written by Edgar Wallace, Wong showed her mettle by challenging the director:

> Interestingly, Miss Wong's ideas about presenting a Chinese woman di-ffered considerably from those of Lee Ephraim, who insisted her stage crossings should be made in short, hesitant steps a la Butterfly. But Anna argued her point that Chinese women did not walk in such a manner and her projection of the tragic Minn (who commits suicide) benefited from her innate knowledge.[40]

The director Ephraim confused supposedly Japanese "butterfly" walking mannerisms with putative Chinese behavior, which Wong refused to allow. Perhaps the hesitant steps referred to footbinding. Regardless, Wong strategically used her ancestry to create the protagonist she wanted to por-tray. Wong played off both her fame and the authenticity ascribed to her by the parameters of Western modernity. In fact, Wong was able to com-plicate modernity by showing the modern—walking steps—embedded in the traditional. Although past scholarship has emphasized how Wong's character's death signified her professional marginalization, what should also matter is the dignity with which her contemporary critics and audi-ences felt she invested in her portrayal of Minn.[41]

Contrasting Anna May Wong with Japanese-born actor Sessue Hayakawa shows how Wong was construed as modern and Western. Often compared to silent-movie legend Rudolph Valentino, Hayakawa's expres-sive facial gestures and smoldering sexuality ensured the success of such films as Cecil B. DeMille's *The Cheat* (1919).[42] In 1931 the fan magazine *Motion Picture* showed how Wong's and Hayakawa's cultural differences were popularly understood:

> Sessue Hayakawa smokes Japanese cigarettes, has Japanese people around him, talks with a completely bewildering Japanese accent, looks oriental, and above all thinks with the oriental attitude. "Never make plan," say Sessue with his difficult accent. "Never plan ahead." Anna May, with Western verbosity, is more explicit in expressing her philosophy.[43]

As the passage shows, the Asian American stars had divergent cultural careers in the 1930s. Even though both worked in Europe, Wong's mastery of British English proved essential to her success in sound motion-picture productions. The above comparison shows the popular belief that Wong was far more cosmopolitan, modern, and Westernized than Hayakawa. The article emphasized Wong's mastery of European languages, including the English accent, as well as her films in Europe. The article further racially differentiated them:

> She is glad to be back.
> She went away a Chinese flapper—and now many tell her that she no longer even looks Oriental.
> He [Sessue Hayakawa] has remained completely Oriental.

Hayakawa's foreign appeal served him well in the late 1910s and early 1920s but not in the 1930s. In a political climate hostile to immigrants, exemplified by the 1924 Immigration Act, it is not surprising that the *Motion Picture* article showed American-born Wong in a far more positive light than immigrant Hayakawa. The inscrutable, unintelligible male "Oriental" was not as palatable as the hybrid, cosmopolitan, Westernized female.

Demonstrating the importance of accent and national origin to claiming modernity, the contrast in the two actors' speaking voices was starkly apparent in a 1931 movie that starred both Anna May Wong and Sessue Hayakawa: *Daughter of the Dragon*. In *Daughter*, Wong's clear, lilting diction rendered all her lines intelligible, whereas Hayakawa's thick accent made him difficult to comprehend. As with many other movie actors in the talking era, Hayakawa's unacceptable voice overshadowed the memorable facial gestures that served him so well in the silent era.[44] *Daughter of the Dragon* became one of Sessue Hayakawa's last major Hollywood roles until the 1957 *Bridge over the River Kwai*.[45]

Although critics praised Wong's lovely voice, she castigated *Daughter* for its negative depictions of the Chinese. In an interview for *Film Weekly* entitled "I Protest," Wong asked:

> Why is the screen Chinese always the villain of the piece? And so crude a villain—murderous, treacherous, a snake in the grass. We are not like that. How should we be, with a civilization that is so many times older than that of the West? . . . I get so weary of it all—of the scenarist's con-

ception of Chinese character, that I told myself I was done with films for ever. You remember Fu Manchu? *Daughter of the Dragon?* So wicked.[46]

Although Wong was quickly lured back into the movies, *Daughter of the Dragon* marks her last "wicked" film role. Throughout her career, Wong not only protested what she considered to be inappropriate representations of Chinese ethnicity but did everything within her power to create her own counterinterpretations and performances.

In her attempts to perform modernity, Anna May Wong was by no means unusual among Chinese American women. For example, cabaret performer Rose Yuen Ow's life story exhibits striking parallels to Wong's. Defying San Francisco Chinatown's behavioral norms, teenaged Ow first sold tickets at a "[moving-]picture place," then passed out refreshments at San Francisco's largest cabaret, the Tait Cafe.[47] Acting on her boss's jest that if she could ballroom dance, he would place her in the show, Ow mastered the fox-trot, waltz, and cakewalk. Maneuvering her boss into making good his jest, Ow eventually ballroom-danced at the cabaret for $200 a week. Similarly, Raymond Hitchcock brought the "Chung and Rosie Moy" novelty show to New York, whereafter the Chinese American dancers continued to work the vaudeville circuit around the United States. The success of other contemporary performers, such as Dorothy Siu in the circus and the dancers in the Forbidden City USA nightclub, show audiences' interest in Chinese American performance.[48] The foreign image of the Chinese Americans drew European American audiences to the paradox of "Orientals" imitating American song and dance. In other words, it is because Chinese Americans had been racially constructed as foreign and non-American that their performance of American modernity proved so striking.

Even though Anna May Wong had worked to create herself as culturally Western through voice and dress, such traits did not ensure free migration through the exercise of her legal American citizenship. Despite her woman-of-the-world travels to Europe, she was still denied the right to cross borders at will. First, in an era that banned Chinese immigration, Wong had to file travel papers upon leaving the United States so that she could prove her citizenship.[49] Second, journeying from California to New York, Wong disembarked at the Detroit train station to chat with friends. However, when she attempted to reboard the train, Canadian immigration officials refused to let her back on, for the train passed through Canada on its way to New York. Wong was forced to spend the night in Detroit to take a train routed through the United States.[50] Like U.S. immigration laws, Canadian ones discriminated against people of Chinese descent. Thus Wong's cultural and legal citizenship did not always convince those who enforced the laws.

Despite the harrowing real-life train experience, one of Anna May Wong's most critically acclaimed roles occurred on a movie-set train. In *Shanghai Express* (1932), Wong and Marlene Dietrich have matching personas as Hui Fei and Shanghai Lily, women of ill repute traveling on the Peiping (Beijing)–Shanghai express train. The reputations of Shanghai Lily and Hui Fei are established at the beginning of the movie through the contrast to and interactions with Mrs. Haggerty, a bourgeois Victorian-moraled lady attired in a white lace blouse with cameo at her throat. Haggerty presents them with cards with the address of her "respectable" Shanghai boarding house. Dietrich asks her, "Don't you find respectable people terribly—dull?" After Haggerty professes shock, Dietrich asks her, while looking at the card, "What kind of house?" Haggerty replies, "A boarding house." Dietrich, pretending that she had previously misheard Haggerty as saying bawdy house, says, "Oh," and arches one eyebrow. Indignant, Haggerty turns to Wong and says, "I'm sure you're very respectable, madam." Wong replies in her best upper-class British accent: "I must confess I don't quite know the standard of respectability that you demand in your boarding house, Mrs. Haggerty." Quivering with outrage, Mrs. Haggerty leaves them together in their train compartment.[51] Wong's and Dietrich's costumes emphasize their characters' symmetry: Wong in light colors with dark straight hair, Dietrich in dark dresses with light fluffy hair. Clothing, hair, and makeup visually accent their characters' analogous dangerous sexuality.

Shanghai Express received critical approval. According to many, Wong's role upstaged Dietrich's, and some claimed that, had there been an Academy Award for best supporting actress in 1932, Wong would have been nominated.[52] In fact, a friend of Dietrich viewed the movie with her and, when Dietrich complained about her own acting, the friend mentioned the magnificence of Wong's performance, which apparently caused a distinct chill in the air.[53] Considered to be one of director Josef von Sternberg's finest efforts, the movie earned him a nomination for an Academy Award.

During the 1930s, three historical shifts laid the groundwork for Anna May Wong's Chinese American roles by changing the way that "Orientals" were portrayed on the screen. The *New York Times* on April 14, 1930, castigated Sax Rohmer's novel turned movie *The Mysterious Dr. Fu Manchu* for its unreal and overly dramatic "mysterious messages, daggers bathed in blood, opiate druggings, and much gun play."[54] Chinese Americans protested the representation of themselves as Fu Manchus.[55] As a result of such condemnations, liberal pressure drove evil Orientals such as Fu Manchu from the screen.[56]

Second, the 1930s gains in "positive" portrayals in racialized cinema were paradoxically assisted by the 1934 Hays Code, which not only prohibited interracial sexual relations but also forbade ethnic typecasting.[57] Chinese American actors noticed the difference that the Hays Code made in their movie parts. According to oral history interviews, Chinese American actors of the era remembered their roles improving in the mid-1930s. Keye Luke, who played Charlie Chan's number-one son, reminisced about his movie career and found that his roles changed in the mid-1930s: "It seems I was always cast as a good guy and only 2 or 3 Oriental parts as nasty since 1934."[58] Even though he was not explicitly asked about the Hays Code, in examining his movie career Luke pinpointed 1934 as a turning point.

Third, and perhaps more important, the Sino-Japanese War, triggered in 1931 by Japan's invasion of Manchuria, resulted in greater sympathy for China and Chinese Americans. The United States sided with China, which also signaled a turn in race portrayals. Thus in the 1930s, as the United States developed the image of China as a good ally, "Orientals" became ethnicity-specific. In films, Chinese and Chinese Americans gained an identity distinct from that of the Japanese. The changing status of China boosted the value of Wong's portrayals of Chinese patriotism. In the 1932 movie *Shanghai Express,* Wong functions as a patriot loyal to the Chinese nation, whereas in *Daughter of the Dragon* (1931) a year earlier, she depicted a woman who did not have national allegiances but swore loyalty to one sinister man, her father.

Shanghai Express would be one of the last movies of the 1930s in which Anna May Wong played a woman of a "lower" class background. In the 1930s, Wong made three acting-role transitions: from sexually disreputable Chinese women, as in *Daughter of the Dragon*; to upper-class women of ambiguous sexual respectability and differing national allegiance, exemplified by *Dangerous to Know*; and finally to her ultimate incarnation in the late 1930s as upper-class, sexually respectable Chinese American women illustrated by *King of Chinatown.*

Anna May Wong performed Chinese American characters in low-budget, second-tier "B" movies such as *King of Chinatown* because "A" movie personnel refused to cast her in the appropriate starring roles. Wong showed her awareness of her symbolic importance as a Chinese American in Hollywood. She rejected one of the most important widely circulating film parts of her professional career because she considered it derogatory. In 1935, *The Good Earth* (1937) had one of the largest budgets in cinematic history, $2 million.[59] It has been argued that the book was the major reason why Americans shifted from demonizing the Chinese to allying with them during the Sino-Japanese War, especially after its author, Pearl S. Buck, won the Nobel Prize in 1938.[60] To many, Wong was the logical choice for the lead role of O-lan. However, MGM thwarted Wong's hopes of becoming a major star in a leading "A" feature by casting Luise Rainer, the actress who won back-to-back Academy Awards for best actress, including one for O-lan in *The Good Earth*. MGM invited Wong to screen-test as Lotus, the second wife who ruins the family. Wong repudiated the role because she did not want to be the only Chinese American playing the only negative personality. She stated for the press:

> I'll be glad to take a test, but I won't play the part. If you let me play O-lan, I'll be very glad. But you're asking me—with Chinese blood—to do the only unsympathetic role in the picture featuring an all-American cast portraying Chinese characters.[61]

Wong declined to depict the evil other and a European actress, Tilly Losch, won the role of Lotus. Wong's refusal to act in such a high-profile movie is significant, for it would have increased her visibility in Hollywood. Given the limited number of cinematic acting parts for actresses of any race, Wong's rejection of the role of Lotus demonstrates her conscious decision-making process in how she wished to shape herself as a professional. Echoing her interview "I Protest," in which she denounced evil portrayals of the Chinese in *Daughter of the Dragon*, Wong condemned MGM's desire to cast her as an evil Chinese instead of as the heroic O-lan. Anywhere between five hundred and two thousand Chinese American actors from Los Angeles worked on *The Good Earth*, including Wong's sister, Mary, but not Los Angeles Chinatown's most famous actress.

Anna May Wong herself took advantage of the improved image of China to pay her first visit there. After *The Good Earth* debacle, Wong's highly publicized tour included visits with dignitaries and cultural sites. Wong commented that the possibilities for motion pictures in China were enormous and that Hollywood should create more China-based films.

Upon her return to the United States, Wong actively worked to develop roles conducive to her understanding of how to perform Chinese American modernity.[62]

Performing Chinese American Cultural Citizenship

During the height of Western colonialism and imperialism, Anna May Wong's ability to exploit the space of agency between exoticism and cosmopolitanism allowed her to become an international star. For a brief moment in the 1930s, Wong utilized that star power to negotiate a contract that allowed her to perform distinctly Chinese American roles in movies such as *King of Chinatown* and *Daughter of Shanghai*. In these portrayals and in her public appearances, Wong shifted the category of American cultural citizenship to include Chinese Americans. Theater scholar Karen Shimakawa argues that in late twentieth-century performance, the category of "Asian American" moves between invisibility and visibility, foreignness and domestication/assimilation.[63] I argue that in early twentieth-century cinema, invisibility/foreignness had been the dominant trope, and that this 1930s moment of Wong's Chinese American roles was the one where visibility/domestication first became a possibility.

Unlike other scholars who argue that Anna May Wong's career peaked in 1932 with *Shanghai Express* and *Daughter of the Dragon*, I believe that her movies of the late 1930s, such as *King of Chinatown* and *Daughter of Shanghai*, merit further study.[64] These Paramount B movies differed from Wong's earlier films for three reasons: (1) she portrayed Chinese American roles, (2) the women she depicted on the screen were elite and respectable, and (3) she received star billing. Since her Paramount B features did not require the same advertising and production budget as A movies, there was enhanced potential for progressive and unusual roles.[65] For B films, studios would be more likely to approve an experimental script, since there was less money riding on the project. These films are especially evocative because they both point to the potential for and absolute impossibility of Chinese American cultural citizenship. Through postmodern hybridizing of both Chinese and American cultural markers, Wong's mainstream cultural practices were transformed into distinctly Asian American female practices. However, although the narratives were potentially radical along the lines of race in opening up the possibility of "Chinese American" as a category on screen, they came at the cost of gender conventionality and middle-class/elite normativity.

King of Chinatown marked the pinnacle of Anna May Wong's Chinese American professional roles. Her character, Dr. Mary Ling, has the medical skills to do what no other doctor can do: she saves the life of gangster and "king of Chinatown" Frank Baturin, played by Akim Tamiroff. His enemies have shot him and there is one chance in a thousand that he will live, hence his survival shows her extraordinary surgical skills. Although *King of Chinatown* is a B movie, it was considered important enough to merit national mainstream magazine attention. In a two-page photo essay, *Click* magazine captured Wong's real-life training, in which she witnessed kidney surgery so she could convincingly "wring every ounce of emotion" as Dr. Mary Ling.[66] In the film, since Ling/Wong has already decided to leave the Bay View Hospital to concentrate on the China war relief, she agrees to become Baturin's personal physician for a month in exchange for generous donations to the fund. Wong has another motive for wanting to keep the gangster alive: she incorrectly worries that her father may have masterminded the attempt on Baturin. Baturin's Merchants Protective Association's extortion has troubled Chinatown, and Wong fears her father has decided to kill Baturin to end it. Believing her father to be a potential murderer signals her Americanness in her rebellion as an ungrateful Chinese daughter.

What makes *King of Chinatown* particularly interesting is that instead of circumventing the threat of miscegenation by killing Anna May Wong's character, a henchman-turned-rival assassinates Baturin.[67] This is in direct contrast to movies such as *Limehouse Blues* and *Dangerous to Know*, in which Wong's character dies—not the white male lead's—in order to avoid the threat of interracial sexuality.[68] Thus *King of Chinatown* marks a significant break from cinematic oblivion as resolution. The very last scene of *King of Chinatown* depicts Wong, hardly dead or marginal, with a wedding ring on finger, seated next to her husband, Bob Li, played by Philip Ahn, while flying to China with medical equipment. Instead of Wong's not-so-dangerous sexuality being contained by death, it becomes controlled in a respectable upper-class same-race marriage. Baturin is the danger, not Ling/Wong, and he gets eliminated.[69] Wong's character enjoys Hollywood's best reward for women, namely, marriage. Marlene Dietrich's question in *Shanghai Express*, "Don't you find respectable people terribly —dull?" beautifully captures the potential banality of upper-class gendered respectability.

In his dying breath, Baturin bequeaths his fortune to Mary Ling's hospital work in China, which was part of a broader Chinese American political effort known as China Relief. Mirroring real-life Chinese American women, Anna May Wong's on-screen work to raise money for China War Relief is valorized and considered completely in keeping with her American patriotism. China Relief was not merely a cinematic device but an important political endeavor for Chinese American women. Dr. Mary Ling's real-life counterpart, Dr. Margaret Chung, was recognized for her outstanding fundraising and even went as far as to "adopt" the "Fair-Haired Bastards," a group of predominantly European American male aviator Flying Tigers, in her efforts to support China against the invasion.[70] Others turned to literary means to champion China's cause. For example, Jane Kwong Lee wrote two plays about China Relief. The first, *Boycott Silk Stockings,* focused on five Chinese American women who resolved not to buy or wear silk stockings as long as Japan was in China. Her second play, *Blood Stains Rivers and Mountains,* told the story of two female college students who became aviators and went to China to "sacrifice for our country."[71] In keeping with Chung's and Lee's patriotic efforts, the real-life Anna May Wong signed autographs to raise money for China Relief.[72] American support for China meant that raising money for China Relief could extend the definition of American cultural citizenship to include it.

As shown through these cultural portrayals, Japanese imperialism in Manchuria and China proved a turning point for Chinese American cultural citizenship. In the 1930s, the mainstream American perception of China changed because of the Sino-Japanese War. For example, *Time* magazine editor Henry Booth Luce championed the cause of China.[73] Thus Chinese American diasporic citizenship became increasingly acceptable, or, if you prefer, less risky, in the 1930s. In other words, it was not an act of treason for Chinese Americans to support China. What was particularly striking about Chinese American loyalty to China was that many in mainstream American society considered it consistent with American patriotism. With the Japanese invasion, China became the "good" American ally, Japan the "bad" enemy, a dynamic that would remain in place until the post–World War II American occupation of Japan and the "fall" of China to communism reversed it.

Daughter of Shanghai *and Chinese American Cultural Citizenship*

King of Chinatown was not the only movie in which Wong played a heroic Chinese American woman. In *Daughter of Shanghai,* Wong assumed the persona of Lan Ying Lin, a filial Chinese American daughter who tracks down her father's assassins and breaks up an illegal alien smuggling ring.[74] Lan Ying Lin's father, Quan Lin, has gathered evidence that will incriminate the leaders of a profitable crime ring that smuggles Asian illegal workers into the United States. Quan Lin's American citizenship is further underscored not only because the movie shows that there are illegal Asian workers in the city but because of his determination to halt that illegal immigration. An importer of rare, beautiful Chinese antiques and a venerable member of the Chinese merchants' association, Lin is one of the most distinguished persons in San Francisco. As in *King of Chinatown,* voice is an important marker of class status and American identity. Mr. Lin and Lan Ying speak perfect American English with no discernible pidgin. Audible traces of her English accent underscore the upper-class inflections in Wong's voice. Both characters are loved and respected by their workers and their wealthy European American customers.

Underscoring their admirable deployment of American citizenship, the movie plot of *Daughter of Shanghai* emphasizes the tragic heroism and honor of both Lins in service of enforcing American immigration laws. Representing a triple threat to the crime ring, Mr. Lin refuses to pay the smugglers extortion money; declines to employ the illegal Chinese aliens; and informs a European American society widow, Mary Hunt, that he will denounce the smugglers to the local and federal authorities. Lin's plan to turn in his accumulated evidence spells his death warrant. As he and Lan Ying ride in a taxi to meet with federal agents, the taxi is driven into a truck and he is assassinated.

The modern American female citizen within the cultural logic of *Daughter of Shanghai* is an active heroine. What is particularly telling is that production notes for the film show that before Anna May Wong signed on, the main character initiated very little action, but once Wong committed to the movie, the screenwriter rewrote the character of Lan Ying so that she instigated the major plot sequence.[75] This runs against her previous "passive" victim roles. Though distraught over her father's death in the taxi, Lan Ying uses her ingenuity to escape the assassins. When the criminals check the cab, she feigns death. As they close the taxi door, she thrusts out her purse to hold the door open. While their backs are turned, she dashes out of the taxi and hides under blankets in a truck. When they lower the truck into the water, she flees to safety. Given the change in Lan Ying's character after Wong agreed to star in the movie, one can infer that these action sequences were prompted and perhaps even initiated by Wong.

As a Chinese American female heroine, Lan Ying's feats break up the crime ring and avenge her father's death. The day after her father's assassination, Lan Ying takes over her father's business and vows to bring the assassins to justice. Traveling to Central America, she cleverly employs subterfuge to enter the crime ring's business without arousing suspicion. Inverting gender conventions, she escapes the group's island location by dressing like one of the Chinese male workers, in black pants and shirt with her hair tucked underneath a large straw coolie hat. Working with Kim Lee, a detective on the case played by Philip Ahn, she discovers that her father was killed by the rich widow, Mary Hunt, who had been one of their store's best customers and who had ostensibly been aiding them by arranging a meeting with the federal agents, but who instead kidnapped and betrayed them. Kim Lee and Lan Ying capture Hunt and bring her to justice. Like *King of Chinatown, Daughter of Shanghai* ends with the promise of Wong and Ahn's future marital bliss. Thus these Chinese American films extended the definition of cultural citizenship to show their ideal citizenship to a national audience via the movies.

This public, heroic, crime-stopping female version of cultural citizenship was publicized in the Chinese American community. Chinese Americans heard about Anna May Wong's Paramount movies before they were released. The *Chinese Digest* reported that Wong had signed a three-year contract with Paramount.[76] In a later edition, it reported that she "has played the villainess for so long now she would enjoy a nice role for a change."[77] Hence, the community knew that Wong felt positively about these new Chinese American film roles.

Gender as the Limit of Cinematic Chinese American Cultural Citizenship

Although the upturn in roles for racial and ethnic minorities spelled opportunity for Chinese Americans, any potential of demonstrating radical cinematic Chinese American cultural citizenship in *King of Chinatown* or *Daughter of Shanghai* was thrown into question by the films' conservative gender ideology. Wong's agency is unique rather than typical. Frequently she is the only woman in a world of men, and the only female Asian American, underscoring her exceptionalness. In *Daughter of Shanghai*, the society woman criminal, Mary Hunt, was played by Cecil Cunningham, an exceedingly butch lesbian.[78] Her draglike portrayal of an older aristocratic woman accentuates Wong's heroic femininity and grace. In *Island of Lost Men* and *Daughter of Shanghai*, Wong searches for her father, and there is no mention of any mother, which removes a potentially powerful female figure.[79]

Gender conventions not only rendered Anna May Wong the only woman in a world of men, but they also affected her ability to show physical might. In action sequences, Wong displays heroic exploits when she is alone, not with men around her. Wong's solo action sequences show the potential for cinematic female physicality. However, when she is paired with Philip Ahn, he, not she, slugs the villains. In the final action sequence, Ahn and the chauffeur Kelly fight the criminals while Wong stands by the wall and screams, showing that Wong requires male rescue.

Likewise, despite *King of Chinatown's* "elevation" of race and class, it is heavily circumscribed by heteronormative gender conventions. Though Baturin falls in love with Ling, the movie only hints at courtship. When Ling informs him that because of his recovery he is now her prize patient, the movie's score and soft lighting intimate romance. Indirectly expressing his growing affection, Baturin asks her if she plans to marry Bob Li, presumably to find out if her affections are engaged. He declares she is beautiful in a tone that goes beyond collegiality but stops short of overt wooing. Implying that his life before knowing her was empty of affection and meaning, he asks her not to go to China and offers to fully equip a local medical practice for her. Throughout these utterances, Ling sidesteps his statements and does not reciprocate his affections.

The lack of overt courtship shows the limits of American cultural citizenship for Asian Americans, namely, the impossibility of interracial romances. Baturin and Ling's romance stalls at veiled conversation because the Hays Code forbade interracial relationships.[80] Named after its creator and implementer William Hays, the new code, self-imposed by Hollywood studios because of pressures from entities such as church groups, teachers, and government agencies, had several goals: "the censorship movement chose several, sometimes contradictory targets: ethnic and racial stereotyping, anti-Americanism, unconventional morality, and the sexual objectification of females."[81]

The Hays Code reflected current antimiscegenation laws, which remained in various states' legal codes until the 1960s and pointed to America's deep racial fears. Though not written into the Constitution, miscegenation laws pointed to racial minorities' second-class citizen status by restricting the right to marry whomever one chose.[82] For Asian American women, marriage and citizenship were particularly fraught issues. The 1922 Cable Act decreed that a woman would lose her American citizenship if she married an alien ineligible for citizenship (Asian immigrant male). With the ban on interracial sexual relationships, the codes aligned Hollywood with miscegenation laws that had been passed by American state legislatures starting in the nineteenth century. These laws banned marriages between whites and nonwhites. For example, by 1880 section 69 of the California Civil Code, which regulated marriage licenses, forbade intermarriage between "whites and Mongolians, negroes, or mulattos, or mixed blood, descended from Mongolians or negro from the third generation." Section 60 of the California Civil Code, which regulated miscegenation, was updated in 1905 to agree with Section 69 by forbidding marriages between Mongolians and whites. Out of the nineteen Far Western states, five targeted the Chinese, two the Japanese, and eight used the term *Mongolians* to cover both. Six states added the term *Malay* to cover Filipinos. The miscegenation laws were declared unconstitutional in California in 1948, and by the U.S. Supreme Court in 1967 in *Loving* v. *Virginia*.[83] Thus Hollywood was relatively late in banning interracial relationships. As actor Akim Tamiroff's (Baturin's) whiteness was in question, he being Russian, the film essentially consolidated his whiteness by making his relationship with Wong forbidden on-screen.

Many have argued that Hollywood cinema of the 1930s, 1940s, and 1950s was predicated on the controlling gaze of the male camera and the male spectator upon the female body.[84] By the time *Daughter of Shanghai* was made, the dancing and costumes in Wong's movies, though in keeping with those of European American actresses, were nonetheless marked by race. Moments of narrative rupture occur. For example, when Wong played showgirls later in her career, as in *Island of Lost Men* or *Daughter of Shanghai,* the story line unfolded that she was really the daughter of a prestigious man masquerading as a dancer and singer in order to find her father and recover the family's honor. Wong's appearance could be interpreted as emblematic of a "New Woman," signifying modern sexuality in the service of heroism.

Although Anna May Wong's fully clothed, sexually respectable surgeon is a breakthrough role in the history of Asian American women and film, examining her interactions with the male characters reveals servile gender behavior. At the beginning of *King of Chinatown,* Wong portrays an exceedingly competent surgeon, but in later scenes with Tamiroff, she acts bewilderingly domestic. While he is her patient in the hospital, she brings him a tray of food with tea and toast, and while in his home, she does motherly tasks such as plumping up his pillow. As he accepts his cup of tea, Baturin informs Ling that he never discusses business with a woman, and she does not challenge his misogyny. Though she cannot be expected always to perform complex surgical operations, replacing the scalpel with a tray undermines her radical potential as an Asian American female surgeon. Although there should not be a contradiction between domesticity and workplace competence, depicting Wong as a cross between a nurse and a maid undercut her authority as a physician.[85]

Anna May Wong playing a surgeon and a wealthy art dealer did not reflect the reality of Asian American women's occupations in the pre–World War II era. Instead, these roles promoted a narrow vision of female Asian American cultural citizenship. In the 1930s, Asian American women could not hold professional jobs for which they had trained. Much like the members of Chi Alpha Delta, young Chinese American women, despite their college education, either worked in their ethnic enclaves or were employed in clerical work far below their educational qualifications.[86] So playing elite professional women opened up possibilities that were yet to be achieved in reality. However, emphasizing the professional reified people with power and privilege in capitalist societies. Thus, such a valorization of the professions would boost the worth and power of those who were already in power. Although Wong's role indeed was a cinematic breakthrough, emphasis on her being a surgeon, wealthy, and well educated foreclosed the possibilities of working-class struggle and resistance. Instead the role normalized hegemonic power and work relations and set the class parameters of female Chinese American cultural citizenship.

Race and Ethnicity in Hollywood

Although Anna May Wong's early success in films and as a cultural icon can be attributed to Western imperialism's fascination with the other, her later ability to play Chinese American film roles needs to be evaluated in the context of a changing Hollywood. In the mid-1930s, changing mores meant newly emerging cultural citizenship possibilities for all racial minorities. Film scholars have argued that depression-era Hollywood, especially with regard to race and gender, was ahead of American society.[87] All of Wong's star power meant that once Paramount Studios green-lighted Chinese American–themed films, she would be the one who would win the starring roles. In other words, Wong was a co-creator in the race and gender realignment of Hollywood.

Scholars of African Americans in film have discovered, as was the case for Chinese Americans, an overall trend of more "positive" portrayals in the film roles of the 1930s. The decade was a turning point for African Americans in movies in that they gained more prominent roles of all types.[88] Though Hollywood continually typecast Hattie McDaniel and Butterfly McQueen as "mammies" and maids, the actresses gained critical recognition for their acting, including Hattie McDaniel's Best Supporting Actress Academy Award for her portrayal of Mammy in the 1939 movie *Gone with the Wind*. Lena Horne, too, gained prominence in mainstream Hollywood during this time.[89] The 1930s films of Oscar Micheaux featured all-black casts in detective stories and dramas, and Micheaux's stories expanded the types of roles that African Americans could play.[90] And when African Americans did not like film portrayals, protests ensued.[91]

Similar "positive" roles were available for Latino/a actors and actresses. In part due to the United States' Good Neighbor policy toward Latin America in the late 1930s, scholar Ana Lopez found, the film roles of Latinos in Hollywood improved: "After decades of portraying Latin Americans lackadaisically and sporadically as lazy peasants and wily senoritas who inhabited an undifferentiated backward land, Hollywood films between 1939 and 1947, featuring Latin American stars, music, locations, and stories flooded U.S. and international markets."[92] Hence stars such as Dolores del Rio, Lupe Velez, and Anthony Quinn enjoyed Hollywood success.

"Ethnic" personnel supported Anna May Wong's stardom. As Jewish Americans "invented" Hollywood, Paramount Studios' Jewish American producer Adolph Zukor backed Anna May Wong's Chinese American movies, such as *King of Chinatown*.[93] Russian American Akim Tamiroff costarred in *Dangerous to Know* and in *King of Chinatown*. Mexican American Anthony Quinn played a Chinese person in the movie *Island of Lost Men*. Quinn also portrayed two European American villains in *King of Chinatown* and *Daughter of Shanghai*. Later in his career, Quinn starred in leading roles such as Zorba the Greek and would win two Best Supporting Actor Academy Awards. Philip Ahn, from one of the first Korean American families in Los Angeles, played Chinese Americans. As many present-day Asian American actors have stated, being cast multiethnically increased opportunities for employment and thus career advancement. Quinn, Tamiroff, Ahn, and Wong filmed several movies together during their Paramount years, and Wong's name led the credits, reflecting her status as the star. Despite the advancement of ethnic actors in the 1930s, however, Wong was the only thespian of Asian descent to be hailed as a star by the movie studios and by the general public.

Chinese American Hollywood

Although tremendous charisma, magnetic appearance, and sheer determination allowed Anna May Wong to become a star, she did not do so in a vacuum. From the 1920s through World War II, Los Angeles' Chinatown had a special relationship to Hollywood and thus to the nation. Since movies were not filmed on location in Asia but in Southern California, Hollywood tapped into the Chinese American community as the source for thousands of extras and other actors. In a modern nation-state predicated on wholeness, Chinatowns function as "authentic" other nations within the nation. As a representative of that alternative nation, Anna May Wong embodied "authentic" Chineseness. However, given the 1882 Chinese Immigration Exclusion Act, Wong and the Chinese Americans who inhabited Los Angeles' Chinatown did not have personal knowledge of China but gained it through their work on Hollywood movie sets. Beautifully demonstrating the contradictions and slippages within modernity that knowledge gained from film work was presented to the nation, and to international audiences, as authentically Chinese. In addition, as Chineseness was at a premium, the community benefited economically during the Great Depression.

Anna May Wong emerged out of a specific racialized performance tradition. Growing up in Los Angeles just outside Chinatown and Hollywood, Wong, like many other Chinese Americans, capitalized on early cinema's fascination with race and otherness.[94] What is unique about the Los Angeles Chinese American community is the degree to which almost the entire population was involved in the motion picture industry. As movies about Asia were filmed around Los Angeles, numerous members of the community were part of Chinese American Hollywood, forming a branch of the Chinese Screen Actors Extras Guild and developing community networks for finding jobs in Hollywood. As a woman Wong was a scarce resource, for in 1910 she was one of 147 Chinese women and one of 77 daughters out of a total population of 2,602.[95] Though one of many Chinese Americans to work in Hollywood, Wong did not have to compete with many Chinese American women.

The new spate of movies about China meant great opportunities for Chinese Americans in Los Angeles to supplement their depression-era incomes by working as extras. With the improved Sino-American relations in the 1930s, movies such as *The Good Earth* and *The General Died at Dawn* marked an upsurge in the recruitment of Asian American actors and actresses. Eddie Lee, an extra and a movie-prop store owner, remarked that the movie work opportunities were viewed favorably by Chinese Americans in Chinatown: "I never heard any criticism of the Chinese roles in the motion pictures. The Chinese were happy to take the jobs and earn extra money."[96] In fact, as was the case for *The Good Earth,* so many movies were made about China that not only could every person in Los Angeles' Chinatown who wanted a role could take one, due to the paucity of actors, movie producers were forced to cast in Northern California.

For Chinese Americans, participation as extras on Hollywood movie sets heightened their Chinese American cultural citizenship. Given years of Chinese immigration exclusion laws, American-born Chinese movie extras felt that their "real" experience of China came on the movie sets.[97] Just as it did for mainstream Americans, the movies allowed Chinese Americans to "understand" Chinese culture. In her article "Night Call—In Chinatown," journalist Louise Leung Larson reported that thousands of Chinese Americans learned how to braid their hair into queues and to wear Chinese peasant costumes while on the set of *The Good Earth.* Such an understading gained from the movie sets highlighted how culturally American those extras really were. Yet, like Anna May Wong, courtesy of their race they performed Chineseness for American audiences.

The Chinese American community of Los Angeles knew Anna May Wong as the most famous Asian American actress of her day. The community admired Wong for her filial piety, local ties, and China Relief efforts. Despite her father's disapproval of her career, Wong put her brothers through college and emphasized the importance of education.[98] Swan Yee, an aspiring actor when Wong was at the peak of her career, held her as a model for his own career in show business and recalled: "Anna May Wong was a pretty good actress. She did not have any competition from other Asian actresses."[99] When Yee arrived in Los Angeles, he went to Wong's home to ask for work but was told by her maid that none was available. Prominent journalist Louise Leung Larson included a photograph of herself with Anna May Wong in her autobiography.[100]

In many ways, Anna May Wong symbolized pre–World War II Chinatown. Eating in Los Angeles Chinatown restaurants, Wong was visible in the community. Lisa See, whose family was prominent in Los Angeles' Chinatown, contextualizes Wong's patronage of the Dragon Den restaurant: "No single person held customers in thrall as much as did Anna May Wong. . . . [D]ressed in silk cut on the bias, with a full-length ermine coat draped over her shoulders, [she] could be found holding court at her own table." As See relates, Wong's behavior was reminiscent of royalty: "She would seductively extend her hand to those who came to pay respects—even those Chinese who scorned and ridiculed her behind her back."[101] Wong headed the parade that opened the new Los Angeles Chinatown, an ethnic community rebuilt after being displaced by Union Station, and planted a willow tree that symbolized her Chinese name, Frosted Yellow Willow. In addition, she headlined community fundraisers.[102]

Not only were Chinatowns places where movie studios sought talent, but they were also locations through which Hollywood movies worked out ideas about race and good and evil. Anna May Wong's Chinese American 1930s Paramount movies reversed the earlier Fu Manchu racial scenarios that had caused her to reconsider her film career. In the Paramount films, Chinese Americans moved to the center stage and European Americans became the villains. In both *King of Chinatown* and *Daughter of Shanghai,* the criminals are European Americans while the Chinese Americans are the heroes. Disorder in Chinatown is not due to Chinese American pathology but caused by persons who do not belong to Chinatown. The heroic actions of Anna May Wong and Philip Ahn restore order to Chinatown, and their marriage will seal familial succession. The resolution of heterosexual nuptials affirms racial purity and class order. Constructing Chinatown as an authentic and pure homogeneous space is paradoxical, for instead of Chinatown and its inhabitants needing to be contained, for fear they would contaminate white society, the situation is reversed.[103]

The worth of Chinese American cultural citizenship was heightened in the 1930s. Chinese identity, versus a pan-Asian "Oriental" one, became a key distinction in the decade. When Japan invaded Manchuria, Chinese Americans publicly began to distinguish themselves from all things Japanese. In a world dominated by European Americans, racial and ethnic groups at the bottom of the hierarchy were pitted against each other.[104] Casting the Chinese as the "good" ethnicity is a variation on the divide-and-conquer strategy, used, for example, by Hawaiian plantation owners, that pitted different Asian ethnicities against each other to prevent labor union solidarity.[105] Thus, in the 1930s, the Chinese were culturally created as the "good" ethnicity. Movies such as *The Good Earth* and *The Bitter Tea of General Yen* made a point of referencing a geographically specific Chinese culture, not an amalgamation of Asian or Oriental cultures.

Anna May Wong used ethnic particularity to highlight her own Chinese identity. As a Paramount press release stated in 1937, after the Japanese military occupation of Manchuria:

> In view of current events in the orient anything Japanese annoys Anna May Wong, Chinese actress.
>
> She had, up to yesterday, occupied an apartment overlooking a Japanese garden. The view was a constant source of vexation to her, particularly as callers were constantly calling attention to it.
>
> Last night Miss Wong moved to a furnished home in another part of Hollywood, far from any landscaping suggesting Japan.[106]

Given that it is a studio press release, the motives in announcing the move may not be Wong's own. However, though relocating to another home may seem trivial, Paramount's care in announcing such a move speaks volumes as to its symbolic importance. Wong's change of residence and Paramount's accompanying publicity show conscious ethnic differentiation between the good Chinese and the bad Japanese. Wong's or the studio's deliberate marking of her star image not only made for a good story or sound politics; it reinforced her image as Chinese at a time when such distinctions were culturally powerful. Such ethnic differentiation allowed Chinese Americans to consolidate their ethnic identity as Americans. Chinese Americans themselves considered such ethnic differentiation important: for instance, Wong's move away from the Japanese garden was reported in San Francisco *Chinese Digest*'s "Chinatownia" section.[107] And, as Wong had participated in China Relief fundraisers and autograph signings, her support for China was corroborated in other, more reliable sources.

Performing Modern Cosmopolitan Femininity

Anna May Wong used modern fashion to claim beauty, humanity, and modernity for Chinese Americans. Such claims allowed her to counteract scientific racism, orientalism, and the "controlling image" of Asians as perpetual foreigners in the United States.[108] Wong's adoption of cosmopolitan fashion gave her greater attention, fame, and therefore power in her career.

Anna May Wong on the cover of *Look* magazine, 1938.

Such markers of gendered modernity were key to claiming belonging to the nation-state. Arguing against anti-Asian groups, missionaries proclaimed that the Chinese could become incorporated into the United States through adoption of modern styles in fashion, hair, and diction.[109] What is perhaps most remarkable about Wong is that she created a new type of "modern" through hybridity. Rather than adopting 100 percent American or Western styles as advocated by those pro-assimilation missionaries, she brought Asian cultural influences and Western tailoring together in contemporary time, thus negating the "exotic," "ancient" costumes that served to mark Asians as backward and nonmodern.

The cover of *Look* magazine crowned Anna May Wong's status as an American icon. As the "World's Most Beautiful Chinese Girl," Wong graced the cover of the March 1938 issue. A closer examination of this issue provides a glimpse into Wong's iconography as understood by the greater American public and the establishment of her American cultural citizenship. Founded in 1937, *Look* boasted a circulation of 2 million and a price of ten cents an issue. Now defunct, the chiefly pictorial *Look* featured topics ranging from glamorous UCLA sorority women to raising quintuplets to exposing fascism.

The pages devoted to Anna May Wong highlighted her glamour, clothing, and, not surprising, given the moniker the "world's most beautiful Chinese girl," her physical attributes. The captions and photographs in *Look* displayed both Wong's Chinese ethnicity and her American citizenship. Underneath a still of Wong from the British movie *Chu Chin Chow,* the pictorial explained that Wong had only recently visited China and that, despite her appearance, she was American-born. In case the point was not understood, the next picture clarified Wong's nationality as a sophisticated American citizen: "Anna May Wong, seen here with one of her brothers, Roger Wong, wears clothes unusually well. In 1934 the Mayfair Mannequin society designated her as the world's best-dressed woman. . . . An American citizen, she has given up plans to retire to China." A picture of Wong wearing a modish Western ensemble—long striped tunic belted over a dark skirt, with a jacket whose lining and length matched the tunic, accessorized with a dark hat tilted at a rakish angle and black high-heeled pumps—beautifully complemented the caption and reinforced the point. Although Wong had planned to spend more time in China, her 1936 trip there showed her her cultural differences with the Chinese and demonstrated to her that her true home was in the West.

Look's feature effectively crowned Anna May Wong as the icon of modern hybrid Chinese American cultural citizenship. One caption read: "Umpire Wong. Last summer Anna May Wong showed how completely American she can be, by umpiring a baseball game, in which Lowell Thomas, with her here, was a player. In the movies, however, Anna May usually is a siren type." For the game, Wong dressed in a dark cheongsam with white wavy lines on it as a pattern, appearing almost like chain mail. Although the text calls her all-American, given her cheongsam, the photograph partly contradicts that. The caption and photograph overdetermine Americanness in the face of visible ambiguity so that they evoke wholesomeness. Such a portrait of Chinese American identity alleviates anxiety over race and acculturation. What is interesting is that the Chinese and the Western coexisted and cosignified each other.

In the final photograph, with Marlene Dietrich and Leni Riefenstahl, Wong's cosmopolitan woman-of-the-world status is highlighted for American audiences. She is clad in a completely Western sleeveless flapper dress in dark material with a chiffon overlay, accented by a knotted long single-strand pearl necklace. Like Wong, Dietrich sports a sleeveless flapper dress accessorized by a multistrand beaded necklace. The caption notes: "If Anna May, seen here between Marlene Dietrich and the German actress Leni Riefenstahl, kisses an Englishman in a movie, the scene is cut out by British censors. Despite this, she is very popular in England, where she has made a number of pictures. She first visited China in 1935, was received there like a princess." Despite the caption's claims, British censors did allow the movie *Java Head* to show a kiss between Wong and a British actor. The caption and photo show Wong's international prominence. Association with Marlene Dietrich, dazzling costumes, being called "princess," and travels to Britain all signified woman-of-the-world glamour and a moneyed lifestyle. As biographies of Dietrich show, despite being the same height, Dietrich called Wong her "little China doll."[110] The phrase is implicitly racist for it places Wong in an inferior, nonhuman status in relation to Dietrich.

Anna May Wong's European-inflected cosmopolitanism conferred elite status upon her star iconography, which translated into class elevation in her movie roles. In the 1930s, in her public life as well as in her screen personas, Wong cultivated sophisticated Europeanized femininity. Wong's fashion savvy was recognized in 1934 when the Mayfair Mannequin Society voted her the best-dressed woman in the world.[111] Based on her introduction of the coolie and Mandarin hats in London and Paris, fashion experts in London, New York, Berlin, Paris, Vienna, and Stockholm ranked her the most sophisticated woman on both sides of the Atlantic. Wong did not merely reflect current fashion trends; she determined them. Her ability to be a modern, hybridized, cosmopolitan woman gave her more class and clout than being elite Chinese or working-class American.

American fascination with race and modernity through the female body ensured the success of actresses who occupied positions analogous to Anna May Wong's, such as Dolores del Rio and Lupe Velez. Together, Del Rio and Velez typified many of Wong's roles and much of her appeal, for del Rio represented the upper class, Velez the working class.[112] Just as the Mayfair Mannequin Society proclaimed Wong 1934's best-dressed woman in the world, in 1933 del Rio won *Photoplay*'s "most perfect feminine figure in Hollywood" search.[113] The sexuality that came through in

Anna May Wong in a coolie hat.

Wong's dancing roles resembles that of Velez, the "Mexican Spitfire."[114] It is striking that in back-to-back years these racial minority actresses were considered more beautiful than their European American counterparts. All three women exemplified Hollywood's and the general American public's absorption with gendered ethnicity and racialized otherness. However, current scholarship shows that Mexican-born del Rio and Velez continually enacted "foreign" women and did not enjoy the equivalent of Wong's American roles.

Like the members of the Chi Alpha Delta sorority discussed in the previous chapter, Anna May Wong deployed hybrid cultural practices such as hairstyles, food, and fashion to highlight newly emerging forms of Asian American identity politics. As she did throughout her movie career, Wong demonstrated cultural citizenship through sumptuous clothing, the wearing of which was a proper and patriotic way to be an American movie star during the Great Depression. In *King of Chinatown,* Wong's apparel accentuates her class status and femininity. Leading Hollywood designer Edith Head concocted wonderfully elegant clothing for her. In every scene, Wong dazzles in a different costume. Postmodern pastiches of both the primitive and the civilized, her hats and jackets are the latest Western fashions with Chinese accents. In the final scene she dresses in a long, luxurious cream silk gown with a short jacket and a sweeping skirt. During the Great Depression, many women went to the movies to escape fears of poverty by viewing their favorite movie stars attired in glamorous clothing.[115] Wong did not disappoint them. Her elegant wearing of Chinese-accented American clothing made such fashions acceptable and desirable in mainstream circles.

Along with clothing, voice is one of the markers of class and American-born status. In all the conversational sequences in *King of Chinatown,* Bob Li (Philip Ahn) and Mary Ling (Wong) speak polished, educated, American English, and Mr. Ling, the traditional Chinese physician herbalist, speaks grammatical English with a slight Mandarin intonation. Wong's deployment of educated American English with British undertones, cultivated during her London sojourn, complicates Renee Tajima's assertion that "Asian women in American cinema are interchangeable in appearance and name, and are joined together by the common language of non-language—that is, uninterpretable chattering, pidgin English, giggling, or silence."[116] Through their voice, dress, and actions, both Wong and Ahn show distinct mannerisms that are upper class and American. Their class position is reinforced by comparisons with others in the movie. For example, Frank Baturin's (Akim Tamiroff's) enemy Mike Jordan, played by Mexican American Anthony Quinn, enunciates in working-class tones that betray his lack of formal education.

Other films of the 1930s show Anna May Wong's hybrid modern fashions. For example, luxurious modern costumes and interiors mark *Dangerous to Know,* a movie that illustrates the second developmental stage of Wong's movie roles: upper-class dress and ambiguous sexual respectability.[117] Based on her London and Broadway role in *On the Spot,* in *Dangerous to Know,* Wong played hostess (the implication being mistress) to gangster Stephen Recka, portrayed by Akim Tamiroff.[118] The deliberate elegance of her upper-class appearance effectively enticed viewers. Wong received Tamiroff's guests in a dark gown with a tightly fitted bodice that draped into a fluid skirt, had a high neck and frog fastenings, and was cov-

Anna May Wong dressed by Edith Head in
Dangerous to Know.

ered by a long, flowing silk jacket that, like a cape, wafted behind her when
she walked.[119] The luxurious Edith Head creation combined the latest
Western haute couture with Chinese overtones. Head, Hollywood's leading clothing designer, subsequently fashioned Wong's costumes for *King of
Chinatown*. Thin and elegant, Wong stood at eye level with her leading
man and towered above her European American female counterpart. With
clothing and height as chief makers of Wong's visual iconography, she
dominated the screen and her dignified and expressive sexuality shim-
mered across to the audience.

Anna May Wong's costumes for *Dangerous to Know* prompted public
dialogue over whether "ancient" or "modern" clothing was more appropriate for her film character. In a poll, "style arbiters" from Hollywood, New

York, London, and Paris unanimously voted that American dresses best suited her. According to designer Travis Banton, who spoke for the group, "I think Miss Wong looks superb in her colorful, exotic, Oriental costumes. But for the role of a dangerous, ultra-sophisticated adventuress it is obvious that her gowns should be those of a reckless, expensively-groomed woman of the world. The Chinese gowns stress a decorative quality, whereas the American gowns which Edith Head is designing for Miss Wong in the film provide the sex appeal men of today look for in women."[120] The fact that it was even worth discussing what types of costumes best suit a modern role speaks to the importance of clothing in situating female film stars. Of course, clothing fashion in China itself was continually changing so that the West was not the only source of modernity in Chinese clothing.[121]

Anna May Wong was by no means the only woman of Chinese descent of the 1930s to attract American public and media attention. The cultural and political impact of Madame Chiang Kai-shek (Mayling Soong) underscored American interest in Chinese feminine modernity. Educated in the United States, as the wife of General Chiang Kai-shek, the Chinese nationalist leader and leader of Taiwan, Chiang's modern, cosmopolitan and Western appearance aided their claims to the true China. Though not Asian American, her image paralleled that of Anna May Wong. In 1937 she and her husband were *Time* magazine's "couple of the year" (in lieu of man of the year). Although he was dressed in traditional Chinese robes, she was garbed in a modern Western business suit.[122] Chinese American women in San Francisco learned from her example, and her speaking was so effective in U.S. Congress that some credit her with the repeal of the Chinese exclusion laws.[123]

As befits those negotiating modernity and cultural citizenship, young Chinese American women showed considerable interest in the latest fashions. As many of their mothers were not up to date with the latest fashions, second-generation women relied upon local and mass media for fashion advice. In a 1937 *Chinese Digest* edition, columnist Alice Fong Yu (the same Alice Fong Yu that appeared in chapter 1 as the president of the Square and Circle Club) reported in "Fashion Tid-Bits" that navy, beige, and gray were the vital colors of the year, and that boleros and redingotes were all the rage. Fong Yu did acknowledge that while the current fashions had skirt lengths from 13 and 14 inches from the ground, "for you 'n me [Chinese American women], 12 or 13 inches are dandy."[124] Although Fong

Yu did report on the mainstream fashions, she modified her reportage to suit her audience's needs.

What is particularly ironic is that when Alice Fong Yu reported on movie-star fashion, she focused on Luise Rainier rather than Anna May Wong. In the same "Fashion Tid-Bits" article, she stated, "Luise Rainier as Olan in the 'Good Earth' does not have to worry about her clothes from one season to another," showing that young Asian American women were attuned to film stars as role models.[125] Had Wong agreed to play in *Good Earth*, or had MGM seen fit to cast her in a "positive" role, Fong Yu could have discussed Wong instead of Rainier. Unlike her Los Angeles counterparts, presumably San Francisco–based Fong Yu was not personally acquainted with Wong.

Perhaps one of the most interesting discussion surrounding Anna May Wong's appearance arrives courtesy of a Paramount press release concerning her hair. To match her Chinese American movie roles, the studio commanded her to cut her hair into a bob, which Wong refused to do. As a Paramount press release ruefully documented:

> Hollywood, accustomed to tailoring its personalities to suit its pictures, met unexpected opposition today when it attempted to de-orientalize the most famous Chinese actress in the world. . . .
>
> Miss Wong refused the "modernization" of a bobbed hair dress on the grounds that her exotic roles call for correct Oriental demeanor and that in most foreign lands where her pictures have a great following women still wear their hair long. . . .
>
> Studio officials made bobbed hair a stipulation of the new agreement because the three pictures they have prepared for the Chinese star call for an Americanized oriental actress.[126]

The press release has implications along an interpretive spectrum. On one end, one could argue that, secure in the knowledge that no other actress could play Chinese American roles, Wong utilized her American leading-lady privilege to defy the studios. As for other Hollywood film icons, her star status meant that officials tried to control her image, but it also allowed her to wield power. Wong won this battle, for in movies such as *King of Chinatown* and *Daughter of Shanghai* her hair remained triumphantly long. For this 1938 Paramount contract, Wong strategically used supposed Chinese culture and fashion to shape Hollywood studio power. On the other end of the interpretive spectrum, it is also possible that, given the source of the information, Paramount Studios used supposed Chinese culture and fashion to generate publicity for their star, which reinforced their hegemonic studio power. Regardless of to what degree either interpretation is correct, two things are noteworthy. First, modernity and appearance were critical to Wong's star persona. Second, Wong, whether or not "really" defiant, was publicly construed as such by her employer.

This long-hair debate provides a contrast to the earlier, 1931 comparison between Anna May Wong and Sessue Hayakawa, in which Wong was portrayed as Western and modern. The change in her performance of modernity may be attributed to a number of factors. With the increasing popularity of China and Chinese movie themes, Wong needed to be both Chinese and American. With the power that accompanied her new studio contract, Wong could express her preferences and thus refuse the haircut. In addition, Wong's act shifted the very definition of modernity to include a cosmopolitan deployment of the foreign embedded in the construction of the term *American*.[127] Wong's (and the studio's) actions were in keeping with those of her community. Made up of second-generation Chinese American women, San Francisco's Square and Circle club, led by its indefatigable president Alice Fong Yu, boycotted silk stockings and had fashion-show benefits for China Relief.[128] The boycott appeared in *Life* magazine. Thus fashion was a key way for women to show political affiliation and activism. Chinese American women's use of fashion was also key to gaining the attention of national American media for their causes.

Conclusion

With the advent of U.S. involvement in World War II, film work for Anna May Wong ended, and, like her movie character Dr. Mary Ling in *King of Chinatown*, Wong officially retired from the motion-picture industry to dedicate herself full time to the China War Relief effort. Reflecting greater American war participation, Paramount Studios chiefly financed war-genre movies that employed male leading characters. Paramount publicized Wong's movie and personal wardrobe auction that benefited the China Relief fund.[129] As befit a hometown legend, in Los Angeles' Chinatown, Wong raised money for Chinese War Bonds by signing autographs in exchange for donations to China Relief.

Anna May Wong's and the Chinese American community's efforts to publicize their patriotism both to China and to the United States was successful. In 1943, favoring China at the expense of Japan resulted in the United States rescinding Asian exclusion by granting China an immigration quota of 105. The cinematic valorization of China alongside China's alliance with the Allied Powers during World War II solidified the relations between China and the United States.

Though Anna May Wong retired from the motion-picture industry, she continued her work in theater and vaudeville. In 1943 she starred in Cambridge Summer Theater's play *The Willow Tree*.[130] Though Wong professed her willingness to continue working as a film actress, studios employed her as a consultant instead. Like many other motion-picture actresses and actors, she entertained the troops during World War II, performing up and down the coast of Alaska.[131]

Anna May Wong was not the only major movie actress to retire during World War II. Other foreign and "ethnic" actresses such as Greta Garbo, Dolores del Rio, and Lupe Velez ended their careers in Hollywood at the same time. For Asian American actresses who played roles as supporting actresses and extras, the war years marked a long hiatus in cinematic opportunities. Focused on masculinity in crisis, the war genre chiefly employed Chinese American men, not women. This was a marked departure from Hollywood of the thirties, when not only Anna May Wong but other Chinese American women such as Soo Yung, Iris Wong, and Lotus Long found regular employment.

Anna May Wong's struggles as the first Asian American actress to play roles featuring women of Asian descent exemplify politicized power struggles over modernity, cultural citizenship, and racialized, gendered performance. In the 1930s, Wong made three acting transitions: from poor, sexually disreputable Chinese women, to upper-class women of ambiguous sexual respectability who held differing national allegiances, to her final stage in the late 1930s playing upper-class, sexually respectable Chinese American women. Wong's negotiations between her Chinese and Western identities showed the limitations and opportunities for racial minority women working in Hollywood.

My historical search for Wong has yielded a complex story of gendered racial production. Wong's life story shows us how the performance of American cultural citizenship changed when constituted by modern European cosmopolitanism, Chinese ethnicity, and hybrid Asian American practices. Over her career, Wong continually negotiated her roles, which ranged from a Mongol slave to a Chinese American surgeon. Though Wong's attempts to shape the cultural production of race and gender were not always successful, for a brief moment her work grappled with the possibilities of an American-born, modern, educated Asian American woman. No American-born motion-picture actress of Asian descent has yet equaled the range and number of Wong's roles. The paucity of Asian American actresses and actors in contemporary major motion pictures points to the ongoing gender and racial inequities in Hollywood.

While the first two chapters of *A Feeling of Belonging* focused on an ethnic-specific group and a different cultural practices, the remaining three chapters traverse cultural practices and Asian-ethnic groups. During World War II and the postwar period, the American-born female populations increased, ethnic cultures collided and merged, and pan–Asian American activities expanded. Joined by other Asian American women and by other practices such as beauty pageants and magazine reading, the stories of Chi Alpha Delta and Anna May Wong continue into the next three chapters.

3

Shortcut to Glamour
Popular Culture in a Consumer Society

How to tell your friends from the Japs: Most Chinese avoid horn-rimmed spectacles.   —*Time* magazine, December 22, 1941

[*Scene* magazine will] help heal the wounds of war—both here at home and across the Pacific.   —*Scene*, July 1952

Dear Sirs: George Ohashi's article on "Short Cut to Glamor [*sic*]" (Scene, April) is just what we have been hoping to find in your magazine. Thanks.   —Rosemary Ono, *Scene*, May 1950

This chapter examines the paradox alluded to in the above quotations: in the post–World War II era, Asian Americans claimed modernity, cultural citizenship, and civil rights through consumer and youth cultures. According to many cultural critics, dominant hegemonic society uses consumer culture to make society accede to its will, not through coercion but by making its power seem natural and legitimate. Why, then, did the language and narratives of Asian American belonging to the nation-state become structured through the auspices of youthful female improvement through consumption as portrayed in Asian American popular culture?

The answer lies in the dynamics that propelled the dominance of American democratic liberalism in the middle of the twentieth century, namely, the United States' economic and political evolution into a consumer society combined with the construction of racial inequality as a matter of denying access to public institutions. For the purposes of this chapter, I define the concept of mid-twentieth-century American democratic liberalism as the ideology of societal progress through individual striving, undergirded by the ideal of equality of opportunity.[1] Liberal-democratic narratives of progress both structured the conception of racial inequality as a lack of access (to schools, lunch counters) due to prejudice and propelled the growth of consumer capitalistic culture and its metaphors as the vehicle through which to promote racial equality. These narratives were further aided and abetted by the Cold War ideological and military battle between the United States and the Soviet Union in the aftermath of World War II, in which American liberal-democratic politics and consumer capitalism were pitted against the Soviet Union's state-planned communism.[2] The Cold War itself is so significant to this era that it is the subject of the following, companion chapter on Cold War beauty culture.

The dominance of American political democratic liberalism intertwined with the growth of American consumer capitalism. Throughout the twentieth century, the U.S. economy shifted from that of a primarily industrial society to a consumer service economy. During the Great Depression, U.S. governmental policies, marked by programs ranging from the Works Progress Administration to the National Recovery Administration, heavily intervened in the U.S. economy.[3] World War II accelerated the U.S. government's turn to a consumer economy in its control of wartime production of goods and rationing of consumption. The fear of a postwar slump and regression to an economic depression propelled active campaigns to consume as an act of patriotism.

These mid-twentieth-century shifts to a politically liberal-democratic consumer society changed categories of cultural citizenship as defined by the interplay between race, citizenship, and belonging. In fact, the discourses of consumption shaped the parameters of civil rights; as historian Lizabeth Cohen has found, mid-twentieth-century civil rights actions were articulated through the right to be a consumer citizen-subject.[4] In other words, racial equality was most successfully framed not through the ideology of natural rights but through the right of free access to consume. Thus civil rights workers agitated for (and won) racial desegregation through the right to accommodation in the public sector, such as the desegregation of Woolworth's lunch counters, of buses, and of schools.

Articles such as "Short-Cut to Glamor" were part of larger Asian American attempts to redress American racism through the deployment of those liberal narratives that advocated the free access to consume and the need to combat prejudice. Published in the Japanese American–

turned–Asian American popular magazine *Scene,* that article and myriad others in every issue showed how Asian American women could display contemporary hairstyles as well as food, fashion, skin-care and recreational activities that would show their modernity, prove their cultural citizenship, and thus lessen racial prejudice and further equality. This was completely in keeping with the times. Works such as Gunnar Myrdal's landmark *American Dilemma* and those produced by researchers trained by Robert Park at the University of Chicago School of Sociology studied the role of attitudes and "prejudice" in negative racialized behavior.[5] Building on those ideas, civil rights activists, politicians, social workers, and others focused on the pedagogy of combating racial prejudice through exposure, normalization, and equal access to public accommodations.[6] Introduced as the prime evidence for the landmark *Brown v. Board of Education* (1954) school desegregation decision, the Clark doll studies best exemplified liberal-democratic ideas around racial prejudice. Using brown and white dolls, Kenneth and Mamie Clark revealed that young children of all races had already learned damaging hierarchical racialized ideas.[7] By showing that racial prejudice had ill effects at an early age, the proponents of *Brown* v. *Board of Education* argued successfully that schools should be desegregated in order to create the liberal goal of equal access to education. According to liberal-democratic ideology, that equal access would level opportunities, create more contact between the races, and thus lessen prejudice.

"Short-Cut to Glamor" and portrayals of "healthy" all-American youth culture were other such weapons in the democratic liberal war on harmful racial attitudes. Asian American communities produced cultural artifacts such as magazines and ethnic newspapers that showed the construction of the Asian American modern liberal consumer-citizen as young and female. To fight racial prejudice and claim belonging in the liberal American consumer nation, cultural citizenship entailed proper participation in modern consumption culture. Propelled by the post–World War II baby boom, youth were the most significant disciples of and players in liberal consumer culture. The United States was not unique in the twentieth-century trend of equating national vigor with youth, for in the 1930s, fascist and communist regimes tended to glorify male youth as the ideal national representative body.[8] Finally, Asian American communities in particular had disproportionately large numbers of youth in the postwar era because of the historical restriction on Asian female migration, which resulted in late community formation.

Like other Americans, Asian Americans grappled with being consumer-subjects. Yet, despite the seductive liberal promise of equality through consumption, the playing field was not level. When were Asian Americans permitted to enter the world of the American consumer republic? During the middle of the twentieth century, Asian Americans were not a marketing category targeted by mainstream advertisers, corporations, or media entities. Hence, to locate Asian Americans in popular culture, one must look not at mainstream sources but to community outlets such as racial minority newspapers and magazines.

In privileging racial minority sources over mainstream ones, this work shows the uneasy relationship between racial minorities and the nation-state. Like much current scholarship, this work builds on that of the Frankfurt school, but it does not follow the latter's condemnation of popular and mass cultures as mere reflections of hegemonic values. Instead, examining liberal-democratic narratives shows how Asian Americans used that language within their popular culture practices to argue for an enhanced place in the American nation-state. In addition, this chapter refutes any notion that participation in mainstream forms of cultural practices reduces racial identity by showing the building of community allegiances, diasporic cultural citizenship, and broader participation in Asian American culture.[9] Moreover, by focusing on racial minority popular culture, this work reveals the unmarked whiteness of the liberal American consumer-subject. Finally, Asian American youth consumer culture imagined an American society where the racial equality promised in liberal-democratic consumer society was put into practice. Through *Scene* magazine and clubs such as the sorority Chi Alpha Delta, young Asian Americans built multiple Asian-ethnic cultural events as well as interracial coalitions.

Crafting Asian American Liberal-Democratic Consumer Cultural Citizenship

Throughout the middle of the twentieth century, wars in Asia against fascism and, later, communism not only consolidated the dominance but inculcated particular aspects of American liberal democracy. The Sino-Japanese War in the 1930s, the bombing of Pearl Harbor and World War II, and the post–World War II occupation of Japan had profound implications in forming American political culture. Asian Americans were able to craft cultural citizenship through displays of patriotism in two particularly interesting ways. First, Asian American communities used the language of liberal-democratic consumer citizenship to combine loyalty to Asian nations with their allegiance to the United States. In other words, Asian Americans worked to reconcile their diasporic affiliations—shared history, cultural heritage, and politics with an imagined homeland—within the acceptable limits of their American citizenship. Second, wartime exigencies highlighted the importance of young Asian American women as patriotic community representatives. Although patriotism and cultural citizenship at times overlap, not all displays of cultural citizenship are patriotic. By patriotism I am referring to an overt, declared allegiance to hegemonic notions of nationalism, usually acknowledged as such by dominant society.

What is particularly fascinating in this era is how Asian Americans used the language and practices of liberal-democratic consumerism to expand the construction of patriotism to include their nation of origin. As discussed in the preceding chapter, Japanese imperialism in Manchuria and China proved to be a turning point for Chinese American cultural citizenship. In the 1930s, the mainstream American perception of China became favorable because of the Sino-Japanese War, for the United States favored China over Japan. Although Japan had been committing acts of aggression in China since 1931, with the Japanese invasion of Manchuria in 1937, previously politically divided Chinese American communities united in support of China.[10] What is really important is that the Chinese American communities were able to cast their support for China in ways that buttressed, not opposed, their loyalty to the United States.

The wars in Asia laid the groundwork for a new formation of Asian American cultural citizenship by setting the stage for young women to become visible symbols of Asian community patriotism as channeled through liberal-democratic consumer culture. In the 1930s, gender and consumerism—or to use Meg Jacob's term, "pocketbook politics"—structured political protests.[11] For example, Chinese American women led the National Dollar Store Strike and boycotted silk stockings to protest Japanese imperialism. This was in keeping with the actions of other racial minorities, such as the black nationalists and socialist-leaning New Negroes who advocated racial solidarity with the marketplace in order to achieve black economic power.[12] China War Relief encompassed those gendered consumer politics through activities such as clothing drives, food donations, and soliciting medical supplies. By 1930 over fifteen thousand Chinese American women, 67 percent of whom were American-born, lived in the United States.[13] Large numbers of those women participated in clubs such as the Women's Patriotic Club in San Francisco; the New Life Association with chapters in Chicago, New York, Portland, Boston, Seattle, and California; and the Chinese Women's Association of New York, all of which formed in response to the war and were dedicated to war relief.

Similarly, for Filipino Americans, World War II signaled an opportunity to demonstrate their fitness for citizenship and to prove the worth of the Philippines' decolonization through the language of democratic liberalism. Filipina American women were instrumental in culturally defining Filipino American roles in World War II.[14] For example, students in the Philippine-Michigan Club at the University of Michigan held a fundraising dance and clothing drive. The group raised over five hundred dollars and twenty-one boxes of clothing.

Democratic-liberal narratives structured declarations of loyalty to America in the face of Philippines decolonization. To initiate the University of Michigan fundraiser, Mrs. Pilar H. Lim spoke on "The Orient Sees America's Vision," in which she "stressed the faith that the Filipinos have in America as defender of their liberty," as well as the "gratitude that our country now has for American armies fighting in the Philippines." In her speech, Lim explained how Filipino Americans had been the beneficiaries of American democracy. Lim extolled the Americans who had "brought education, commerce, better methods of sanitation and agriculture, and democratic government to the Philippines."[15] An "American" (presumably European American) gentleman declared that although America did not fully merit Lim's praise, her words created enormous goodwill and international friendship. If they could show they were people who recognized and practiced liberal democracy, Filipinos could then prove their ability to self-govern after decolonization.

Another interesting development that would carry over into the postwar period is that in the struggle to prove American cultural citizenship during the war years, Asian American communities relied on young female figureheads. Since soldiers are overwhelmingly marked as male, women during wartime functioned as safer representatives of racial minority community loyalty. Given the racial conflation of Asian American with Asian, male Asian American bodies in drum corps uniforms marching down Main Street might raise the specter of a hostile invasion. Women thus more safely represented Asian American patriotic loyalty to the American nation-state. Indeed, as we shall see later in this chapter, gendering of patriotism and cultural citizenship figured well into the post–World War II era.

Asian American communities used young women as especially compelling symbols of American patriotism to further claims of American cultural citizenship. For example, the Mei Wah Girls club started a drum corps to promote China War Relief. As Mei Wah means "American" in Chinese, this naming process beautifully illustrates how, through cultural citizenship, a group tries to claim both racial difference and mainstream national belonging. The twelve women that constituted the Mei Wah Girls Drum Corps choreographed their routines and designed their own costumes.[16] Modeled on military band uniforms, their garments showed hybridity between American and Chinese fashions. In allegiance to their Chinese heritage, their shirts bore frog fastenings and cheongsam-type collars and sleeves, which they paired with American white pants and shoes. For the most part, the women sported fashionable permanent-waved, shoulder-length hair and resplendent smiles. As exemplars of community, the Mei Wah Girls personified gendered patriotic Asian Americans in ways that proved so popular that they were asked to perform at Los Angeles citywide events such as the Santa Claus parade and the opening of Union Station.

Chinese Americans were not the only Asian American ethnic group to gender patriotism in order to claim American cultural citizenship; Korean Americans did so as well. Although before World War II there were not many people of Korean descent in the United States, Dora Yum Kim's autobiography shows how Korean American women symbolized their community. Kim remembers 1942 as a turning point because, for the first time, Korean Americans were asked to participate in San Francisco's American Day Parade. She reminisced that "we wanted to have a bunch of girls walking as a group in the parade. We didn't have enough girls in San Francisco so we got Korean girls from all over California."[17] Since Kim lived in San Francisco's Chinatown and knew the parade route, she was asked to lead the Korean American women's march. As loyal Americans participating in the American Day Parade, Korean American women wanted to prove their communities' cultural citizenship.

Parallel to these Korean American and Chinese American women, being female rendered Anna May Wong's patriotic displays suitable for mainstream consumption. Wong used her celebrity status to raise money and support for China War Relief. As seen in the preceding chapter, "I

Protest," in the movie *King of Chinatown,* Wong played a physician who gave up a prestigious surgical career in the United States in order to go to China to lead an ambulance corps. In real life, Wong's public demonstrations of cultural citizenship were considered part of her American patriotism, for she aided war relief both in mainstream venues and Chinese American enclaves. Like celebrities, Wong entertained the troops by performing with the United Service Organization (USO) camp shows up and down the Pacific Coast, even to Alaska. Given the war in Asia, using a female performer of Asian descent to entertain American troops was symbolically important in breaking down the mutable racial hatreds. As was the case for the Mei Wah Girls and Korean American women, deploying female performers was critical. The long history of the "yellow peril" and fears of the Asian contagion combined with images of Japanese militarism would render alien and threatening American male performers of Asian descent.

The construct of liberal-democratic consumerism propelled the dismantling of institutional racism, for racial segregation contradicted America's democratic war aims. On a practical level, the need for additional bodies in the war industry prompted presidential decrees such as Executive Order 8022, which forbade discrimination in federally funded defense industries. Thus World War II signaled the beginning of the end of state-sanctioned institutional racism and segregation in the wage-labor market. For racial and ethnic minority groups other than Japanese Americans, and for women of all races, the wartime labor shortages facilitated the move into better jobs that had not been open to them before the war.[18] For Chinese American women, the war ushered in a dramatic improvement in status.[19] As historian Judy Yung has discovered, World War II marked a turning point for Chinese American women in terms of wage-labor opportunities and public roles. Chinese American women took jobs in the armed services, defense factories, and the private sector, and in the public sector worked in war relief. These jobs, in turn, provided them not only with the money to be consumers but access to a world predicated on the work–leisure divide.

For Chinese Americans, these avid displays of cultural citizenship through patriotism, combined with political developments, resulted in the reinstatement of immigration rights. In 1943, because of the need to placate China as an ally and to secure the consent of Chinese Americans, the U.S. government rescinded the decades-long policy of Chinese immigration exclusion.[20] And Chinese American men at this time were partially integrated into the armed services, unlike African American, Filipino American, and Japanese American men, who served in segregated units.

Internment

Japanese American internment, however, shows how race contradicted the American creed of democratic liberalism. The outbreak of World War II and the subsequent tragedy of the internment of Japanese Americans chronicled the failure of the American government and the American public to see Japanese Americans as American citizens. The story of Chi Alpha Delta, the predominantly Japanese American sorority chronicled in chapter 1, demonstrates not only the failure of American democratic liberalism but also how the future of Japanese Americans as Americans necessitated learning and displaying cultural citizenship as channeled through democratic liberalism. As Chi Alpha Delta sorority member Toshi Miyamoto reported, with the bombing of Pearl Harbor on December 7, 1941, "[the] atmosphere [at UCLA] really changed. I was scared and didn't want to be seen too much. I felt so conspicuous because I was Japanese and I didn't want to venture out onto campus."[21] As Miyamoto's interview and many other personal narratives have documented, first- and second-generation Japanese Americans fell under scrutiny and suspicion.[22] The UCLA school newspaper, the *Daily Bruin,* documented the slow abrogation of the students' rights, from suspicion to curfew to internment.[23]

The beginning of World War II highlighted Chi Alpha Delta's citizenship under fire. On December 8, 1941, the current members' dinner meeting was "cancelled due to the national crisis."[24] In early February, sorors attempted to maintain a semblance of normalcy by continuing sorority events even though school had been disrupted "because of the present unusual conditions."[25] However, on February 19, 1942, President Franklin Delano Roosevelt signed Executive Order 9066, which gave the secretary of war the power to designate military zones and exclude any persons from them. With the Executive Order, Los Angeles became part of the Western Regional Defense (WRD) zone, which meant that the military had the authority forcibly to relocate into concentration camps people of Japanese ancestry living within the zone's boundaries, the majority of whom were American citizens.

Given the internment order, Chi Alpha Delta sorors had to improvise in order to cope with their imminent departure to an unspecified location

for an unknown duration. The members of both the active and the alumnae groups stored their minutes, records, and scrapbooks at the home of
one of their European American advisers, Mrs. Bernice Nelson. On March
13, 1942, the active members decided that if the chapter did not reorganize
three years after the war had ended, then the house fund and any additional money would be converted to a Japanese American scholarship
fund.[26] In all likelihood, as told in chapter 1, had the Janss brothers not refused to sell the chapter-house property in Westwood to the Chis, the
sorors would have either had to give it up for quick sale or lost it to another form of de facto confiscation.

Despite American cultural citizenship practices such as the Chi's Barnyard Frolics and Organdie Dances, Japanese Americans' claims to Americanness were ignored. In one of the greatest violations of twentieth-century American liberal democracy, the U.S. military summarily interned
more than 110,000 people of Japanese descent, including approximately
twenty-five hundred college students. A University of California question-
naire showed that most students wanted to continue their education and
that they prioritized it over remaining with their families in relocation
centers.[27] All in all, internment forced 244 Japanese American students to
leave UCLA.[28] Though the sorority archival records do not show any
wartime activities in the internment camps, the speed with which the
sorority reestablished itself after the war demonstrates that, at a minimum, the members maintained contact with each other.

The relocation of the approximately twenty-five hundred Japanese
American college students who lived in the Western Regional Defense
zone raised the specter of military sabotage and racial uprisings through
interracial coalition building. For starters, the war relocation authorities
had to identify universities outside the WRD zone that were willing to
accept Japanese American students.[29] For example, the University of
Chicago accepted Japanese American students but restricted them from
defense project sites.[30] Led by Fisk president Thomas E. Jones, adminis-
trators at African American colleges such as Fisk and Howard warmly
welcomed Japanese American students.[31] However, at first the National
Japanese American Student Relocation Council, the government organization in charge of supervising the removal of Japanese American students, refused to send Japanese Americans to black colleges, fearing that
placing indignant Japanese Americans among angry African Americans
would cause multiracial civil rights uprisings. Later, the council partially
acquiesced by saying it would not be "sending the sort who would col-

laborate with negro student agitators in causing a troubled situation."[32] One can only speculate as to the potential for cross-race student coalition agitation for civil rights. Catholic, Protestant denominational, and small liberal arts schools tended to be the most welcoming of Nisei students.[33]

The internment camps forced Japanese American participation in democratic liberalism that propelled the Nisei generation into community leadership roles. Internment camp schools taught courses on "common ideals of democratic citizenship," as did Americanization classes and English lessons for the immigrant Issei.[34] In addition, model governments within the camps ensured the prevalence of American liberal democracy. As the camp authorities privileged those with English-language skills and a knowledge of American liberal democracy, the young Nisei generation assumed disproportionately greater community leadership roles than they would have had they not been interned.[35]

Indeed, while in the internment camps, all Japanese Americans were forced to answer a direct citizenship test. The war relocation authority forced all internees to answer a "registration" petition that not only required them to declare loyalty to the United States but also made those men of military draft age who declared themselves loyal to register for the military selective service. Those who refused to declare their loyalty were threatened with deportation or sent to the "troublemakers'" Tule Lake highest-security concentration camp. John Okada's 1957 novel *No-No Boys* memorialized such acts of refusal.

The war accelerated the Japanese American participation in American culture that had begun in the 1930s. As historian Valerie Matsumoto argues, the war had a significant impact on the status of Japanese Americans, and on women in particular.[36] Clearly, internment was a horrific event that disrupted every aspect of Japanese American life on the West Coast. However, analogous to the situation of African American women under slavery, whose men were also subject to white male patriarchal control, Japanese American women were able to gain status relative to the men in their community because in the internment camps, regulations undermined patriarchal authority within the ethnic community.[37] Women in the camps were paid low but equal wages for equal labor and had increased leisure time to devote to recreational activities. For the second generation, dating was not as supervised by parents; young men and women had many more opportunities to socialize. Thus, youth cultural activities would explode in the postwar era.

Although internment targeted Japanese Americans, other Asian-ethnic groups were misidentified as Japanese and thus were also racialized by internment. Korean American Mary Paik's lived experience, for example, showed how all Asian Americans were potentially subjected to violence. In her autobiography, Paik explained: "They just assumed that all Orientals were Japanese; they didn't even bother to find out before committing violence."[38] To avert that violence, Chinese Americans famously donned buttons proclaiming their ethnicity.[39]

American popular culture participated in the ethnic differentiation that resulted in the spurious demonization of the Japanese. After the attack on Pearl Harbor, *Time* magazine published an infamous article on how to tell Chinese friends from Japanese enemies that included cultural "evidence" such as Japanese wearing horn-rimmed glasses.[40] This eyeglass example shows how mainstream culture looks to consumer articles for racial identification cues. Given the atmosphere and racialized violence, there were strong incentives for Asian Americans to perform Asian-ethnic specific cultural citizenship. On that same date, *Life* magazine published its version called "How to Tell Japs from the Chinese." Much more heavily indebted to anthropological comparisons derived from scientific racism, the *Life* magazine article included annotated photographs. For example, *Life* declared that "the Japs" betrayed "aboriginal antecedents in a squat, long-torsoed build, a broader, more massively boned head and face, flat, often pug nose, yellow-ocher skin and heavier beard."[41] As enemies, the Japanese were considered more primitive and warlike than the Chinese, who "wear [the] rational calm of tolerant realists." In the postwar era, the task, then, was for Japanese Americans to craft suitable counternarratives of race through liberal-democratic consumer culture.

Postwar Asian American Liberal-Democratic Consumer Subjects

A closer examination of *Scene*, a leading Asian American magazine published in the postwar era, shows how the political need to prove cultural citizenship in the aftermath of World War II compelled the display of the young, wholesome, female, all-American citizen-subject. Produced in Chicago from 1949 to 1953, *Scene* magazine provides a marvelous glimpse into the creation of an Asian American consumer-subject that at first focused on Japanese Americans and later incorporated other Asian-ethnic Americans, such as Chinese and Korean Americans. Magazines have heavily intervened in the political economies and cultures of race, gender, class, and nation.[42] It is the very fact that *Scene* was not an explicit youth or female magazine that makes its emphasis on female and youth cultures so striking. Modeled after *Life* magazine, *Scene* included features on international politics and had Japanese-language feature articles and advertisements. Yet *Scene* editors almost always placed young women of Asian descent on the magazine's cover and the majority of issues focused on women and youth activities. Thus, building upon World War II female exemplars, the good Asian American citizen was young and female. In the pictures accompanying the articles, *Scene* indirectly promoted female improvement, for the women were very well dressed, which demonstrated that knowing appropriate class-inflected clothing and makeup for each occasion was crucial to social success. Through features on food and fashion, *Scene* could create a national and international "imagined community" of culture by instilling in its readers the desire to buy the most appropriate products, as well as offering lessons in how to display appropriate Asian American cultural citizenship.[43]

Scene and its contemporaries, *Nisei Vue* and *East Wind,* were by no means anomalies in the history of Asian Americans and print media.[44] Demographic factors influenced when and where the magazines emerged. After World War II internment and resettlement, Chicago's population of Japanese Americans skyrocketed, from 320 in 1940 to 11,233 in 1950.[45] The changing political economy meant that increasing numbers of Japanese Americans had the income to buy the magazines and to participate in cultural activities similar to those portrayed in the magazines.

Though women were the subjects and objects of the overwhelming majority of the features, *Scene* magazine was edited, produced, and written chiefly by men. The first editor of *Scene,* Robert Ozaki, published the August 1949 edition. The staff changed the subsequent year to publisher James Nishimura and editor-in-chief Togo Tanaka, who would guide the magazine until its demise in 1954. These men were Nisei who were prominent in the extensive Japanese American periodical world. Togo Tanaka, for example, had previously been the English-language editor for the *Rafu Shimpo* (the Los Angeles Daily News) and was imprisoned by the FBI immediately after Pearl Harbor.[46]

Scene aimed at nothing less than to eradicate the social and cultural damage inflicted by World War II. In a July 1952 editorial, Nishimura and Tanaka explained the motivations for the founding of the magazine: "[to] help heal the wounds of war—both here at home and across the

Pacific."[47] Racial hatreds between the United States and Japan tapped into particular manipulable anti-Asian racial narratives in order to build support for the war at home, which had resulted in a particularly bitter Pacific war as well as in internment.[48] For Japanese Americans, internment caused postwar wounds of dislocation, unjust accusations, and economic and social upheaval. An integral part of the war, the production of cultural knowledge of the "other" ranged from war pamphlets, to the *Time* magazine article stating the differences between the Chinese and the Japanese, to Ruth Benedict's anthropological studies of the Japanese. The publication of *Scene* magazine was the Japanese American community's attempt to produce cultural knowledge consistent with liberal-democratic consumer values.

The magazine's founders wished to lessen racial prejudice through demonstrating proper belonging in American democratic-liberal consumer culture. *Scene*'s April 1952 issue linked the production of an Americanized cultural citizenship to Japanese American internment and implied that it was a way to prevent future incarceration. An article entitled "So Let's Americanize . . . Whom?" explained the reasons for adopting cultural behaviors as follows: "The U.S. Commissioner of Indian Affairs is a kindly man who ran the relocation camps of World War II. Niseis remember his message: *Go ye forth from these barbed-wire camps, back into the mainstream of American life. Americanize yourselves.*"[49] Since many of the internment camps were on former or present-day Native American reservations, it is apt that the man in charge of the camps later became the U.S. Commissioner of Indian Affairs. By dressing like people portrayed in *Scene* and participating in activities profiled in the magazine, Japanese Americans could prove not only to themselves but, more important, to the larger society how American they really were.

Mainstream resistance to *Scene* magazine proved how magazines were contested terrain for racial attitudes. Even in 1950, Japanese Americans continued to bear the brunt of America's World War II resentment toward Japan. Non–Japanese Americans' puzzled and angry responses to *Scene* showed they did not accept Japanese Americans as Americans. *Scene* magazine profiled an episode where a reporter, a non–Asian American woman judging by her name, tested the public's reception of the magazine. In the September 1950 article, Florence LaFontaine Randall documented the conflation of Japan with Japanese Americans and the lingering race hatreds of the average American toward Japanese and Japanese Americans:

Gathering together all the copies of SCENE I had I entered a Midwest hotel and laid the copies on a lobby table within easy reach of roving guests.

"I never saw a Japanese magazine before. It's funny they would allow such a thing."

I asked, "Why not? They're Americans, aren't they?"

"I doubt it, after the last war. I hate the ———."

... "All I know is that they're killers, dope fiends and war mad."

... out of 15 observations, all but 4 like that one.[50]

The above quotations illustrate the inability of most of the fifteen respondents to categorize people of Japanese descent as legitimate American citizens and show the perpetual demonization of them as World War II enemies. *Scene*'s pictures and stories of Americanized activities attempted to address such people's fears and misunderstandings of Japanese Americans and, through the images and narratives of liberal-democratic American consumer culture, to show the general American public that Japanese Americans were indeed "good" Americans who partook of cultural practices such as sports and beauty contests.

As befit an era that defined civil rights as the access to public accommodation and the right to consume, the magazine promoted buying a subscription as a patriotic act and urged its readers not only to subscribe but to give gift subscriptions as a means to gain allies, presumably among non–Japanese Americans. Thus beneficiaries of *Scene* gift subscriptions could see that Japanese Americans were Americanized, not aliens. *Scene*'s cost, twenty-five cents per issue, three dollars per annual subscription, was right in line with other contemporary American magazines.

Scene created not just a national imagined community of readers but an international one as well. From its inception, *Scene* circulated in a global economy and in some ways can be considered one facet of a cultural Marshall plan for Asia. A year after the magazine's first issue in August 1949, in September 1950 the editors announced subscription information that showed the magazine reached audiences around the world: "Starting in October, subscription basis. 25,000 copies of Scene each month to readers throughout the United States, in Canada, Alaska, Mexico, Central and South America, the Hawaiian Islands, and Japan." *Scene* magazine was particularly concentrated in countries that had significant Japanese populations. Although readers lived primarily in the United States, judging by letters to the editor, *Scene* was of great interest overseas. Given that in countries such as Peru the U.S. government had pressured the national government to intern its citizens of Japanese descent, American cultural citizenship practices were doubtless of great interest there as well.

Despite (or perhaps because of) its Americanization focus, *Scene* also demonstrated cultural citizenship that went beyond nation-state borders. Not only did *Scene* want to reach out to the Japanese diaspora, but the magazine's larger goal was to target the entire Asian diaspora: "*Scene* intends to become America's outstanding magazine of Asia."[51] By 1952, as shown in this chapter's section on pan-Asian ethnicity, readers viewed and read about the activities of other Asian-ethnic groups such as Korean Americans and Chinese Americans. By 1953, *Scene* changed its focus enough to merit a change in subtitle from "The Pictorial Magazine" to "The International East-West magazine." Like Chinese American youth such as Jade Snow Wong, the Japanese American second generation could act as a bridge between East and West.[52] As "the East" grappled with issues ranging from American military occupation to the new Cold War politics, *Scene* magazine offered a vantage point as to how Asians within a global superpower were performing American cultural citizenship.

Scene *and the Asian American Consumer Culture*

As Asian Americans stood outside mainstream consumer marketing categories, ethnic newspapers and magazines such as *Scene* reveal the making of the Asian American consumer subject. The incredible productivity of the American post–World War II consumer economy had profound societal implications. Postwar abundance meant so much more than a washing machine in every home. Instead, such riches were linked to democratic political freedom. Just as the goods would supposedly be evenly distributed throughout society, so would political rights.[53] *Scene* aimed to become the Asian American consumer cultural bible, adherence to which would allow one to become the ideal postwar liberal-democratic consumer subject.

Like most magazines, *Scene* adhered to a relatively standardized format from month to month. The cover featured a young Asian American woman with an appearance considered to be attractive. Her profile would be featured in the first few pages of the magazine. When letters to the editor appeared, they tended to be placed near the beginning. The "Feminine

Scene" column did not appear in every issue, but when it did, readers could find it toward the back of the magazine. The bulk of the pages were devoted to features such as "Miss Bussei of '53" and "Most Glamorous Mother." Photographs and advertisements appeared throughout the magazine.

From an economic-structural standpoint, *Scene* occupied a very different niche from mainstream periodicals. Almost all of its advertisements for goods and services targeted Japanese American local or national audiences. In fact, there were very few advertisements compared to mainstream magazines of the time such as *Life* and *Time*. There were no national mainstream corporate advertisements such as those for dish soap or automobiles. In almost every issue, Japanese corporations placed a few brand-name advertisements for items such as soy sauce and cameras.[54] Other advertisements targeted Japanese Americans by listing travel to Japan. Some of the advertisements that did not directly target Japanese Americans were placed by the Chicago Publishing Corporation, which promoted mail-order books such as "How to Talk More Effectively."[55] One might speculate that, since *Scene* did not have many advertisements, let alone mainstream ones, they were more able to respond to audience demands and publishers' imperatives.

What is very striking about *Scene* magazine is that, directly counter to its features and covers, advertisements usually did not feature Asian American bodies. Often they depicted objects rather than the people who used them. For example, in an advertisement for Kikkoman soy sauce, the picture showed two bottles of soy sauce with a flag and "Nippon" on the left and a saucepan on the right. A boat drawn over an arrow connected the soy sauce and the saucepan.[56] The layout was meant to be a sketchy representation of the world; Japan had soy sauce on the west/left and America had the saucepan on the east/right. Above the boat was the caption "Japanese flavor for your dinner table," and below the saucepan "For Sukiyaki Kikkoman Soy Sauce." Another strategy for advertising to Asian Americans without using Asian American models was employed by the Chicago Publishing Corporation. When they advertised their "Magic Dress Pattern Maker," they used a drawing in which the pattern maker was held by a hand rendered feminine by nail polish and bracelets. However, the drawing did not include a body, thus circumventing the need to race the body.[57]

In conjunction with its diasporic and global ambitions, the growth of Chicago's local middle-class Japanese American population can be seen through the Chicago-area Japanese American insurance and real-estate agents who advertised in *Scene*. Chicago merchants placed many local advertisements, which allowed the community to take economic shape. *Scene* put those advertisements in a special section entitled "Chicago Advertisers." Almost all the restaurant advertisements came from Chinese restaurants, such as the Golden Star Restaurant, which boasted the "Best Chinese Food in Chicago" and a "Special Cantonese Chef," and Wah Mai Lo, with its chow mein, barbequed pork, egg roll, sweet and sour ribs, Hong Kong noodle, and Ding Hoe chop suey.[58] For Japanese Americans, Chinese restaurants were the places to celebrate special occasions, for in an era of segregation, racial and religious minorities frequently found themselves unwelcome in European American restaurants.

As the Asian American consumer markets were underdeveloped, it is possible that the editorial staff had some space for promoting a particular vision of Japanese Americans and United States–Japan relations because their funding came mainly from subscriptions, not advertisers.[59] There were not as many advertisements that targeted women as one would expect given the feminine nature of the magazine's articles and given women's roles as chief consumers in American society. One reason for the paucity of advertisements can be attributed to the demographics and economics of the Asian American communities. Unlike African American communities, which made up a substantial portion of the American population, or Mexican American communities, which could also market to Mexico and Central America, advertisers targeting Asian Americans did not have a large enough audience to justify mounting a campaign that targeted Asian Americans/Asian American women. Though infrequent, when the magazine carried advertisements with images of Asian women, the ads used Japanese women. *Scene's* August 1953 issue carried an advertisement for Juju skin cream featuring screen star Michiyo Kogure of Japan as a model to give the product glamour.[60]

Given the focus on youth and youth activities, one might expect advertisements targeting young people, featuring entities such as clubs, meetings, or recreational activities. However, *Scene* did not have such advertisements. In all likelihood, clubs could not afford to advertise in *Scene,* a monthly spot would be too infrequent to meet their needs, and they received free publicity through *Scene's* profiles anyway. Unlike European American youth in the 1950s, Asian American youth were too small a group to attract the attention of Madison Avenue advertising firms.[61]

Hence there were no advertisements for "youth" items such as hula hoops, chewing gum, or clothing.

Japanese American Liberal-Democratic Youth Culture

As could be expected, postinternment Japanese Americans had the most to gain from proving American cultural citizenship, and *Scene* magazine and Japanese American youth clubs were primary weapons in their demo-cratic-liberal war on negative racial attitudes. Newspaper articles on Chi Alpha Delta rush events and *Scene* magazine articles such as "Beauty Basi-cally Speaking" and "A Nisei? Well, Yes and No" showed the construction of the idealized Japanese American modern liberal consumer culture as young and disproportionately female. *Scene* was not a teenager or youth magazine, nor were youth the only age demographic. Yet the images, pic-tures, and activities of various communities were replete with healthy, vig-orous female youth. Building on the lessons learned from World War II, editors hoped that such exemplars would lead the way to a racially equi-table society. During an era of racial segregation, one of many civil rights aims was to claim space in consumer culture by showing and practicing ideal citizenship. Although the focus on youth culture was in keeping with postwar mainstream American society, the emphasis on its female practi-tioners was particularly Asian American. This section focuses on two as-pects of Japanese American youth culture.[62] First, it examines the details of gendered Japanese American youth culture. Second, it investigates how Japanese American participation in youth consumer culture was not just a sign of assimilation but marked them as racialized subjects. In other words, it signaled social practices that marked Asian American distance and differences from mainstream society, and thus the constitution of Asian American culture.

Chi Alpha Delta's swift reorganization attested to female youth culture's tremendous salience. During the first school year after the cessation of the war, 1945–1946, Japanese American college students returned to the for-mer Western Regional Defense zone, and 632 attended West Coast univer-sities and colleges.[63] Chi Alpha Delta regrouped well within the allotted three years and paid to have their photograph included in UCLA's 1947 yearbook. The official meetings of both the active and alumnae chapters recommenced in 1946. The rapid reestablishment of the undergraduate chapter of Chi Alpha Delta can be attributed to the support of the well-organized alumnae chapter. As Paula Fass and Beth Bailey have demonstrated, collegiate life was a prime location for learning good citizenship.[64]

Chi Alpha Delta's activities demonstrated American cultural citizenship during the age of consumer democratic liberalism so well that they were profiled in *Scene* magazine. Although their activities were very similar to those of the prewar era, exposure through forums such as *Scene* normalized their activities for a national and international audience and created a national Asian American culture. After reorganizing in 1946, they continued rituals that had taken place in the prewar era by holding a formal dance to honor the women who had most recently agreed to join the sorority. As in the prewar era, the sorority designated which members were new, "virgin" ones by asking them to wear white gowns. The Chi Alpha Deltas invited all alumnae, the new pledges, and the *Rafu Shimpo* newspaper staff, including renowned columnist Mary Oyama, to the dance.[65] The women announced their presence at UCLA by participating in campus Greek events such as Mardi Gras and Spring Sing. While reestablishing the sorority, the women of Chi Alpha Delta found much to discuss with each other, sometimes to the detriment of their study habits. Belying any silent Asian female image, in 1946 they talked so animatedly that they were "asked to refrain from sitting together in the library and making too much noise!"[66]

Young Japanese American women demanded inclusion in *Scene* magazine as exemplars of the ideal postwar citizen-subject. *Scene* featured several young women's clubs organized for social activities. These numerous Chicago clubs consolidated under an umbrella organization and held an annual dance and queen contest. Young women around the country noticed the attention received by the Chicago women, for many identified with the young women and enjoyed similar club activities. An April 1953 letter to the editor in *Scene* from San Francisco Bay Area readers said: "Dear Sirs: The pictures of the girls' clubs of Chicago in the February issue made it certainly one of the best. . . . We'd like to make a suggestion. There are quite a few girls' social clubs in San Francisco and the Bay area (Jynx, Sigma Rho, Dhyanas, to mention a few). It would be real swell if you would print an article and pictures of these clubs."[67] The editor replied that if they sent in photographs and a description, the magazine would try to print some of them.

Members of Theta Gamma Psi, a young women's social club formed in the East Bay of the San Francisco Bay Area, responded to the editor's April

1953 invitation to submit materials to the magazine. Two months later, in the June 1953 issue, *Scene* profiled the club in an article entitled "Club for Fun" and explained the club's founding as follows:

> A covey of California girls living in contiguous Oakland, Berkeley and Richmond woke up, a little over a year ago, to the fact that they were seeing an awful lot of each other.
>
> "Heck," one of them chirped at their umpteenth hen session, "if we're going to keep this up, we might as well set up a club."
>
> And so the girls did.
>
> It was refreshing, for a change, to see the sprouting of a club that unabashedly pretended to nothing but the pursuit of social pleasure.[68]

Although the magazine agreed to profile the club, the tone of the article trivializes its importance; the use of birdlike words like *hen, chirp,* and *covey* convey the impression that these women are not full human beings but lightweight and animal-like. The use of those words might have given readers the sense that the club was frivolous.

Despite the trivializing language, the article did explain that the women in the club picked out Greek letters for their name, Theta Gamma Psi, and had regular activities with each other and with young men. Like the UCLA sorority Chi Alpha Delta, the Theta Gamma Psis had a European American adviser, in this case Mrs. Naomi Goldstein. In 1953, fourteen young women were members of the club. To celebrate their first anniversary, the young women held a dinner at the Tonga Room Restaurant in San Francisco's exclusive Fairmont Hotel.

The club members' desire for publicity is significant for three reasons. First, it speaks to the women's desires for publicity and fame as the idealized postwar citizen-subjects. Second, it shows public acknowledgment of Americanized identities. Third, it demonstrates that the contents of the magazine were shaped not just by the editors but by the female readers. The submission of materials shows a desire to gain an authorial voice. Even if, as cynics might claim, the event was staged by the editors, nevertheless it gave the illusion that readers were engaged in dialogue with and participation in, rather than passive readership of, the magazine.

Scene was not a youth magazine, nor was it a women's magazine. Yet gendered culture continually appeared in its pages. Magazines such as *Scene* normalized "American" food for parties and provided daughters of immigrant women the knowledge of how to prepare and present such foods. In *Scene*'s September 1949 issue, the monthly column entitled the "Feminine Scene" showed readers—ostensibly female ones—how to make party sandwiches.[69] The article pointed out: "Preparing pretty party sandwiches is an easily acquired art and one that shows off, to a very good advantage, the cooking prowess of a clever hostess."[70] The story profiled a number of different sandwich combinations shaped into various forms, which included "avocado-pineapple sandwiches, raisin-peanut butter pinwheel sandwiches, celery seed breadsticks, cervelat (sausage) flash bars, cream cheese-jelly cube sandwiches, deviled ham-peanut butter star sandwiches." It was not only the wealthy women who were entertaining; many others did as well. However, what is particularly noteworthy is that while such an article highlights domestic labor, that activity was in honor of entertaining others, not in service of the nuclear family. *Scene* was not alone in advising youth how to entertain; *Seventeen* magazine published food columns three times a year in which they explained socially critical knowledge such as how to put together double-decker sandwiches that could be served when bringing "the gang" home after the movies.[71]

Scene's sandwich article underscored the importance of "American" food products—products changing due to the American stakes in a global political economy—when entertaining in the postwar era. As the above list of sandwiches shows, one effect of World War II was the prevalence of preserved-meat sandwiches, for the column did not include any ideas for fresh turkey or roast beef sandwiches. The inclusion of warm-climate ingredients such as avocados and pineapples were a result of growing populations in, and awareness of, California and Hawaii, plus improved U.S. food distribution networks and advertising that made such ingredients familiar, affordable, and desirable to the middle classes of all races.[72] This reflected how American consumer culture broadened its definition of acceptable American middle-class tastes. Japanese American adoption of those warm-weather climates marks their immigration and labor history growing pineapples in Hawaii and avocados in California. The differing shapes of the sandwiches such as pinwheels, stars, and cubes showed an interest in further developing domestic skills through showing clever presentation.

Asian American participation in consumer culture was not a sign of their assimilation to mainstream society but instead marked their difference from the mainstream white European American consumer subject. Adoption of forms with differences is key to cultural citizenship and hybrid racialized modernity. Female participants in youth culture have different restrictions and expectations placed on their lives; hence resistance is not an adequate measure of their subcultural potential.[73] Rather, subtle but telling differences in translation from mainstream culture mark not only Asian American distance from it but Asian American culture itself.

Japanese American youth transformed quotidian items into distinctively Asian American ones. Collective youth identity is embedded in consumer culture yet transforms it, for youth subcultures transform material objects in order to express their political affiliations. Dick Hebdige concurs that subcultures revolve around commodities such as fashion and music that have a symbolic value infused with political meaning not obvious to the casual outsider.[74] The following passage from "Teen-Age Fads" from a 1949 issue of the magazine *Nisei Vue* beautifully illustrates Hebdige's notion of youth subculture:

> Although the cartridge cases and sailor caps are basically alike, they don't look anything alike after the girls have worked on them for a while. For instance, they think a girl is a schmoe if she doesn't scribble all kinds of things on her case—such as the names of her favorite fella, songs, clubs, etc. No two purses look alike after all this scrawling! With the caps, it's the same story.[75]

This passage shows how Japanese American female youth acted as a subculture in relation not only to the adult population but also to European American youth. Customizing cartridge cases and sailor hats to denote favorite clubs and "fellas" marked the women racially as Japanese American. Those marks reworked war surplus, in part intended for the war effort against a Japanese enemy, into a local, alternative consumer product. Indeed, female accessories have been important markers of social location.[76]

What is particularly striking about modern consumer culture is the extent to which young women of all races turned to peers and magazines as arbiters of taste and style instead of relying on advice from their mothers.[77] In postwar displays of cultural citizenship, Asian American women found numerous occasions to display peer-driven "modern" and Western fashion and food choices. The women of Chi Alpha Delta, for example, used fashion to promote the sorority and as a pedagogical tool in showing how to clothe the ideal postwar citizen. The local Los Angeles Lanz-brand clothing store not only provided free loaner clothes for sorority fashion shows but would arrange for clothing fittings and accessories, would develop the program of appearance, and would either host it or type out comments for the sorority's choice of speaker. Chi Alpha Delta's 1959 fashion show used

Lanz clothing and sorority-member models. To make the event professional, the sorors rented a ramp from the Hollywood Dance Studio and hired Mrs. Merijane Yokoe, who had hosted similar events at the annual Japanese American Nisei Week festival, as their announcer. The organizers noted that the models would have to go for clothing fittings and practice their modeling, and that member Momoyo Ohara had had experience doing so. The Chi Alpha Deltas planned to write to Los Angeles–area newspapers such as the *Kashu Mainichi* and *Rafu Shimpo* for advance publicity and observed that they would have to provide their own photographs of the event, for the *Rafu* did not have a photographer to send.[78]

This Chi Alpha Delta fashion fundraiser shows how participation in consumer culture was fraught with class dissent. Using the Lanz name and fashions would appeal to the undergraduate female or "co-ed" population, thus heightening Chi Alpha Delta's prestige. Since Lanz provided the clothing for free, it was possible to hold the event as a fundraiser. However, some of the sorors believed that the Lanz brand line cost too much; thus it made no sense to hold a fashion extravaganza that featured clothing that many could not afford. This points to the desires and aspirations of young women as opposed to the reality of what they could afford. Sensitivity to the price of the clothing belied any notion of commodity culture being available to all. Thus consumer culture marginalized working-class women and those barely with a toehold in the middle class.

Racialized beauty and body standards in particular show Asian Americans' distance from European American hegemonic norms. Although theoretically anyone could adopt Western clothes and show American cultural citizenship through clothing purchases, manufacturing reality showed that the fashion industry privileged women of northern and western European extraction as having the normative body. Many Asian American women have had difficulty finding clothes that fit them, for, despite 75 percent of the entire U.S. female population being 5'4" and under, most dress manufacturers make clothes for taller women. *Scene*'s July 1950 issue addressed petite clothing needs:

> Even in these days of tall willowy models and matching dress creations, the petite milady is not entirely forgotten. Dresses and suits just as smart and exciting as those worn by her taller sisters can be found in stores which are devoted exclusively to dresses for the petite figure, such as Chicago's Pint-Size Shop which furnished the dresses on this page. You need not encounter the familiar "Please go to the Junior Miss Section" brushoffs.[79]

Scene showed its readers that petite women could find age-appropriate clothing at stores such as the Pint-Size Shop. Although the name of the shop sounds more like a children's boutique, supposedly women who shopped there would be treated as women rather than as girls. This advice echoes Alice Fong Yu's advice from the 1930s *Chinese Press* fashion column about modifying fashion to fit Asian bodies. At times, *Scene* magazine carved out a space for Asian American women to participate in consumer culture, despite obstacles posed by white standards of normative bodies.

How best to display contemporary hairstyles that would show their modernity, prove their cultural citizenship, and thus lessen racial prejudice and further equality fascinated Asian Americans all over the United States. Los Angeles reader Rosemary Ono reported that the beauty article "Short-Cut to Glamor" in *Scene's* April issue was what "we have been hoping to find in your magazine."[80] Ono's use of "we" implies either that she and others, such as friends and relatives, looked at and discussed the magazine together or that she was invoking a readily imagined community of female readers. Women could alleviate their gender anxieties about appropriate public appearances by following the tips in the article. For busy mothers and working women, the shortcuts offered in the article saved precious time and energy. They also constructed a raced, classed, and Americanized being. According to the magazine, this being was female, middle-class, and interested in same-sex social activities, fashion, beauty, and fun.[81]

It is precisely through disputes over issues such as beauty that groups delineate the boundaries of their values, and hence themselves. Despite Rosemary Ono's endorsement, Mineko Chado's latest American hairstyle, portrayed in "Short-Cut to Glamor," generated controversy in many parts of the United States among both men and women. "Short-Cut to Glamor" was a two-page pictorial that featured a hairstyle makeover on a young woman named Mineko Chado, complete with before and after photos. This feature on female improvement was completely in keeping with liberal-democratic consumer culture. For example, Buster Shibata of New York City wrote: "My sister says that Mineko Chado's 'new look' hairdo (SCENE [*sic*], April 1950) makes Miss Chado more attractive. I can't see it. . . . The 'before' [pompadour] hairdo makes her look better to me."[82] The letter reveals that Shibata and his sister were interested enough in the magazine and in the hairstyle to discuss it and to write in right away, so that the letter could be published in the subsequent month's edition. Whether or not the latest fashion in hair was suited to Asian American women was considered an important enough issue for Shibata and his sister to argue over it.

BEFORE her new hairdo, Mineko Chado, of Denver, has her hair set in the pompadour style. Long hair makes head look bulky.

AFTER trimming, the new look, gives trimmer appearance and slenderizes plump girls although pretty Mineko is slim enough.

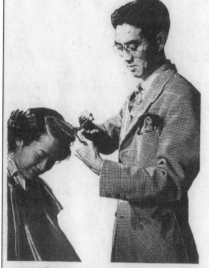

HAIRDRESSER OHASHI cuts the hair to longer than six inches and as short as a quarter of an inch at the neck. The average is about two and one-half inches.

46

Short

By George Ohashi
SCENEfotos by Carl Iwasaki

(George Ohashi has been a hair-dresser since 1937, opening his own shop in 1939 at the Hotel Del Mar, Del Mar, Calif. At the time of the evacuation, he had three shops in Southern California and had 30 beauty operators working for him. He now has a shop in Denver and one in Sacramento. He has won seven first places and numerous other awards in competition for original hairdos.—ED.)

SO YOU are a Nisei girl. And nature didn't endow you with the tall, slim build so stylish these days.

Well, be of good cheer, girls. The new trend in coiffures—shorter and shorter for '50—is just the thing for you.

Here's why. Most Nisei girls not only are chunky, but have too much hair. Unless some of the hair is trimmed out, any kind of hairdo has the tendency to make the head look too large and bulky. Ergo, accentuating built-to-the-ground illusion.

す。お好みで如何ようにも変わります

(五)これは短めで参考までに致しますが

(四)短かく刈った後の髪型の組み方

(三)この型は刈ったばかりの所

(二)は刈り込み中の所

(一)日本人の組んだ髪型です

しい髪かたちが左右されます。顔の大きさを御紹介致しますが、御信じになって、御手入れ致します。顔の形や頭の型によって美

紹介の仕方

"Short Cut to Glamor."

The shorter style demands that the hair be no longer than six inches at the longest—about two and one-half inches on the average—and as short as a quarter of an inch at the neck.

This short hair is tailored close to the contour of the head in wide, natural-appearing waves. Or if you prefer, the same short hair can be fluffed or combed sculptured for formal wear.

At any rate, the result is a slimming, flattering appearance that is becoming to Nisei girls.

Actually, there are few women who cannot wear short hair styles. If you have a problem, take it to a good hair stylist. He'll know how to adapt your hairdo to fit your personality and make the best of your good points.

Nothing can alter your appearance so quickly and dramatically as hair styling. Sometimes, all you need to achieve an interesting change is a different part. If you have been wearing your hair brushed off your face, try combing it forward.

Swirl bangs, fluffed or flat, are popular. You can wear them high or low depending on the shape of your face.

In experimenting with various hairdos, a good hair foundation is a "must." This consists of well-proportioned and personalized hair shaping, plus a good professional permanent wave to serve as the basis for sculptured curls.

Professional permanents are preferable. It can be timed perfectly and the hair blocked and executed so it will best suit the particular person. Home permanents usually turn out with the curls too tight or too loose in the wrong places. Shaping also is usually too long or too short so that even the best stylist cannot produce a good coiffure. But it is inexpensive.

In picking a suitable hair style, try analyzing the coiffures of other women whose faces are of the same general type as yours, then copy a style that strikes your fancy. Wear it a few hours, no matter how strange or absurd it may seem—you may discover an interesting new effect that helps your appearance and personality.

Cut to Glamor

VARIATIONS can be made of the short haircut. Here, bangs are swirled downward. Bangs may be worn high or low to match the face.

CASUALLY SCULPTURED hairdo goes well with formal wear. In experimenting with various styles, a good hair foundation is a "must."

47

Yet a closer look at the haircut so praised by Rosemary Ono and Buster Shibata's sister reveals blatant embrace of racial standards of white beauty. The hairdresser who performed the transformation on Mineko Chado, George Ohashi, owned three hairdressing shops in Southern California, one in Denver, and one in Sacramento and had won numerous hairdressing competitions. In the article, he offered tips on how one could style hair in different ways. However, the article itself disparaged the supposedly typical attributes of Japanese American women in comparison to the unnamed physical standard of European American women. Consider the opening sentences: "So you are a Nisei girl. And nature didn't endow you with the tall, slim build so stylish these days." According to this formulation, young Nisei women, by racial definition, are deficient. To add insult to injury, the article declares: "Most Nisei girls not only are chunky but have too much hair. Unless some of the hair is trimmed out, any kind of hairdo had the tendency to make the head too large and bulky." According to that logic, the wrong hairstyle will make not only the head too large and bulky but will accentuate the "chunky" body.

Hence, the barrage of letters that followed in subsequent issues might be read as a veiled commentary on the European American standards of beauty that *Scene* was promulgating, and in fact on the racial paradoxes of liberal consumer citizenship itself. It is not surprising that Japanese Americans refused an improvement that overly valorized a white standard of beauty. From the opposite side of the country, Ruth Iseri of Portland, Oregon, wrote in her opinion, "Dear Sirs: My vote is for the pompadour," which was the "before" hairstyle; a view that gender-unspecified J. Noda from Philadelphia shared.[83] Through these race-specific mass media channels, Japanese Americans all over the United States, especially from major metropolitan areas, could debate the symbolic feminine body and to what degree it should be Western and modern.[84] Although these contestations proliferated after World War II, they continued the networking started by 1930s Japanese American newspaper columns.[85] What is important is that they show community being formed around debates over consumer culture.

Indeed, Asian Americans demonstrated profound ambivalence to newly emerging middle-class gender roles both in terms of the family and in terms of consumption. U.S. governmental policies and programs such as the Federal Housing Authority and Federal Highway Act structured these economic and societal shifts to suburban consumer society.[86] A move to the suburbs entailed stocking a single-family dwelling with consumer goods such as cars and washing machines, and one could show cultural citizenship through the proper acquisition of such products. Given those economic imperatives combined with Cold War ideology, the domestication of sexuality was a key ideological move throughout U.S. society.[87] Yet such domestication was different for Asian Americans than for mainstream Americans.

Given the 1950s dichotomy in gender roles, what is astounding is that the Asian American men featured in *Scene* magazine appeared far more domestic than their counterparts in mainstream magazines. Although men were profiled in stories with far less frequency than women, on September 1951 the periodical featured "Lo$ Angele$" wonder boy Taul Watanabe, who became wealthy through brokering million-dollar real-estate deals in Los Angeles. Such an article would convey the message that while for women the most desirable trait was a middle-class, European American–influenced physical attractiveness, for men the most desirable trait was economic power. However, what is particularly noteworthy about the photographs accompanying the essay is that Watanabe is portrayed as not only a family man but a domestic man. In one picture, he is sitting next to his pigtailed three-year-old daughter, playing the electric organ. On the last page of the feature, Watanabe stands alone in his kitchen at the stove, with a patterned apron tied around his neck and waist, saucepan and frying pan in front of him, preparing the evening meal. Similarly, auto salesperson Frank Hirashima, one half of *Scene's* featured "Model Couple," stands alone in his kitchen, preparing food. Likewise complicating postwar gender-role dichotomies, his wife, Margie Hirashima, works outside the home as a bookkeeper.[88] Unlike the European American families studied by historian Elaine Tyler May, it is striking that Hirashima also uses domestic appliances for domestic tasks. These characteristics suggest that gender-role equality was a greater imperative than any separation into male and female public and private spheres.

Race and Racialization

In the quest to combat racial prejudice through the right to be a consumer citizen-subject, Asian Americans broadened the scope of cultural citizenship by developing pan-Asian and cross-racial communities. During the age of liberal-democratic civil rights, multiracial and multiethnic groupings took shape because of the increased salience of racial categories in political discourse. Although interethnic and interracial socializing and work culture certainly had been prevalent among working-class Asian Americans for decades, for middle-class youth culture this interracial crossover grew in the postwar era. Most scholars examine pan-Asian ethnicity and the growth of the Asian American movement from the late 1960s onward.[89] However, in the 1950s consumer and mass cultures show the growth of Asian American and cross-racial awareness. Chi Alpha Delta membership rolls and articles from both *Scene* and the *Philippine Star Press* document the growth of pan-Asian culture and multicultural events. What this showed was that Asian Americans were holding the United States to the promise of liberal-democratic consumer culture, namely, that racial equality could be achieved in the consumer marketplace. Although this was not necessarily a radical move, it was extraordinarily significant because liberal democracy was a concept, not a practice, in American society.

In the last years of its existence, *Scene* focused on Asian-ethnic groups other than Japanese Americans. This reflects the increasing numbers of second-generation Asian Americans, the moving out of ethnic enclaves, and the strengthening of pan-Asian awareness.[90] The attention to other Asian-ethnic groups also points to the magazine's need to broaden its audience and increase its circulation.

In a profile of Korean American singer Florence Ahn, *Scene* identified her as a Nisei, meaning a second-generation person, in order to attract the attention of the predominantly Japanese American audience. The article presented her Asian-ethnic identity as something of a puzzle. The large typeset caption that accompanied a photograph of Ahn read: "Los Angeles is her home, her husband studied at Waseda university and, looking at her, you would assume she's a comely Japanese-American. Then why haven't more Niseis heard of this big-time singer." Thus the caption set the stage for the puzzle of Ahn's identity.

The article, whose headline read "A Nisei? Well, Yes—and No," explained:

> She sang on Arthur Godfrey's first television show. Since then, she has been a featured performer at the Roxy theater and the St. Moritz hotel in New York, at the China Doll and the Palace in the same city and at practically every famous eastern fun spot you can name.
>
> In short, she's a fixed star in the big time. And she's a Nisei. Yet, few Nisei's have heard of her.

That's puzzling, but not too much. The singer in question is a Nisei all right, but a slightly different kind. She's Korean-American.

She looks like a Japanese-American, but Florence Ahn isn't even a professional name. It's the name the singer's parents gave her when she was born in Honolulu.[91]

The article heralded Ahn as a second-generation Asian American whose career should be of interest to *Scene*'s audience. Ahn exemplified a kind of success and social acceptance to which they, as second-generation people, might aspire. Given that "Asian American" was not yet a term in use, the author instead employed Japanese American vocabulary as way of trying to create a pan–Asian American identity.

The same year that Korean American identity issues began to be covered by *Scene,* letters from readers show how Chinese American topics began to be covered by Chinese American writers employed by *Scene.* On July 1953, a letter to the editor expressed a reader's interest in starting a Chinese American magazine in Los Angeles: "Dear Sirs: We . . . are planning to publish a picture magazine like SCENE, but for the Chinese populace. . . . [W]e would appreciate answers to a few questions. . . . Gerald Jann, Jade Printers, Los Angeles, Calif."[92] Little did Jann know when requesting information that, instead of founding a Chinese American pictorial magazine, he would be soon be hired by *Scene*: four months later, letter writer Jann was invited to join *Scene* as a reporter. A November 1953 feature entitled "Behind the Scene" explained why Jann had been hired:

Chinese-Americans have always been counted among SCENE's readers, but we had trouble landing a Chinese-American writer until we began work on this issue. So we feel especially good about being able to introduce Gerald Jann. His initial contribution is the profile of Judy Dan (Miss Hong Kong of 1952) that makes this November issue some sort of landmark.[93]

Scene editors were themselves aware that the inclusion of a Chinese American writer and story was a break with the way the magazine had been conceived. For both economic and political reasons, the editors were eager to embrace a pan-Asian focus and readership. By including Chinese American readers, the magazine could increase its circulation and scope. Politically, the category "Asian American" was beginning to take shape, and *Scene* could promote those new political coalitions.

Beauty queens such as Judy Dan and Mary Lew, the "Winter Flower Queen," were not the only Chinese American women to receive attention in *Scene*.[94] In the July 1953 issue, months before the profiles on Dan and Lew, the magazine featured an article on another Chinese American woman, Polly Bemis.[95] Bemis's life in nineteenth-century America has been well documented from her coming to America, to her life as a prostitute, to her subsequent marriage and work life.[96] *Scene*'s four-page article featured pictures and a brief story about Bemis's life.

Scene's reportage of Japanese performer Chiemi Eri with the African American Delta Rhythm Boys suggests interest in intercultural themes: "After shuttling across to California where she recorded 'Gomen-nasai' for Capitol Records, Chiemi returned to complete swing around Hawaii. Pair of Delta Rhythm Boys, with whom she teamed for hit engagement, chat with her backstage at Honolulu Civic Auditorium."[97] One wonders what kind of reception Eri and the African American Delta Rhythm Boys might have received had they toured other segments of the U.S. mainland. Florence Ahn and Eri were by no means anomalies but were part of the larger trend of hundreds of "girl" bands and women performing jazz in the forties. During that era, bands such as the International Sweethearts of Rhythm featured multiethnic members, including Willie Mae Wong on the tenor saxophone.[98]

In keeping with that interest in intercultural themes, *Scene* profiled Japanese American artist Misaye Kawasumi, who performed not only Japan-themed but Mexican and Native American dances. The article explained that Kawasumi was "a front line star with [the] young but brilliant Lester Horton dance group of Los Angeles."[99] Though Kawasumi was a third-generation Japanese American named Bernice, the article showed that Kawasumi assumed a Japanese first name, Misaye, as her stage name.[100] In honor of her Japanese ancestry and to express the horrors of atomic warfare, Kawasumi created a dance called "Hiroshima Revisited." The magazine explained the creation of the dance: "The Hiroshima atom bomb was an idea for the 1953 season. Horton 'blocked' out the dance and suggested the basic meanings. Then it was Misaye's turn to complete the expression within her own understanding. The result was form and color worked out to a dance in a white kimono and dance patterns of terror, anguish, desperation, hope, and creation."[101] One might imagine that Kawasumi's Japanese heritage was key to the success of "Hiroshima Revisited." Kawasumi was not limited to Asian-themed dances. As the article explained, "Horton is planning two new works for Misaye this fall, ballet ideas on Mexicans and American Indians."[102] Thus Kawasumi portrayed multiple races and ethnicities on stage.

In keeping with the burgeoning civil rights movement, *Scene* presented a vision not only of harmonious black–Asian relations but also of a multiracial society. *Scene* profiled a church group from New York that boasted multiethnic membership: "The group is the Christian Youth Fellowship. Its officers are Eugene Inouye, president; Thomas Moshang Jr., vice-president; Madeline Sugimoto, secretary; and Barbara Komine, treasurer."[103] The members included European Americans, Puerto Ricans, Chinese Americans, and Japanese Americans. Given the rise of civil rights movements, such groups held out the possibility of multiple racial groups working together.

Asian American youth groups reflected consumer-culture trends toward increasing multiethnic membership. In the 1950s, Chi Alpha Delta's membership became increasingly pan-Asian.[104] Women with non–Japanese American last names appeared more and more frequently on the membership rosters. After World War II, more Asian American students from non-Japanese backgrounds entered UCLA.[105] In 1958, Chi Alpha Delta listed Doris Loo as a member, and in 1960 they pledged three women with non-Japanese last names: Betty Leong, Sylvia Lew, and May Tang. Despite attracting non–Japanese American women, those members did not earn the highest office, for it was not until the late 1980s that the Chis had a succession of non–Japanese American presidents.[106]

Similarly, the *Philippine Star Press* reported increased friendship between Filipino and Chinese youth: "Nowadays, we see among our social affairs the Chinese youth groups mingling with our Filipino youths. They really get along smoothly. They are all a bunch of wonderful kids, Filipino and Chinese alike."[107] Although historically the Chinese and Filipino laborers had been pitted against each other, the postwar second generation voluntarily affiliated with each other.

Korean American youth also mingled with the Chinese Americans. As Dora Kim Yum's life story shows, since there were so few Korean Americans in the United States, they reached out to the Chinese American community. Although she went through high school and college in the thirties, Kim's life history is revealing. She not only lived in San Francisco's Chinatown; she socialized there as well. Poignantly, Kim tells of how she and other Chinese American women went to a school dance attended mainly by European American students. To their humiliation, she and her friends were ignored, while all the European American women were asked to dance. Recognizing the reality of racial prejudice and segregation in dating practices, after that she and her friends attended citywide Chinese American dances every Saturday night, then as a group went out for *jook* (rice porridge) afterward. In college at the University of California, Berkeley, Kim joined the Chinese Students' Club.[108]

Conclusion

Young Asian American women became demographically and symbolically important in their communities in the postwar era. They were prominent in civic events such as beauty pageants, in youth organizations, and in widely circulating magazines and newspapers. The postwar rise in consumer culture created new cultural citizenship practices for all Americans, not just Asian Americans. Asian Americans were not merely trying to keep up with the European American mainstream; rather, they participated in tandem with it. Utilizing culture in gender-appropriate ways, these women could demonstrate modernity, progress, and American cultural citizenship to their own communities and to mainstream American society. As the decade of the 1950s went on, issues of multiethnic Asian and American cultural citizenship were brought to the forefront.

The next chapter, "Contested Beauty," is a companion chapter to this one and focuses more closely on the issue of beauty introduced in this chapter, highlighting its importance during the Cold War civil rights era. Local Asian American pageants and *Scene* magazine articles concerning beauty show its centrality to proving modernity through the display of the ideal liberal-democratic female subject.

4

Contested Beauty

Asian American Beauty Culture during the Cold War

Nearly five thousand people enjoyed a July 4th picnic at picturesque Adobe Creek Lodge here under the auspices of the Chinese American Citizens Alliance, and watched the crowning of "Miss Chinatown, 1950." The attendance . . . was the largest single gathering of Chinese in America ever.   —*Chinese Press*, July 1950

CDA [Caballeros de Dimas Alang] Popularity Contest Looms As One of the Biggest Events of Its Kind

Popularity Contest of Manila Post 464 for "Miss Manila" Now in Full Swing   —Los Angeles *Philippine Star Press*, Sept. 11, 1950

In the post–World War II era, leading Asian American civil rights groups such as the Chinese American Citizens League and the Caballeros de Dimas Alang centered their annual meetings on beauty pageants. As the above Asian American press excerpts show, beauty pageants enjoyed tremendous salience. Other contemporary queen contests ranged from the one that selected the Cotton Queen to the Miss Portrait of Spring of Chicago, and from the Seattle Seafair Queen to the Page One newspaper queen. The prevalence of this peculiar institution at this historical moment speaks to the convergence of particular imperatives of politics and community. The ability of a racial minority and/or postcolonial community to select an ideal female citizen through a beauty pageant demonstrated modernity, the fitness of colonial subjects for self-rule, and,

Miss Portrait of Spring.

in this particular era, Cold War liberal capitalist politics. Hence it is not surprising that at this time not only do we see the proliferation of Asian American beauty pageants, but African American and Caribbean pageants also multiplied, and the international pageants Miss World and Miss Universe emerged as well. For groups for whom racialized appearance had everything to do with being able to claim social rights, beauty pageants allowed them to negotiate both their community and the nation-state. It is precisely that negotiation that makes beauty pageants volatile yet subject to longevity through the continual need for reiteration and renegotiation of values.

When embarking on this project, I did not intend to scrutinize Asian American beauty culture. Instead, I had envisioned that this chapter would focus on ideal women as portrayed in Asian American presses and periodicals. However, as happened for almost all the scholars in the landmark anthology *The Beauty Queens: On the Global Stage,* community sources directed my attention to the centrality of beauty culture.[1] Analyzing beauty pageants has been especially tricky because the "second wave" of feminism was willed into being through concerted opposition to the 1968 Miss America pageant.[2] Despite that, the newly emerging scholarship on beauty pageants argues that issues of race and postcolonialism render the events more complex than the second-wave feminist focus on exploitation and commodification allows.[3] Scholars have located racial minority and postcolonial beauty pageants as sites that invoke historical countermemories, imagine alternative futures, or claim a place in the nation.[4] In addition, pageants can signify a method by which supposedly anachronistic peoples are brought into temporal and spatial alignment with the modern world.[5]

This chapter focuses on ideal female citizenship as promoted by civil rights organizations and mainstream Asian American periodicals that were consciously trying to fight racial discrimination. The post–World War liberal Cold War civil rights era signaled an opportunity for racial minorities to claim civil rights, but only in particularly narrow ways. Thus, under a Cold War liberal democratic ethos that rewarded displays of all-American citizenship, Asian American beauty culture became a site for its gendered display. My analysis begins with an exploration of how Asian American civil rights groups' beauty pageants, ranging from the Filipino American–sponsored Fourth of July queen pageant to the Japanese American Citizens League Nisei Week queen festival, allowed communities to reinterpret history and imagine their place in the nation-state through negotiating the symbolic of their ideal female citizens. Beauty and ideal citizenship by no means constitute a consensus, and disagreements and alternatives show the parameters of the possible. Yet beauty culture could also affirm community while negotiating the nation-state.

Cold War Civil Beauty Rights

> In America's treatment of the colored races in her own population is her Achilles Heel in Asia. Communist propaganda has drummed into the ears of Asiatics the charge that no person of Asiatic descent is treated with decency in America.   —*Scene*, editorial

Why did Asian American civil rights groups center their annual meetings on beauty pageants? For Asian American communities, beauty culture became a site for Cold War politics that played out through displays of ideal female citizenship. Although past scholars have focused on traditional political histories of the Cold War, new critical attention is being paid to cultural issues.[6] The Cold War was of special concern to Asian Americans because Asia was a primary site for these battles: witness the Korean War, the Vietnam War, and the "fall" of China to communism. For Asian American communities, the very conditions of the Cold War body—American, beautiful, and female—were under debate and negotiation. Given that racial minorities still had not been accepted fully into the American body politic, not only did the terms of the debate have to be forged but also inclusion into the realm of citizen-subject had to be proven. Yet, paradoxically, given the U.S. need to prove its superiority to the Soviet Union, the Cold War allowed claims of racial discrimination to be selectively heard. The Soviet Union's assertion of the lack of racial progress in the United States as proof against the fairness of a capitalist democratic political system provided an unprecedented opportunity for Asian Americans (and other racial minorities) to claim a place in the nation.[7]

Within modern nationalism, women in particular are produced by and within cultural narratives, typically of a past whose negotiations with the present of a new nation centrally require the reconfiguring of gender relations.[8] The Cold War realigned gendered nationalisms into the Soviet asexual female worker drone versus the hyperfeminine consumer American mother or sex kitten. In other words, the Cold War polarized the image of the ideal female citizen into either an American feminine girl/mother or the masculinized Soviet worker-producer. The Soviet ideology of womanhood resulted in the powerful image of the female factory worker breaking all production records.[9] The ideal Soviet woman was a worker, mother, and wife, and to be beautiful was to be "bad." Thus beauty pageants, with their antiwork overtones, were inconsistent with Soviet Cold War gender ideology.[10]

Debated and circulated in media such as *Life* magazine, the hallmarks of realigned Cold War American values, in contrast to Soviet ones, included heterosexuality, family life in the suburbs, middle-class propriety, and whiteness.[11] In the ensuing hypermasculine political culture, what is now recognizable as a corresponding superfemininity emerged. Brassieres, *Playboy* magazine, Marilyn Monroe, Jacqueline Kennedy, and Barbie all became icons of American femininity.[12] These icons built upon the female "pin-up" posters of World War II that supposedly reminded men why they fought and, in the Cold War era, could continue to remind. Lady-like, sexual yet innocent, and determinedly marked as female, this new construction of beauty required inculcation via cultural forms such as magazines and beauty pageants.

The Nixon–Khrushchev debate underscored the importance of beauty to Cold War political ideology. In 1959, American vice president Richard Nixon traveled to Moscow and met with Soviet premier Nikita Khrushchev at the American Exhibition.[13] The American Exhibition contained, among other things, a model American kitchen fully equipped with the most up-to-date consumer goods. The two men proceeded to dispute the merits of their respective political and economic systems through the pros and cons of this kitchen. The "Kitchen Debate" ended with a discussion of the beauty of the women of each society. American reportage of this visit underscored the link between female beauty and political-economic systems. The popular news magazine *U.S. News and World Report* claimed that Soviet women desexualized themselves through work and political activism and that Moscow was "a city of women— hard-working women who show few of the physical charms of women in the West. Most Moscow women seem unconcerned about their looks."[14] Through Western eyes, female appearance was linked to economic and political ideology. Beauty through the appropriate use of consumer culture signified the superiority of the Western democratic capitalist way of life.

The Cold War both narrowed allowable channels of protest and permitted selective racial minority claims to be heard. The McCarthy witch hunt for supposed Communist subversives in American government and society and the ensuing decimation of the political left precluded socialist and communist means of racial protest.[15] The House Un-American Activities Committee (HUAC) highlighted just how important it was to be American in order to avert charges of disloyalty and all the economic and political problems that such a charge entailed. Yet there were also substantial rewards for proving American loyalty. For Asian Americans in particular, decolonization of the Philippines, immigration quotas being lifted, and naturalization bans being eliminated signaled political gains. The McCarran Walter Act of 1952 gave the right of naturalization and property ownership to all Asians and accorded a nonquota status to wives of Asians who were permanent residents, but it retained the national origins quota system of 1924.[16] One way to prove loyalty and to earn those rewards was through civil rights sponsorship of all-American beauty pageants.

In the middle of the twentieth century, racial segregation rendered American beauty pageants a civil rights issue. The liberal framing of civil rights as individual access to white institutions through racial desegregation made glaring the whiteness of mainstream pageants such as Miss America. For racial minority women burdened by the double discrimination of race and sex, success at mainstream national beauty pageants was impossible. The Miss America pageant was founded in 1921, and "Rule Seven" of the pageant allowed only "whites" to compete. In the 1930s, pageant rules stated that contestants must be "of good health and of the white race." Until at least 1940, contestants had to complete a biological form that outlined their racial "heritage." As leading Miss America pageant scholar Sarah Banet-Weiser has convincingly argued, a racially marked body acts as a "specter—the marked other—against which the ideal (white) female citizen is defined."[17] Functioning as that specter, the first African American woman did not advance to the national Miss America pageant until 1970, and none won until Vanessa Williams in 1984.[18] Thus, while for white women the 1968 pageant jump-started the women's movement because it represented the exploitation of women's bodies, for black women the very same pageant represented the continued segregation and marginalization of black women's bodies.[19]

Despite the absence of African American women until the 1970s, it was during the 1940s that the Miss America pageant first reflected racial and ethnic shifts. In 1941, Mifauny Shunatona, a Native American from Oklahoma, was admitted to the pageant. Bess Myerson's 1945 crowning as the first Jewish Miss America was viewed as a blow to anti-Semitism. The first Puerto Rican and the first woman of Asian descent to be admitted to the Miss America pageant came within the larger framework of testing out territorial status, potential statehood, and issues of race and representation. The first Asian American woman to compete in the Miss America pageant achieved that distinction by accident. In 1948, Yun Tau Chee actually placed as the runner-up in the Miss Hawaii contest, but when the winner was disqualified, Chee represented Hawaii at the pageant.[20] The same year, Irma Nydia Vasquez from Puerto Rico was the first Latina to compete at Miss America. It is significant that in the same year racialized contestants from Hawaii and Puerto Rico competed at Miss America. On the one hand, their participation can be interpreted as breaking the color barrier. On the other hand, their participation can be interpreted as the United States gaining Cold War legitimacy for colonial possessions in Hawaii and Puerto Rico. As these women represented territorial possessions, it could be viewed that America did not completely exploit their lands but allowed them a limited place in the body politic. Chee's participation in Miss America was an aberration rather than a trend. It was not until well after the end of the Cold War that the first Asian American woman, Angela Perez Baraquio, won the Miss America title in 2001. In the middle of the twentieth century, since Asian Americans did not participate in significant numbers in the Miss America pageant, attempts to prove American cultural citizenship occurred at community or theme pageants, not at the mainstream national pageants.[21]

Asian American community civil rights agendas met the American liberal-democratic society creed of individual opportunity and achievement squarely at the beauty pageant. Asian American communities used beauty pageants to foster an imagined "nation within nation," as a way to constitute themselves internally as a viable political entity.[22] In addition, in an era of racial segregation and uneven rights ascribed by race, Asian American civil rights groups used beauty pageants not only to imagine themselves belonging to the nation-state but to show their ability to stage their community's model citizenship to the larger American public. The beauty pageant was an all-American way to show how Asian Americans could stage individual opportunity and achievement through competition and arrive at an ideal female American citizen. Hence the beauty pageant enabled them to show that they knew and could distinguish ideal citizenship and ideal community, and thus were capable of exercising full American citizenship rights and privileges.

As has been argued throughout this book, all Asian American groups had to prove Americanness to counter the image of the historical alien-foreigner constructed through immigration and naturalization restrictions. Specific Cold War–era political challenges differed among the groups. For Japanese Americans, healing the distrust fostered by wartime internment and postwar resettling into communities was a significant issue. For Chinese Americans, the major hurdle was proving they were not communists like the Chinese in the People's Republic of China. For both Philippine nationals and Filipino Americans, Philippine independence challenged them to define themselves not as colonized subjects or nationals but as people with a distinct national origin and identity.[23] If they modeled themselves after the United States, then independence would be compatible with noncommunist American liberal values of egalitarianism, self-making, and progress.

Civil rights organizations' sponsorship distinguished Asian American beauty pageants from the mainstream ones of the period. Asian Americans were not the only racial minority group to hold beauty pageants; African American and Latino/Chicano groups also held queen pageants as focal points of civil rights meetings.[24] By contrast, the main sponsors for European American beauty pageants—clubs such as the Jaycees, Elks, and Rotary—promoted beauty contests to normalize the standards for middle-class white femininity.[25] Beginning in 1948, a major civil rights group, the Chinese American Citizens Alliance (CACA), held patriotic queen contests. Such contests sought to demonstrate the community's identification with and loyalty to the United States. As the focal point for the annual San Francisco meeting, the CACA queen presided over Fourth of July festivities and was given the title "Miss Chinatown." In 1950, the display of all-American culture would provide an antidote to the recent Cold War "fall" of China to communism. Beauty pageants became a way that the Chinese American community could show its Americanness and, especially after 1949, when China turned communist, its anticommunism.

The Chinese American Citizens Alliance (effective 1929, just like the sorority Chi Alpha Delta) was based on an organization that had been started in 1895 as a direct response to the anti-Chinese immigration laws: the Native Sons of the Golden West (NSGW). The CACA restricted membership to American male citizens of Chinese ancestry who were twenty-one years of age or older, of good character, and capable of self-support; it did not admit women until 1976.[26] The preamble of the group's constitution noted that their ideals were "to quicken the spirit of American patriotism, to insure the legal rights of its members and to secure equal economical and political opportunities for its members."[27] Thus, as befits a civil rights organization, rights and equality were its chief aims. The first and foremost of the CACA's cardinal principles was "[t]o fully enjoy and defend our American citizenship."[28] In fact, members had to vote in American elections or CACA fined them.[29]

As a way of enjoying and defending that American citizenship, on May 26, 1950, the San Francisco *Chinese Press* solicited competitors from all over California to participate in the third CACA beauty pageant, which would be held during the organization's annual meeting. Though open to all young women, the contest organizers' initial strategy was to drum up candidates from college organizations. They promised that if college students showed up in significant numbers, in the future the prizes would be scholarships. The attempt to attract college students shows that, like Miss America Bess Myerson, the organizers envisioned the ideal candidate as a middle-class, well-educated, accomplished young woman.

The contest organizers attempted to reform the contest and make it more respectable and middle-class than the previous years' contests not only by soliciting college students but also by changing how the contest was publicized. Many local Chinese American women had been reluctant to enter the contest because they did not believe it an event appropriate for respectable young women. The organizers hoped to attract more local entrants by banning the publicity shots of the queens in bathing suits that had caused controversy, and by barring professional models from the competition.[30] Anybody who wanted to inspect the bathing-suited queens would have to attend the actual pageant and CACA conference.

The Chinese American community was not the only one to hold their major community gathering on the Fourth of July in order to signal their Americanness. The Filipino American community in Los Angeles also held an Independence Day celebration centering on the crowned queen and her court. As the *Philippine Star Press* reported on May 7, 1948: "With the anticipation of a big dual July 4th celebration, the Filipino Community of Los Angeles is sponsoring a queen contest, the purpose of which is to choose a queen to reign during the celebration. Vying for the covetous honor are five lovely girls, the pride of the Filipinos in Los Angeles County. They are Misses 'Cookie' Tenchavez, Trinidad Padilla, Catharine Edralin, Martha Canlas and Elizabeth Domingo Rigor."[31] As was the case for the Los Angeles Japanese Americans and the California Chinese Americans, the queen competition allowed the Los Angeles Filipino American community to gain publicity.

Political considerations prompted the establishment of patriotic Filipina American queen contests. As women were visible symbols of gendered national identity, societal destabilization wrought by the Philippines decolonization could be managed through an all-American queen pageant for women. Filipino Americans in Los Angeles, Salinas, and other communities held Independence Day celebrations centered on the crowned queen and her court. The Miss Philippines beauty pageant signified not only the local Los Angeles community but also the Filipino American community in California and the United States. In addition, through its quest for the woman who best exemplified Maria Clara, Filipino nationalist Jose Rizal's ideal woman, the pageant invoked anticolonial struggles in the Philippines as well.[32] In fact, before decolonization in 1946, the Independence Days had been named Rizal Days. Beauty-queen competitions were key forums through which Philippine national identity was debated and forged, via the construction of idealized gender roles.[33] Beauty pageants were ubiquitous in Filipino communities.[34] In the 1920s and 1930s, since there were so few Filipinas, the queens and princesses were typically the white girlfriends of single Filipino men. Between the late 1930s and 1965, Filipina newcomers and daughters of earlier couples took crowns.

Likewise, Japanese American political and community organizations held numerous queen pageants after World War II. As responses to Japanese American internment, these pageants emphasized participation in American culture. One of the oldest continuous and most well-known of those contests has been the Los Angeles Japanese American Nisei Week festival.[35] Begun in 1934 as a way for the second generation to make its mark, Nisei Week was also a means for merchants and community leaders to promote Little Tokyo, the business district just east of downtown Los Angeles.

The Nisei Week festival was sponsored by the Japanese American Citizens League (JACL). Founded in 1930, the civil rights group JACL championed causes ranging from demanding that the U.S. government grant American citizenship to the Issei immigrant generation, to rescinding the 1922 Cable Act.[36] Until the 1960s, when Japanese corporate sponsorship prevailed, local Little Tokyo merchants sponsored Nisei Week. Nisei Week built up the Japanese American community and served as a means for outsiders, predominantly European Americans, to tour and spend money in Little Tokyo. Such festivals and queen pageants could "stage" the community not just for insiders but for outsiders. Thus local pageants were one significant means by which outsiders could understand the communities' quintessential worthiness.

Performing the Cold War Civil Rights Body

Cold War politics, modernity, ideal citizenship, ideal femininity, and community values could all be negotiated through the performance of a beauty pageant. A welcome corrective to mainstream presses that ignored the presence of people of Asian descent in the United States, Asian American communities' print media put the women in unusually prominent positions. This reportage provided evidence of ideal citizenship for a community, Asian American and otherwise, larger than those who had attended the pageant. Since Asian Americans were eager to mark their modernity, progress, and American cultural citizenship, they frequently featured accomplished young women in their periodicals' pages, with particular attention paid to those attending universities. Asian American magazines and newspapers engaged in the production of a modern gen-der-differentiated middle-class Asian American culture through the pre-sentation of female role models who included athletes, entertainers, and beauty queens. The construction of race through proper gender ideology, as well as claiming gender roles denied to them, was not limited to Asian Americans; African Americans did so as well. Although nowhere near as extensively as in Asian American print media, sources such as the NAACP's *The Crisis* regularly featured young accomplished African Amer-ican women.[37]

Bess Myerson's Miss America victory showed that education was criti-cal to this new female ideal citizenship, and student culture provided rich sites for its display. To show their community's modernity and fitness for decolonization, Filipino American newspapers featured prominent young women. For example, Josephine Rapada was featured on the front page of the *Philippines Star Press* as "the only Filipino girl in the United States who is majoring in International Relations. She remarked smilingly that some day when Philippine independence is granted she may be able to serve her country abroad."[38] Filipina role models demonstrate community values of vivacity, outgoingness, and educational accomplishment. In addition, Ra-pada's statement that when Philippine independence would be granted, she might be able to serve her country abroad, indicates her serving as a bridge between the United States and its former colony, as well as her hopes for decolonization.

A closer examination of the University of California at Berkeley's "Queen of the Seventh Annual Spring Informal" shows the importance of education and respectability to displaying ideal womanhood. College queens were of such interest to the San Francisco–based *Chinese Press's* widely dispersed readership that the paper assigned a special UC–Berkeley correspondent to report on the school's pageants. The queen-contest bi-ographies almost always discuss hobbies and activities, for the clues to their victory lie not in measurements but in recreational and career prefer-ences. In the 1950s, one needed to be outgoing and have feminine profes-sional aspirations. As the *Press* reported: "Although very serious in her goal at becoming a pharmacist, Miss Liu says she loves meeting people, and 'I'm really honored to contribute my efforts for our Cal club.' College life, roller skating, dances (sources report she's a terrific Charleston critter!)— these show up the likes of this hard-working candidate." Queen contes-tants, as representatives of their community's middle-class ideal, were required to be active.[39] As the type of activity they selected corresponded to social status and possibilities for status mobility, the candidates' activities indicated who had the best chance of winning the crown.

For some candidates, such as Nancy Toy, the manager emphasized personality traits as markers of fitness to become a queen. Note the "explosive" nickname:

> Jack Din, manager for Nancy Toy, sums up his protégé's personality: TNT —the culmination of these three letters aptly describes Nancy Toy, a candidate for Spring Informal Queen.[40]

The reference to an explosive compound as a metaphor for women's sexuality was by no means unusual during the Cold War. The naming of the bikini bathing suit came about because of the comparison between the power of female sexuality and the power of atomic testing in the Pacific Bikini Islands.[41]

The description of Toy provided clues to her poor chances in the contest:

> She's a package of friendliness, sparkling humor and pert vivaciousness all rolled into one. A sophomore, she hails all the way from Phoenix, Arizona. Studying oriental law at Cal., Nancy likes the pleasures of life—eat, sleep, and play!

Toy had an outgoing personality but lacked the necessary achievement markers to be an effective queen. Although studying "oriental law" was a plus, she does not appear to have participated in a wide variety of student and community activities, instead preferring the pleasures of life. She was also from out of state, which meant that she did not have the base of support developed in high school that local candidates would have.

Not surprisingly, Joanna Liu was declared victor over Nancy Toy and the other candidates. Liu's victory was announced by the club president, sealed with the tiara and dance, and glorified with consumer goods: "Before a capacity crowd, in an aura of suspense, Tom Woo, president of the U.C. Chinese Students' Club, announced Miss Liu as the candidate chosen. She was crowned Queen Joanna, her Majesty of the 1950 Spring Informal. Manley Wu, chairman of the evening, presented her with a wrist watch, gift of the Tommy Company of San Francisco."[42] Crowned with a tiara, Liu led the waltzing. As was customary for other pageants, there was no king, so Liu and the court danced with sponsors and managers. Underscoring the importance of the queen's community and family ties, Liu's parents were presented to the crowd. In keeping with the Nisei Week contestants' displays of female modesty, Liu was said to have thought she had no chance of winning.

As can be seen in the newspaper victory photograph, though Liu was not necessarily the candidate with the facial features that most closely conformed to mainstream standards of feminine beauty, her accomplishments and birthplace determined her victory. Although Liu had won the overall crown, she had neither sold the most tickets to the dance nor won the popular vote. As the paper reported: "Determination of the lucky girl for queen was by sales of tickets and popularity vote. Helen Wong topped the girls by selling $1300 in tickets, while Nancy Toy placed highest in popularity votes among the members of the Chinese Students' Club."[43] Since both popularity and ticket sales determined who became queen, one would have to assume that the winners of each category, Helen Wong and Nancy Toy, must have scored low in the category that they did not win, and that Liu did well in both. Coming from Berkeley, Liu had the hometown advantage over the other candidates. Given all her attributes, Liu best represented the 1950s all-American university woman.

Through beauty culture, Asian Americans demonstrated their fitness for belonging to the American nation-state. During the early Cold War era, "American" signified middle-class fashion and style. Not only had more Americans achieved that economic status during the postwar boom, but Americans felt compelled to display appropriate identity markers. As opposed to the "drab" socialist or communist proletariat, the middle-class American possessed the consumer goods, such as the telephone and living room furniture, that showed faith in a capitalist society. Conformity to capitalistic values required an emphasis on gender specificity, such as being able to distinguish the correct shade of lipstick and wavy hair. Although ethnic whites were achieving social mobility, racial minorities were only beginning to make inroads.[44] So for all who were striving to appear middle class, or for those newly arrived, performing appropriate class status was crucial.

A closer look at the 1952 Nisei Week queen contest selection process further reveals the middle-class American fashion knowledge and manners that were crucial to performing the Cold War–era feminine body. Take, for example, this line from the *Rafu Shimpo*: "The 10 Nisei Week Festival queen candidates . . . chewed on juicy barbequed spare ribs, sipped coffee, and chatted with hostesses, judges, and guests."[45] This one moment shows many of the balancing skills vital for post–World War II social-prestige events, such as sorority rushes and debuts, not to mention business functions and in-law meals.[46] Although the excerpt reported that the women were at ease, it would have been extraordinarily difficult for them to have been comfortable eating as they talked to the judges. A contestant who spoke with her mouth full of spareribs, who had barbecue sauce on her lipstick, and who fumbled with her coffee cup would probably be marked lower. A smart candidate might have tried to avoid the food, but then she could be rated lower for not being an obliging guest who partook of her host's refreshments.

The month-long reportage of the multiple elimination rounds in the front-page, lead articles ensured that the process of selecting an ideal female citizen would be known to all. According to one such article, to find out if they had successfully charmed the judges while eating the messy spareribs, the Nisei Week contenders had to wait by their telephones at an appointed hour. The previous day's competition had whittled down the field to five finalists, who would then participate in the final queen's contest. Being one of the finalists was an honor and obligation, for all five would make up the queen's court and have official duties.

The language the *Rafu Shimpo* used implied that all the young women —competitors and readers alike—desired to become a queen, and it painted a genteel portrait of Cold War middle-class family life: "When the resounding bell rang in the quiet of their living rooms where all the girls were 'asked to stay until we give you a buzz. . . .'" This was a life without noise, chaos, or family violence, and with enough affluence to accommodate a house with a separate living room, complete with appropriate consumer goods such as a telephone. The paper conjectured that the women who had been eliminated "took the news with maybe a sniffle or a disillusioned sigh."[47] Since half the nominated young women had declined to run, a sigh of relief may have also been a response.

Through their reactions, the candidates displayed modesty and graciousness that dovetailed with gendered Cold War American values. In many beauty pageants, surprise and sisterhood were the major elements reported by the Nisei Week queen contestants in hearing the news that they had been chosen. The *Rafu Shimpo* called each of the finalists immediately after notification, so they could report the contestants' emotions to the readers. "'I am very grateful to be within the five, but am still "plumb shocked." I had little hope of getting in,' said Miss Kawasumi who enrolled last week at the General Hospital School of Nursing." Other candidates, such as Miss Abe, expressed sisterhood with the other queen contenders: "She said she was of course thrilled but thought all the others deserved to be in the finals too."[48] Since many of the young women came from similar class and educational backgrounds, they likely developed empathy for one another through the ordeal of the competition.

The five queen finalists not only showed appropriate mannerisms such as poise and modesty but sported all-American styles. All five had "American" first names, whereas three out of five women eliminated had Japanese first names, such as Yoko and Toshe. Although the press photographs of the finalists were in black and white, it was apparent that they conformed to mainstream American ideals of femininity. The finalists wore almost identical tea-length gowns with similar dark pumps. The contestants appeared to be the same height, with bright white smiles highlighted by lipstick-rimmed mouths. Although some women of Asian descent have naturally curly hair, the majority do not, yet all the finalists exhibited perfectly waved hairstyles. Indeed, they fit in beautifully with the stylized femininity depicted in *Scene* magazine. Highlighting the reciprocity between the magazine and the pageant, *Scene* devoted space to coverage of local pageants such as Los Angeles' Nisei Week queen pageant in Little Tokyo.[49]

Young women had ample resources to discover how best to perform ideal female citizenship. On the page after the skin-care profile "Beauty, Basically Speaking," *Scene* ran an advertisement for four beauty-product distributors: Mrs. Mary Suzuki, Mrs. Mae Noro, Mrs. Masai Maeda, and Mrs. Tatsuko Hino. The advertisement showed photographs of the young, attractive women and labeled them "your Chicago counselors."[50] The beauty consultants were all married—which was surprising, for one might expect that marriage would end their wage-paid labor. Perhaps the women's success in marriage would lend credibility and respectability to their claims of knowing makeup and beauty.[51] Japanese American women were not the only ones to find paid work in the beauty industry; African American women did as well.[52] With the assistance of experts, Asian American women could select, purchase, and correctly apply beauty products, and thus achieve modernity and ideal femininity.

Consumer culture not only worked to show Asian Americans how to perform beauty culture for themselves; it also showed mainstream society "Asian" beauty tips. Chinese American actress Anna May Wong as beauty purveyor popularized supposedly Chinese beauty customs for presumably European American audiences. Well after her cinematic heyday, in 1947,

Chinese American actress Anna May Wong worked as a spokesmodel for Lentheric's Shanghai perfume. As part of the publicity campaign, Wong gave lectures on "Chinese Beauty Customs" in places such as New York's Plaza Hotel and Stern's department store.

In her talks, which occurred before the "fall" of China to communism, Anna May Wong spoke on how Chinese women cared for their hair and their makeup use.[53] Wong's American lecture tour offered the following "Chinese" beauty tips:

> To beautify the eyes spend half an hour or so a day watching goldfish swim.
>
> To beautify the hands, try rolling a walnut in the palm of each hand daily as regular exercise.
>
> To beautify the feet, practice concentrated toe wiggling.
>
> And to tighten the skin of the face, instead of using all kinds of cream, try covering it with a mask of egg-white.[54]

Though these tips were not particularly Chinese, as befit an era that displayed interest in women of Asian descent and beauty, they were marketed as such. Anna May Wong's national beauty tour signals the beginning of women of Asian descent being increasingly feminized and commodified in mainstream society. As chapter 5, "Riding the Crest of the Oriental Wave," shows in greater depth, Hollywood films and international beauty pageants shifted the mainstream gendered construction of Asian American women to hyperfeminine.

Clothing showed one's mastery of modernity as a basis for the Philippines independence.[55] Fashion as emblems of women's modernity preoccupied Filipina Americans. The *Philippines Star Press* published columns such as "Salinas Tid-Bits" by Trudy and Glo and "As I Was Saying" by editor-in-chief Elizabeth Aquino Campbell. In these venues, the Filipina American authors would relay "news, gossip, and juicy tales" to the far-flung community of women who avidly read the columns. Newspaper chat and gossip columns written by women for women allowed the pedagogy of modernity through fashion to be transmitted to Filipina American subjects throughout the United States. Through these forums, in a post–World War II era of increasing middle-class prosperity, Philippines independence, desegregation, gender conventions, and ethnic identity would be debated and behavioral norms formed.

In "Salinas Tid-Bits," for example, Trudy and Glo congratulated young women on their mastery of Christian Dior's "New Look." Not only did they validate the young women's fashion savvy; the columns also acted as pedagogy in how to be an ideal modern young woman. These columns are striking for their intimacy and friendliness; readers felt drawn into the community and could identify with the concerns. The columnists described various community members' Easter fashions in loving detail. For example, here is Trudy and Glo's description of Riz Raymundo's Easter outfit: "very elegant, very feminine look of spring fashion in a gray suit of Fortman's wool. It was very outspoken in compliments to her figure. Her hat was that New Look of black shiny straw with a black satin ribbon with net encircling the hat. All her accessories were of black felt. Her shoes were of black suede trimmed with gold."[56] That particular feature continued with four more descriptions of other young women's Easter ensembles of equal detail and length. French haute couture designer Christian Dior's New Look was one of the most influential styles of the time. New Look suits had broad shoulders, nipped-in waists, and skirts that flared out from the waist. Thus a New Look suit had an exaggerated female silhouette. Such cultural competency in appropriate gendered appearance countered stereotypes of Filipinos as "our little brown brothers" or as loincloth-clad headhunters.

Part and parcel of ideal female citizenship during the civil rights era was the idea that performing it in appropriate ways would break down racial barriers. The reportage of Asian American women's victories at interethnic/interracial pageants reflects the editors' and writers' belief that they signaled greater acceptance of Asian Americans, which portended changes in American race relations in the postwar era. In California and Hawaii, many young woman of at least part-Asian descent won intercollegiate beauty contests in which women of other races participated. The *Chinese Press* on September 29, 1950, heralded one such victory: "Queen Elizabeth Pa, 19-year-old University of Hawaii co-ed, waves to 15,000 spectators who crowded the sidewalk during the 'Football Festival' in Berkeley, California, recently. Miss Pa, who is part Hawaiian, part Caucasian and part Chinese, was crowned 'Miss Football of 1950' in a contest with pretty co-eds from nine universities."[57] After having won the University of Hawaii's title, Pa won the Football Festival crown over contestants from eight other campuses. Judging by the photograph published in the paper, all the women who became her court were of European American descent.

Judging the Ideal Citizen

Asian American civil rights groups used beauty pageants not only to imagine themselves belonging to the nation-state but to show their ability to stage their communities' model citizenship to the larger American public. The beauty pageant was an all-American way to show how Asian Americans could stage individual opportunity and achievement through competition and arrive at an ideal female American citizen. The beauty pageant enabled them to show that they knew and could distinguish ideal citizenship and ideal community and thus were capable of exercising full American citizenship rights and privileges. Asian American communities arrived at the ideal female citizen through an evaluation process that privileged Cold War liberal capitalistic values.

Since the pageant organizers were often connected to small businesses and knew the sponsors, young women who appealed to business owners were most likely to become finalists. For Nisei Week, substantial prizes were donated by Little Tokyo merchants who would act as sponsors for the festival by their contributions, such as an expensive television set for the winner.[58] These prizes allowed the contestants to display appropriate consumer-cultural citizenship. As a reward for best embodying the Chinese American community, Miss Chinatown 1950 won a grand-prize boat trip from San Francisco to Los Angeles. Indeed, community beauty pageants of all types frequently favor young women who fit small-business owners' definitions of femininity, such as suitable achievement and appropriate grooming.[59] It can be argued that there was a teleology of progress implicit in the idealized notion of femininity articulated by the small-business owners. If women can conform to particular ideals of femininity, then democratic capitalism and modernity can be secured. Displays of proper femininity signify societal order as well as a market for consumer goods.

The Cold War era marked a significant shift in how the Nisei Week pageant was judged, for the sponsors elicited judges from outside the community. These noncommunity judges could ensure that young Japanese American women had mastered Cold War gendered appearance and behaviors. Whereas in previous years the queen contestants earned points by selling tickets to the festival, this year it was solely up to the judges to select the final five candidates, according to the criteria of "personality, poise, charm, and character, as well as her looks."[60] Since all the judges were given a criteria chart and a standard numbering system, ostensibly this method would be more "objective" than other ways of evaluating queen candidates.[61] The contest had become even more complex and sophisticated than in the previous years, for there would be four elimination rounds. The organizers incorrectly assumed there would be so many women entering the contest that the best way to choose the winner would be through extra competition rounds. Whereas the first three rounds involved community judges, the fourth and final event would be the actual selection of the queen by outside judges.

By enlisting judges from outside the community, Asian American norms and values could be evaluated against those of mainstream society. In contrast to the prewar Nisei Week pageants, which had secret judging panels, in 1952 the *Rafu Shimpo* named the ten judges, including the Japanese consul general, Kenichiro Yoshida. Most judges were outsiders to the Japanese American community and were European Americans considered to be experts in the world of business or the world of feminine beauty. In this particular case they included a makeup artist, a Northwest Airlines flight-attendant executive trainer, the society editor for the *Los Angeles Mirror,* and a United Press Hollywood correspondent.[62] This privileged hegemonic values over ethnic community preferences. Although there was no controversy over the final decision, the opinions of the external judges versus those of the community could potentially cause disagreement over standards of femininity.

One of the European American female judges for the Nisei Week festival queen pageant explained her criteria for judging "winning" Japanese American femininity as a hybrid between Japanese and American, which demonstrated why Japanese American women became such potent symbols of femininity in the postwar era. A supervisor of stewardesses, Carolyn Miller explained: "In personality, the Japanese American girl has developed well her ability for creative thinking, independence, and American know-how. Yet she has not lost the gracefulness, poise, and esthetic love of natural things which has made the beauty of the women of Japan so internationally famous."[63] Miller's categorization renders "masculine" traits such as independence and know-how "American," and "feminine" traits such as poise and grace "Japanese." Thus Japanese American women could be lauded for appearing both feminine and Americanized, whereas Japanese American men would not be valorized for "Japanese" traits such as poise and grace.

The very definition of beauty and ideal citizenship relied on the successful mastery of the liberal capitalistic business practices. As a judge, Carolyn Miller observed that the Nisei Week candidates "will more than hold their own in the American business or social world." Miller's remarks underscore the point that women who are successful in pageants are the ones who have social skills and educational achievements that can be put to use in a variety of public settings. Having access to the American business world was still very new for women of color, who a mere decade earlier had been largely excluded. This highlights the convergence of gender and race for female narratives of progress in the context of capitalism and its struggles against communism. Mastering acceptable hegemonic social graces thus could spell individual advancement under a liberal capitalistic ethos. Domestic American narratives of assimilation to mainstream culture were propelled by these Cold War imperatives. By showing their competency in Cold War manners, the contestants, and by association their sponsors and communities, could demonstrate their fitness as capitalists for a larger American audience.

Like the *Rafu Shimpo*, the *Chinese Press* was particularly eager to explain the judging criteria and process of selecting the ideal female citizen and, in doing so, revealed the Cold War linkage between patriotism, beauty, and consumerism. To explain to the Chinese American community how beauty contests operated, a few days before the pageant the *Chinese Press* published a lengthy article entitled "How to Become a Queen." As an exemplar, the paper profiled multiply crowned queen Janet M. O. Chun. Not only had she been the Junior Prom Queen at her high school, in 1948, fitting in beautifully with Cold War beauty culture, the Chinese Civic Association of Hawaii crowned Chun the Chinese Beauty Queen at their July 4 celebration.[64] Indeed, the paper had had a long-standing relationship with Chun, for consumer capitalism factored into being a Chinese American community queen. The paper revealed: "On the same day that she was crowned the Chinese Queen of Hawaii, the first postwar copies of CHINESE PRESS were flown over to Honolulu by Pan-American Clipper. Miss Chun's first official act was to receive the CHINESE PRESS [o]n behalf of Honolulu's Chinese community."[65] By linking the *Chinese Press* with Chun, the newspaper linked beauty queens with the *Press*'s mission of displaying American patriotism.[66]

Contested Beauty

Although beauty pageants gave communities forums to debate and celebrate ideas of femininity, pageants were also sites for dissent from mainstream as well as community values.[67] From the vantage point of mainstream culture, Asian American beauty culture reveals contestations over racialized standards of beauty. It also shows alternatives to liberal individual competition, such as selecting more than one queen or drawing queens by lots. From the perspective of the community, beauty pageants show that the community is not monolithic but contains multiple opinions, for not all members agree upon the traits of its perfect representative. And, not surprisingly, numerous young Asian American women contested the notion that being a community beauty queen was a worthwhile achievement by refusing to participate in its selection.

Asian American women utilized beauty culture to contest the prevalent racialized standards of beauty. Since the constitution of the racialized body as human was a necessary precondition for the enactment of the liberal-democratic citizen-subject, beauty as proof of humanity became a contested issue. Asian American forums such as *Scene* focused on women's bodies in an attempt to circumvent racialized standards of beauty that castigated non–European American women as ugly and subhuman. Claiming the beauty of nonwhite races was a way to counter Social Darwinism and scientific racism that had posited nonwhite races as subhuman and thus not beautiful. In the June 1953 edition of *Scene*, the editors featured a letter from a young college fraternity man with Cold War–necessitated military experience in Asia, who wanted to prove to his classmates that Asian women were beautiful:

> Dear Sirs: I have returned from 18 months' duty in Korea with the U.S. Air Force, plus another year in Japan. . . . Here at school, I have been telling my friends that the Japanese women are very beautiful, but none of them will believe me. I noticed a few copies of SCENE [*sic*] in the college library, and they interest me very much. I also noticed on your January, 1952 issue, on the cover a picture of Kathleen Asano. . . . I was wondering if it would be possible to obtain an 8x10 glossy copy of the photo to show the boys that I am right. Elwood Schweer, Theta Sigma Tau, Ripon College, Ripon, Wis.[68]

Scene reported that Kathleen Asano's all-American cover generated an unprecedented number of requests for further information and photographs. People like Schweer's friends denied the humanity of Asian American women by refusing them the possibility of beauty. Thus it was empowering for Asian American women to be seen and to see themselves

Kathleen Asano.

as beautiful. Other research bears out that African American communities also strove to prove that their women were beautiful.[69]

Female beauty as a means to counter racialized standards of beauty fascinated Asian Americans all over the United States. In articles such as "Beauty Basically Speaking," women could alleviate their gender anxieties about appropriate public appearances by following the tips in the article. For busy mothers and working women, the shortcuts offered in the article saved precious time and energy. They also constructed a raced, classed, and Americanized being. According to both the beauty pageant officials and the magazine, this being was female, middle-class, and interested in same-sex social activities, fashion, beauty, and fun.[70]

Most important, in opposition to national events, community events provided a forum for nonmainstream standards of femininity to triumph. Women who did not fit certain beauty conventions nonetheless won local pageants and were featured in community-specific publications such as *Scene.* For example, at the "Portrait of Spring" contest, one member of the queen's court wore glasses.[71] The queen herself, though in possession of a lovely smile, did not physically emblemize an Asian American Marilyn Monroe. Instead, she displayed a look and body type to which the majority of Asian American women could aspire. Thus the local and the particular allowed room for counterhegemonic beauty.

Not all beauty pageants reflected the individualist ethos of the time. Students at the University of Hawaii enjoyed a unique multicultural solution for choosing among candidates: they elected queens from six different racial groups. As *Scene* reported on July 1950: "Since 1936, a gala annual event in Honolulu has been the beauty contest held by the U. of Hawaii. Unlike most universities, the U of Hawaii selected queens from six different racial groups represented in the student body. The girls on these pages and on the cover were this year's winners."[72] The fact that the majority of the queens were of Asian descent reflected the predominance of people of Asian descent in Hawaii.

The array of queens could more fittingly represent the racial and ethnic diversity of Hawaii's labor-immigration history.[73] Historically, Hawaii's multiracial labor communities had been separated according to ethnicity, and the University of Hawaii's pageant reflected those ethnicities with a Filipino Queen, a Chinese Queen, a Japanese Queen, a Caucasian Queen, a Korean Queen, and a Cosmopolitan Queen. That year, the Cosmopolitan Queen was Caroline Lee, who was "Chinese, Hawaiian and English. Born and raised in Hawaii, she is a junior at the U. of Hawaii majoring in sociology."[74] Since a cosmopolitan queen was a mixed-race queen, Caroline Lee's mixed heritage was considered not only acceptable but beautiful by Hawaiian standards. In the 1950 contest, most queens were born in the territory of Hawaii. And, perhaps because the contest was judged by the international swimming star Esther Williams, many of the queens mentioned that swimming was one of their favorite sports. Though there may have been competition to become the representative of a specific ethnic group, there was no divisiveness among the six ethnic groups. As the array of ethnicities shows, aside from the Caucasian queen, the other queens represented multiple Asian American communities.

One civic pageant, Seattle's International Queens Ball, is noteworthy because it was multiracial and contested the notion of having to select a queen through competition. This may have reflected Seattle's working-class communities' desire not to have to select a queen from any particular ethnic group. Begun in 1950, the city of Seattle founded Seafair as its largest civic celebration. Sponsored by the Chinese American, Filipino American,

Japanese American, and African American communities, the International Queens Ball launched the Seafair celebration.[75] Members of different racial minority groups came together to work on civic uplift. What is particularly striking is that even though this event was a local, Seattle one, it was considered important enough that Los Angeles and San Francisco Asian American papers such as San Francisco's *Chinese Press* covered it.

To promote racial harmony among ethnic minorities in Seattle, instead of dividing people along racialized lines because they would vote for the candidate who represented their community, the queen was chosen in a noncompetitive way. Each of the four sponsoring racial minority communities sent their local queen to represent them at the festival. From these four, one princess would be chosen to represent the international district at Seafair, competing with the thirty other district representatives to reign over the entire festival.[76] However, what was revolutionary about this queen contest is that judges did not choose her. Rather, "Lilyan Mar of the Chinese community drew by lot at the Ball the right to represent the district as Miss International Centre in King Neptune II's royal court of princesses of Seafair."[77] Thus, instead of fostering competition among the women and their communities through judging their physical characteristics, the contest was arbitrary in its results.

People have varying notions of ideal womanhood, and thus its representation can cause contestation within a community. Since the winner of a beauty pageant signifies her community—composed of many generations and class tastes—to mainstream society, her victory opens up its values to public scrutiny. The results of the 1950 Miss Chinatown pageant proved to be controversial.[78] Given the ambiguity in the judging standards, the 1950 Fourth of July Miss Chinatown contest points were very close—the winner had only seven more points than the runner-up and ten more points than the third-place finisher.[79] As could be anticipated by the closeness of the race, not everybody agreed with the official judges' choice. The *Chinese Press* reported: "As Cynthia [Woo] stepped forward unbelievingly, she had all she could do to blink back the tears. The hubbub increased of applause (not unmixed with a few scattered boos), congra[t]ulations, the presentation of many awards, the whirring of the newsreel cameras and the clicking of shutters, and shouts for the crowds to stand back."[80] Clearly, not everybody believed that she best exemplified Chinese American femininity.

As the *Chinese Press* explained, part of what was at stake in the beauty pageant was the ever-changing notion of beauty, which is inextricably linked to politics and culture. The controversy over Cynthia Woo's victory occurred because of the clash between American and Chinese femininity. The paper noted the Americanized version of Chinese beauty displayed at the pageant: "And a note on stature: the height of the eleven young ladies averaged 5 feet 4 1/2 inches, tall for Chinese girls. Long stemmed Chinese-American roses, you might say, with other measurements to match."[81] Height was also an issue for Japanese American women. As befit an organization and event designed to show the Americanness of the community, the women themselves were hybridized emblems of Chinese American femininity.

Yet alongside the Americanized ideals of feminine physical appearance was a Chinese beauty aesthetic that existed in the minds of some community members. The *Chinese Press* columnist commented that the pageant marked a strong difference between American and Chinese beauty aesthetics, the latter epitomized by the T'ang emperor's court favorite Yang Kwei-fei:

> She turned and smiled, there bloom her hundred charms,
> Rendering colorless all the painted girls of the Six Palaces.[82]

Given the vagueness of both beauty standards, and given that it was one of the community's first contests, it is not surprising that the community did not come to consensus over which woman would best represent Chinese Americans. What the pageant does show is the invested interests of community members in beauty, beauty contests, and the cultural construction of citizenship through such events.

Despite all the incentives to be the "beautiful" ideal citizen, numerous young women contested that role by refusing to run in community pageants. Ten out of twenty of the young women nominated for the 1952 Nisei Week festival queen declined to run.[83] Some women may have refused to subject themselves to continual public scrutiny. Others did not have the time to participate in the exhausting competition rounds or in the winners' activities. The competition may have been too costly for some families.

Likewise, young Filipina women did not always want to represent family and community in beauty pageants. In 1942, a young Filipina signaled her resistance to competing in the Stockton, California Caballeros de Dimas Alang pageant by refusing to wear the Maria Clara dress.[84] Since her father insisted that she participate, Angelina Bantillo did not costume herself in an elaborate Maria Clara costume but instead wore a somber black dress. In an oral history interview, Bantillo reported that competing in the pageant made her feel as if she were in mourning; hence wearing that dress signaled her resistance.

Some Chinese American women were similarly reluctant to compete in community pageants. In 1951, the CACA queen contest organizers solicited participation from all over California. Since the CACA was based in San Francisco, the sponsors and community were dismayed that women from San Francisco declined to enter the contest. In the battle over feminine representation of locality and ethnicity, civic boosterism, prizes, and national attention were supposedly reasons why local contestants should discard "false" modesty and enter the contest. The *Chinese Press* exhorted: "Remember, girls, your cooperation adds to the general upsurge of good community spirit. And besides, even without these wonderful prizes, local pride alone should be enough challenge. In short, is or isn't the San Francisco Chinese girl the most beautiful and charming?"[85] The quotation reveals some of the multiple meanings around Chinese Americanness and local chauvinism. Thus, if a San Francisco woman won the contest, it would prove the superiority of San Francisco and its Chinese American community.

Although the *Chinese Press* editorial downplayed the impropriety of being judged according to physical criteria, its emphasis clearly indicated that many young women in San Francisco refused to enter the contest because of their concerns over appearing in public in a bathing suit. It is quite probable that the combination of the bathing-suit portion of the competition and the boos that greeted Cynthia Woo's 1950 victory prompted young Chinese American women watching the pageant to eschew future pageants. That year, confirming the sponsors' fears, a non–San Franciscan, Dorothy Lee, won Miss San Francisco Chinatown 1951.[86]

Affirming Community

Local beauty pageants in general serve different purposes for racialized communities in the United States than do mainstream national ones. Although some aspects of "ethnic" beauty pageants replicate larger American national and state pageants, they simultaneously articulate alternative cultural practices that counter the dominant discourse from which they are excluded. Filipino American community scholar Rick Bonus calls local beauty pageant spaces "alternative sites" because they go beyond main-stream politics and pageants and instead are sites where Filipino American communities are constructed.[87] In addition, racial minority beauty pageants may take forms and elements from mainstream American culture, but in making these their own, they claim belonging in the nation-state and perform an act of cultural citizenship. Thus Asian American beauty pageants are acts of cultural citizenship because they create a cultural practice that simultaneously claims racial difference while agitating for inclusion into the nation-state.

Even in an era when Cold War imperatives channeled bodily displays into all-American ones, beauty pageants could serve as affirmations of racial and ethnic identities. For Asian Americans, although much about the form of beauty pageants was derived from mainstream American culture, both bearing Asian faces and performing markers of racial heritage transformed the beauty pageant into a racially marked one. While the beauty pageants aimed to assimilate racial difference, that process is imperfect.[88] Despite the political expediency of showing a mainstream American appearance, community values and customs allowed for partial Asian-ethnic culture to emerge. Pageants are compelling to racial minority communities because they allow them to enact revised histories and to imagine alternative futures.

Young Chinese American women affirmed the *Chinese Press*'s coverage of the 1950 San Francisco Miss Chinatown pageant. By June 9, 1950, the organizers had been successful in their attempts to publicize the Chinese American Citizens Alliance Miss Chinatown contest and, with the help of the newspaper, had garnered interest and support from all over California. Marion Lowe, the president of the Oakland Chinese Young Women's Society, wrote: "The CACA activities have been always noted with interest, especially your annual Bathing Beauty Contest. Best of luck for a bigger and more successful picnic."[89] Young women, and men, were interested in the models of femininity shown to be successful in the beauty contest. It is significant that Lowe refers to the queen contest as a "bathing-beauty contest."

Cultural producers from *Life* magazine to Miss America pageant organizers to the editors of *Scene* insisted that the representative American body was young, female, single, and American-born. For young Asian American women, creating a new racial minority normative beauty through community contests or *Scene* profiles allowed them to negotiate their communities and gain power. First, just as the senior prom queen signaled the most popular girl in high school, winning a community event or being featured in a magazine could "crown" the social power of a particular young lady.[90] Second, pageants acted as "GI Bills" for women in that they provided economic incentives such as cash prizes, scholarships, and gifts, and the beauty industry provided jobs. Third, the grooming process of the pageant and the photo shoot taught young women public poise, polish, and the skills to operate in the public sphere, including that all-important business world cited by Carolyn Miller. Fourth, the beauty-pageant contestant or model gained status in her family and community. She demonstrated that her parents and extended clan nurtured ideal young ladies through impeccable social reproduction. Fifth, the pageants and magazine profiles functioned as debuts in which young women would be introduced to society as eligible for dating. As a woman was deemed "beautiful," her "dating worth" skyrocketed. Sixth, the excitement and glamour of being at center stage, like a movie star or royalty, at a time when women had very few opportunities to get public attention, was an incentive.

Clearly, not all the prestige elements listed above would be in operation for all people at all times. However, though many young women adamantly refused to participate in public beauty culture because one or more of the prestige elements did not hold true for them, many women did partake.[91] As Filipina poet, activist, and scholar Emily Lawsin has explained, young Filipina Americans' families pressured them to enter beauty pageants as a way to show family prominence and to raise money for the community.[92] In fact, often the audience for beauty pageants was less preoccupied with physical beauty per se than with raising money for community projects and expressing political agendas.

A harmonious queen pageant such as the 1952 Nisei Week queen contest can affirm community values and norms. Since there was consensus within the community as well as between the community and the judges over who would win, the results of the contest on August 16, 1952, were anticlimactic. The *Rafu Shimpo* explained that one hundred couples attended the semi-formal coronation ball and that "the scene lacked the usual tension and anticipation. For many of the dancers, the pre-ball favorite Miss Kato gaining the tiara was taken almost 'as a matter of fact.'"[93] It was apparent to all the observers that Emily Kato best fit all the queen criteria, for she was an active member of the community through being president of her local chapter of the Young Buddhists Association, and she had middle-class parents, an outgoing personality, and fashionable hair and attire. For the coronation, the queen and court wore full-length white ball gowns.

The young women selected as Nisei Week queen and court affirmed the Japanese American community for sponsors and for the greater Los Angeles community. The community sought a safe and acceptable way to present themselves that showed that internment was a mistake. Despite the imperatives for 100 percent Americanness in clothing, 1952 Nisei Week queen and court showed Japanese dress with Western hairstyles in their public "face," demonstrating hybridity and the possibility of calling attention to hegemonic power relations and showing the extent to which cultural citizenship could accommodate difference.[94] Like a movie star or actual royalty, Emily Kato and her court wore kimonos as they rode in a convertible and waved to the public on their way to delivering the official invitation to Nisei Week to the mayor of Los Angeles.[95] Escorted by pageant sponsors, the kimono-clad queen and her court thanked the Little Tokyo merchants.[96] As was the case for European-ethnic community queens, the Nisei Week queen was expected to bring favorable attention to her community.[97] In addition, the queen and her court attended various public activities that linked multiple communities, including ones that were not Japanese American.[98]

Multiple expectations circumscribed the choices available to Japanese Americans, which helps explain why the 1952 Nisei Week candidates wore kimonos when inviting the mayor to the festival. This act indicated the imperfection of translating mainstream criteria into ethnic pageants.[99] For Japanese Americans in the postinternment era, it was a delicate balancing act. On the one hand, at times they had to satisfy mainstream American desires for mastery and exoticism through orientalism. On the other hand, they continually had to prove their American status. And, especially for the older generation, wearing kimonos could signal ethnic pride. Other Japanese and Japanese American women felt similar pressure to wear kimonos. Sponsors mandated that the 1950 Miss Japan Miss Universe contestant and her court had to wear kimonos during their six-week goodwill tour of the United States, despite their preference for modern Western clothing.[100] Similarly, a Seattle restaurateur had difficulties recruiting Nisei women as kimonoed waitstaff. Apparently the young women "seemed overly eager to cast off the old world culture" of wearing kimonos.[101] For the Nisei Week contenders, the symbolism of public ethnic affiliation proved stronger than the Western fashion worn in the elimination rounds and the coronation ball. Since the court was marked by other cues of

Western modernity, such as hairstyles and the convertible, partial displays of Japanese fashion signified their ethnic heritage to the mainstream. Clothing choices for women held contested meanings for the women themselves and for the different communities in which they presented themselves.

Like the 1952 Nisei Week competition, the 1948 Miss Philippines pageant affirmed community and was settled amicably. The *Philippines Star Press* reported each tabulation of the queen ballots every week leading up to the contest and reported the winners on July 3. The *Star Press* announced Frances Tenchavez's victory in a close battle for the title with Catherine Edralin and Elizabeth Rigor. It was so close that "[d]uring the last counting of votes, there was doubt as to the final outcome of the contest." A Los Angeles City College co-ed, Tenchavez won the right to reign as Miss Philippines, queen of the nation, whereas the other contestants represented individual islands: "Miss Tenchavez will be 'Miss Philippines' and will reign as queen during the July 4th celebration. Miss Edralin will be 'Miss Luzon.' Miss Rigor will be 'Miss Mindinao,' and Miss Padilla will be 'Miss Corregidor.'"[102] Like the Nisei Week queens, the Filipino American Fourth of July queens presided over the celebration as visible symbols of gendered national identity.

One reason why beauty pageants were so popular among Filipino Americans is that they could invoke anticolonial struggles and suggest possibilities for a postcolonial future. Organizations that had originally formed to combat colonialism sponsored beauty pageants. For example, in 1898 the Caballeros de Dimas Alang (CDA) overthrew Spanish rule in the Philippines.[103] In the United States, the CDA became one of the leading Filipino American mutual aid societies. The CDA queen symbolized Maria Clara, the ideal woman invoked by Jose Rizal, a CDA and one the leading anticolonial Filipino nationalist martyrs.[104] Thus selecting a young woman who best embodied the traits of Maria Clara publicly reworked the memory of anticolonial struggles and acted as a basis for group cohesion. In addition, the nineteenth-century anticolonial struggle against Spanish imperialism was a safer one to commemorate than the current, twentieth-century one against U.S. imperialism in the Philippines. This move to memorialize history and imagine a future through beauty pageants was not confined to Filipino Americans. For example, the 1921 Mexican India Bonita Pageant, put together after the Mexican Revolution, inscribed indigenous history onto the body of the queen candidate and thus reworked and reinscribed historical memory.[105]

Filipina Americans in the 1948 Miss Philippines contest modeled Maria Clara gowns with Western and Filipina influences. In the publicity photographs, three out of the five candidates wore "modern" Filipina dress. Trinidad Padilla's dress was styled with puffed sleeves and a V-neck, as was Elizabeth Rigor's, which added fur trim. Winner "Cookie" Tenchavez's sleeves and V-neck were far more subdued.[106] Thus Tenchavez's gown best emblematized a hybridized cultural appearance of restrained American taste united with a Filipino sensibility.

The invocation of Maria Clara, anticolonial martyr Jose Rizal's ideal woman, and her continual reembodiment in the queen contest placed the memory of Philippine independence struggles at the center of community celebrations. Yet the performance of the Maria Clara type was not static but one that changed over time. Filipinas commemorated the changes that the Filipina dresses had undergone since the advent of American colonialism. For example, in 1951 the Maria Clara Lodge, the female auxiliary of the Caballeros de Dimas Alang, organized a fashion show that highlighted the "evolution of Filipina Dresses from 1898 to 1950." The "modern style with panuelo" echoed the main features of the 1948 Miss Philippines contest winner's gown.[107] Historian Barbara Posadas documents that in the United States, the Maria Clara outfit comprised a *baro* blouse of fine embroidered white material, a *panuelo* of the same fabric, and a long, shirred skirt of checked or striped black and white material.[108] In the 1930s, the sleeves of the *baro* were shortened to elbow length and flattened against the arms while standing stiff and "butterfly-like" above the shoulders. By the 1940s, these separate elements were combined in one gown called the *terno*, which, over time, has been modified to reflect current fashion. The Maria Clara gown symbolized the continual visual renaming of history yet also signified the flexibility to change into current fashions. The Maria Clara costumes would create a connection to the Philippines, for women, especially in the post–World War II era, frequently ordered their costumes to be made in the Philippines.

Given the Cold War imperatives and the "fall" of China to communism, it is not surprising that, out of all these Asian-ethnic groups, the Chinese Americans felt most compelled to affirm their communities' 100 percent Americanness in early Cold War beauty culture. Queen contestants did not dress in cheongsams until the late 1950s. Instead, bathing suits and the singing of "The Star-Spangled Banner" were part of fervent attempts to counter the Cold War expulsion of Chinese "subversives."[109] For example, before the 1950 Miss Chinatown pageant, patriotic speeches were made, then "Lieut. Col. Chang Wah Lee gave a stirring rendition of the Star Spangled Banner in leading the gathering in that national anthem."[110] For Chinese Americans in the throes of the Cold War, beauty pageants provided a stellar means of affirming American patriotism.

Conclusion

Asian American civil rights groups used beauty pageants not only to imagine themselves belonging to the nation-state but also to show their ability to stage their community's model citizenship to the larger American public. The beauty pageant was an all-American way to show how Asian Americans could stage individual opportunity and achievement through competition and arrive at an ideal female American citizen. The beauty pageant enabled them to show that they knew and could distinguish ideal citizenship and ideal community and thus were capable of exercising full American citizenship rights and privileges. Asian American communities arrived at the ideal female citizen through an evaluation process that privileged Cold War liberal capitalistic values. Beauty pageants were so popular in the post–World War II era that young Asian American women participated in forums ranging from the Page One newspaper ball to the Miss Portrait of Spring to the Cotton Queen to Miss Football.

Local beauty pageants in general serve different purposes for racialized communities in the United States than do mainstream national ones. Although some aspects of "ethnic" beauty pageants replicate larger American national and state pageants, they simultaneously articulate alternative cultural practices that counter the dominant discourse from which they are excluded. As alternative sites, they go beyond mainstream politics and pageants and instead are sites where racial minority communities are constructed.[111] In addition, racial minority beauty pageants may take forms and elements from mainstream American culture, but in making these their own, they claim belonging in the nation-state and thus enact cultural citizenship. Hence Asian American beauty pageants are acts of cultural citizenship because they create a cultural practice that simultaneously claims racial difference while agitating for inclusion into the nation-state.

In the post–Cold War era, beauty is still central to ethnic communities. The Nisei Week, Miss Chinatown, and Miss Philippines contests all continue today. They have been joined by numerous other pageants—the winner of the Nisei Week pageant goes on to attend the Miss Nikkei contest in Brazil; Los Angeles has its own Miss Chinatown pageant. Other Asian-ethnic groups have developed pageants, such as the Vietnamese Hoa Hau Ao Dai contest and the Miss India Georgia pageant.

Though by no means a complete or comprehensive shift, the next chapter, "Riding the Crest of the Oriental Wave," focuses on how American culture shifted into a new form of "orientalism." Wars in Asia, the later stages of the Cold War, American liberalism, and shifting race relations form the backdrop for the sudden visibility of women of Asian descent in mainstream American eyes.

5

Riding the Crest
of an Oriental Wave

Foreign-Born Asian "Beauty"

In the span of a little over a year (1958–1959), Miyoshi Umeki won an Academy Award for best supporting actress, France Nuyen graced the cover of *Life* magazine, and Akiko Kojima was crowned Miss Universe. As Los Angeles' Japanese American newspaper *Kashu Mainichi* observed, "in many fields of the arts the U.S. is riding the crest of an Oriental wave."[1] What distinguishes the late 1950s from the early Cold War era is that in the later period foreign-born Asian women gained international fame in mainstream cultural venues such as beauty pageants and movies, whereas earlier, American-born women of Asian descent gained local fame in community events. Thus, by 1959, a certain type of Asian femininity—foreign-born, slender, and coy yet sexual—was mainstreamed for the first time in American history. Why did this shift in public culture from American to Asian occur?[2]

The crest of the oriental wave occurred at a critical juncture in American history, in a narrow band of time between the end of the Tokyo Rose treason trials in 1949 and the onset of serious U.S. involvement in the Vietnam War in the early 1960s.[3] These events coincided with the beginning of the civil rights era as well as the consolidation of American empire. Anxieties around racial integration within the United States and American imperialism in Asia were alleviated through mainstream media's integration of these foreign-born women of Asian descent. The oriental wave utilized these women to act as symbols of current domestic racial integration and to incorporate empire in reassuringly nonviolent ways that negated the appearance of empire in a rapidly decolonizing world. It brought Asian women into national prominence and normalized the increased migration of Asian war brides. Yet it did so at the cost of effacing the century-long relationship of Asian Americans as the working class of the U.S. Pacific Coast. Instead, Asians became reracialized as newly arrived female foreigners.

This new oriental wave was distinctly different from the classic construction of orientalism because it deployed female beauty and interracial marriage in order to disavow racism and renounce empire. As discussed in chapter 2, in the classic formulation of orientalism, the Orient was a necessary construction against which the West (Europe) could create itself.[4] In the particular case of the United States, the Orient in the guise of the Pacific came into sharp relief with the colonizing of the Philippines in 1898. The postwar occupation of Japan and the Cold War military jousting that resulted in the Korean War fueled the mid-twentieth-century "oriental wave."[5] It is not accidental that female, not male, Asian bodies became prominent during the rise of America's Pacific empire. The United States' unease about its emerging superpower status and growing imperialism courtesy of military bases ringing the Pacific emerged in national consciousness through figures such as France Nuyen, Akiko Kojima, and Miyoshi Umeki. Through the figure of Asian women, these narratives about Asia constructed a seeming equality between Asian nations and the United States through appreciation of beauty and interracial romances, while eliding the power differentials of race and nation.[6]

The dominant liberal discourse during an era of decolonization and civil rights did not promote an overt narrative of oppression and domination. Instead, the new relations with Asia explored in these cultural venues were replete with emotional understanding and reciprocity. However, those seemingly benevolent attitudes supported U.S. power in Asia.[7] Although many scholars have argued that interracial love has been the major structure of feeling that allowed the United States to be an empire without conquest or colonies, I would argue that of equal importance was the display of the beauty and thus humanity of the women of Asian descent.

This chapter explores the significance of foreign-born Asian "beauty" in the political context of liberal-democratic American race relations and Cold War American empire-without-colonies in Asia. The first segment examines how Miss Japan not only emblematized modernity and beauty but sparked Japanese American hopes for favorable international relations in the aftermath of World War II. The second segment scrutinizes the hallmarks of the new type of Asian femininity. The third section examines how the rise of the Asian "beauty" underscored existing racialized standards of beauty. The final and most important segment shows how Asian

American communities interacted with the oriental wave, and how those interactions changed how Asian Americans such as the women of Chi Alpha Delta performed cultural citizenship and modernity. Conjoined with the growth of ethnic and racial pride movements, the oriental wave reinforced diasporic cultural citizenship. Thus it became more politically acceptable for Asian Americans to display their Asian heritage.

Beauty, Modernity, and International Relations

> Merely by drawing the admiration of newspaper readers and newsreel viewers around the globe, Miss Ito (Miss Japan 1953) probably has done more to create a favorable attitude toward Japan than all the pronouncements made by the Japanese foreign office since V-J Day.[8]
>
> —*Scene* magazine, September 1953

Asian American periodicals viewed Asian beauty queens as potent symbols of foreign political relations. As the above quotation shows, in 1953 one provocative *Scene* magazine editorial interpreted Kinuko Ito, Japan's third-place finisher in the Miss Universe pageant, in terms of Japan–U.S. foreign policy relations.[9] As discussed in the preceding chapter, during the Cold War era charges that Soviet women were unfeminine and not beautiful were used to prove the inhumanity and inferiority of the communist system, while conversely, the beauty of women from Western democratic nations showed the superiority of capitalist societies. In this era, women from Asian countries with American military bases won international beauty pageants such as the Miss Universe contest. Since the United States hosted the Miss Universe pageant throughout the 1950s, Cold War politics affected who was invited to the pageant, how women represented their countries, and who won. Through beauty, the issues of modernity and femininity came to the forefront. In particular, racial minority communities, newly decolonized nations, and those under military occupation had stakes in the proper performance of female modernity. For Asian American communities, diasporic cultural citizenship, which signified their identification with "home" Asian nations, meant that the performance of Asian female modernity was linked to Asian American female modernity.[10]

Scene's exegesis that beauty pageants were international affairs coincided with the views of the Miss Universe pageant organizers, who hoped that the competition—women from forty-two states, twenty-two countries, and three territories—would foster "international understanding." That year, 1953, all the international candidates arrived in Los Angeles together and lined up in front of the plane for publicity photographs. According to *Scene,* Ito's stature caused considerable comment and contradicted the prevailing notion of Asian women as petite. As the caption that accompanied the photographic evidence stated: "Stereotype visions of a diminutive 'Madame Butterfly' vanished on Miss Japan's arrival at Los Angeles. Standing 5 feet 6 inches, she was at eye level with most candidates."[11] No longer was Miss Japan "Madame Butterfly," the sign of Japan as a feminized nation tamed by the West. Being on eye level with candidates from other countries can be read as analogous to Japan's desire, after World War II defeat, to be on the same political and economic level as other countries. Given that *Scene* was the source of this information, one can infer that it reflected Japanese American desires to be on the same level with Americans. The pageant was designed to foster improved relations between Americans and other nations, and the pageant organizers paired Americans and foreigners in roommate assignments.[12] The setup fed into the American myth of liberal equality among nations.

In the post–World War II nation-state power realignment marked by gender reconfigurations, beauty pageants were forums for international contentions over modernity and progress as signified by fashion and beauty. Western styles of fashion and standards of physical appearance determined Kinuko Ito's victory in the competition. The differing ways of describing Ito's height can ultimately be attributed to the authors' attitudes toward Japan's place in the world: tall as powerful, short as negligible. During the pageant, the contestants did not have their body measurements made public, nor did they engage in a talent contest, but they did model clothing: bathing suits, formal wear, and "native" dress. Ito's appeal stemmed from her height and tasteful Western formal wear. In the *Scene* magazine article, she was described as "[t]rim-legged, average tall even by U.S. standards (5 feet 6 inches) slender and warmly gracious." A Tokyo fashion model, the twenty-one-year-old Ito proved her popularity, for she "got tremendous roars of approval from capacity audiences watching the Miss Universe contest semi-finals and finals at Long Beach's Municipal auditorium, July 16 and 17."[13] Ito's Japan-designed Western-style evening gown with roses painted on the skirt won tremendous audience plaudits. Ito's modern gown stands in marked contrast to 1950's Miss Japan's "traditional" kimono attire, signaling a shift to displaying modern cultural citizenship. Although there are numerous ways that this would affect Japanese

American cultural citizenship, Miss Japan's performance of modernity would further normalize similar ones by Nisei women.

Asian American commentators framed the 1953 Miss Universe beauty contest as emblematic of the participating nations' social and political progress. One *Scene* journalist actually used the word *democracy* in describing Kinuko Ito: "Not a smashing, breath-taking beauty in the fluffy or fashion-glamor sense, Kinuko has fragile Oriental beauty with an added asset, perhaps reflective of a new democratizing Japan. This quality is that of a woman intelligently capable of making judgements for herself. One doesn't expect to see her disappear behind a fan."[14] Thus, at least to one Nisei writer, the beauty pageant equaled political progress. As Miss Japan, Kinuko Ito represented a modern woman in the Western sense of the word, who symbolized modern Japan. Modernity and femininity have been linked in international beauty competitions, for as scholars Colleen Cohen, Richard Wilk, and Beverly Stoeltje argue, "beauty contests emerge as tools for articulating different political positions in rapidly changing social and political climates. Many of the studies also find a strong connection between beauty contests and notions of social progress. . . . [O]rganizing a beauty contest now often functions as a badge of civilized, modern status."[15] Modernity could be proven, for ostensibly, the better one's candidate did in the international competition, the more civilized and modern one's nation appeared.

As mentioned earlier, commentators cast the Miss Universe pageant as an allegory for foreign relations between the United States and Japan. A *Scene* editorial entitled "A Lesson in Legs" presented Ito's success in Long Beach as a model for Japan to emulate. The Japanese American author noted Ito's popularity with the local audience: "The entry from Japan, lovely Kinuko Ito of Tokyo finished a close third behind the French and U.S. candidates. Our southern California reporter, whose eye is especially good when covering these things, swears that Miss Ito would be 'Miss Universe' today had the judging been based on audience response. He says she drew more applause than any other candidate at the final judging."[16] According to the editorial, Ito's appeal crossed ethnic and national borders.

The writer attributed Ito's success to a physical appearance pleasing to Western viewers. Since Japanese women are usually short, the editorial author believed Ito's height critical. Though he asserted that beauty does not conform to natural, universal, or international standards, he nonetheless acknowledged the importance of Western beauty standards: "Japanese women have an attractiveness that their nation can be proud of. But as a rule, they are not physically built to conform to the standards applied at American or European bathing-suited beauty contests. Their beauty, by and large, is not the leggy sort." Thus the author put together the second part of the political moral: that Japan sent women to contests who were not "average" and "normal" for Japan but those who measured up to Western standards of beauty. The editorial continued: "As soon as 'cheesecake' photos of Miss Ito began appearing in the papers, it became apparent that she was among the exceptions to the rule. She was taller than the average Japanese woman." Apparently, the previous year's Miss Japan had also been unusually tall and thus a Western-style beauty. The editorial continued: "So we detect a pattern. Whoever in Japan picks the girl sent to the annual 'Miss Universe' hoopla in Long Beach, Calif., obviously have adopted the criteria in force in the West. And just as obviously, they applied that criteria with good effect in the case of Kinuko Ito." The deliberate strategy of pleasing the West worked.

The editorial concludes that if a candidate such as Ito can win because she appeals to Western tastes, so can Japanese business and politics. "The moral that emerges from all this—especially from Miss Ito's personal assets—is this: Japan's recovery from the horrible misjudgments of her former militarist rulers is largely dependent upon how she makes out in her relations with the West, especially with its leader, the U.S. It would seem, therefore, that a first rule for Japan to follow is to consider the standards by which opinions and decisions are made in the West."[17] The author believed that if the Japanese wanted to be successful in the United States, they would benefit most by following American standards: "Public relations in Japan likewise is at least 40 years behind the American pace. It seems to us that a serious effort to catch up is overdue, and that a good way to start is to consider the moral in Kinuko Ito's body beautiful." If Japanese business could use American standards to the same degree and effect as beauty officials, then Japan could regain international power. Though scholars such as Cynthia Enloe argue that foreign relations take place in overseas settings when "first world" powers disrupt "third world" ones, this segment suggests that engagement with international relations occurs in numerous forums, including beauty pageants.[18]

Despite *Scene's* hopes for favorable politics attributed to Ito's success, Western stereotypes of Asian "smallness" and "shortness" persisted even when there was evidence to the contrary. The contrast between how the mainstream *Los Angeles Times* viewed Miss France and Miss Japan exemplifies this. Though the Asian American source, *Scene,* emphasized Ito's height as a key to her success, the *Los Angeles Times*'s opinion was radically different. The *Times* described Ito as "Miss Japan, petite Kinuko Ito."[19] What makes the *Times*'s designation of Ito as petite even more striking is a comparison to the newspaper's description of Miss Universe, Christine Martel of France. Though 5'3", Martel is never described as petite. Instead, she is "the shapely Parisienne" and "the winsome mademoiselle."[20] The newspaper quantified her physical appearance but did not classify her as diminutive: "What caught the judges' eyes was 125 pounds of beauty, standing 5 feet three inches and measuring 33 inches at the bust, 22 at the waist and 35 1/2 at the hips."[21] The *Scene* article claimed that Ito was 5'6" and hence, far from being petite, Ito should have looked three inches taller than Martel. When one looks at the *Times* photograph of the five finalists who are all standing, Martel appears slightly taller than Ito does. That greater height might be due to Martel standing slightly in front of the other finalists, or perhaps her heels were higher than Ito's, or perhaps *Scene* exaggerated Ito's height, or the *Times* played down Martel's. The differing ways of describing Ito's height can ultimately be attributed to the authors' attitudes toward Japan's place in the world: tall as powerful, short as negligible.

The Oriental Wave: Asian Beauty in the Public Eye

In the post–World War II era, whole cultural industries revolved around exploring the place of Asia in relation to the United States. Best-selling novels by James Michener, blockbuster Broadway musicals, Hollywood films, and tourism brought Asia, the Pacific, and Hawaii to mainstream American attention. Securing domestic consent for empire through culture enjoyed earlier precedents. For example, from the turn of the century onward, World's Fairs were prime sites for peopled Philippine Villages and displays of raw goods from territories won from the Spanish-American War of 1898. And Hawaiian hula shows toured throughout the United States, bringing a particular vision of Hawaii to the broad American public.[22]

In their various guises, these narratives about Asia and interracial relationships won critical acclaim, prizes, and audience accolades. The first prominent novel about Asia that featured interracial relationships, James Michener's *Tales of the South Pacific,* won a Pulitzer Prize in 1947. The Broadway musical version won numerous prizes for Richard Rodgers,

Oscar Hammerstein II, and Joshua Logan, including the New York Drama Critics' Circle Award for best musical of 1948–1949. In addition, *South Pacific* was transformed into a movie in which France Nuyen played the young native Tonkinese island woman named Liat. Although *South Pacific* was not about Hawaii, nonetheless given the debates over whether or not Hawaii should be a state given its predominantly Asian-descent population, and given that *South Pacific* was filmed in Hawaii, the film was a test case for the racial issues surrounding Hawaii's integration into the American nation-state. *Sayonara, Teahouse of the August Moon, The World of Suzie Wong,* and *The King and I* were just some of the many narratives that allowed the United States to imagine its interests in Asia.

Beauty was a key device to the sentimental bridging of racial, national, and cultural difference. Though acknowledging women of Asian descent as beautiful hardly seems earth-shattering in today's era of multicultural advertising, in the middle of the twentieth century it was a very different story. As World War II demonized the Japanese in order to justify war brutality and detonating atomic bombs, American popular novels of the immediate postwar era portrayed women of Asian descent as unattractive and barely human. For example, in the novel *Sayonara,* upon first seeing Katsumi, played by Miyoshi Umeki in the movie version, Major Gruver (Marlon Brando's character) recoils because he considers her ugly and unfeminine. Similarly, while looking at a painting of a famous Japanese beauty, he thinks, "It was disgusting," and cries out, "Why she's ugly!"[23] As Sojourner Truth's cry "Ain't I a woman" attests, patriarchal racializing castigates nonwhite women as inhuman and thus as not worthy of privileges granted to white women. Thus, to establish cultural citizenship, one first had to establish humanity, which could be done through beauty. Given the mainstream racialized slippage between Japanese and Japanese American, as well as the diasporic identification fostered by mass media, this issue was also relevant for the Nisei.

When the early novels did acknowledge Asian women's humanity, it was presented as a revelation. In her first film, *South Pacific,* France Nuyen played Liat, a woman who has an affair with a white American soldier, Joe Cable. In James Michener's novel, after having sexual relations, Cable justifies the relationship to himself by reasoning that Liat descended from an old civilization and had certain physical traits that were as good as white: "She was clean, immaculately so. Her teeth were white. Her ankles delicate, like those of a girl of family in Philadelphia."[24] Liat did not conform to his notion of what an "uncivilized," "dark," "dirty" person was like.

France Nuyen.

She physically bore the markers of class and status that he associated with elite American women, or his attraction to her racialized her closer to white in his mind. James Michener's revelation of Asian women's attractiveness to a skeptical audience evokes that of Elwood Schweer, fresh from military duty in Korea, who lobbied to show his friends at Ripon College in Wisconsin that women of Japanese descent were attractive.

The ascendancy of actresses like Miyoshi Umeki and France Nuyen signaled a changing of the guard as well as a new aesthetics of beauty. As the next set of actresses of Asian descent to gain starring roles since Anna May Wong retired in 1941, they displaced European American women playing yellowface: Katherine Hepburn in *Dragon Seed* (1949), Angie Dickinson as Lucky Legs in *China Gate* (1957), and Jennifer Jones as Han Suyin in *Love Is a Many Splendored Thing* (1955). They also displaced Anna May Wong as the ultimate figure of Asian "beauty." As for many actresses of both the past and present day, roles for "older" women like Anna May Wong were far fewer than those for ingenues. Though Wong retired from the movies, she came back after the war: "I'll be glad to be doing a movie again," she said, "instead of being a technical adviser, as I seemed to be during the war years. But I'm only going to take roles I like."[25] Acting roles were few and far between and were not of the caliber of her prewar films. For example, Wong played Lana Turner's maid in *Portrait in Black* (1960). She did star in a television show, *Gallery of Madame Liu-Tsong* (1951), for the Dumont network as a gallery owner/detective, reminiscent of her role in *Daughter of Shanghai*. However, the series was canceled after eleven episodes.

Miyoshi Umeki and France Nuyen represented distinctly different types of women than did Anna May Wong. Umeki gained fame as the ultimate war bride, while France Nuyen and, later, Nancy Kwan portrayed the long-haired cheongsam-wearing innocent sexual siren. Foreign birth is a key aspect of this distinctly new type of femininity. Hong Kong–born Kwan replaced Japanese American Pat Suzuki in the Rodgers and Hammerstein musical *Flower Drum Song*, while Umeki, not Miiko Taka, won the Academy Award for *Sayonara*.

Miyoshi Umeki: The Uber–War Bride

Twenty years after playing a supporting acting role to Anna May Wong in *King of Chinatown*, Anthony Quinn presented the 1957 Academy Award for best supporting actress to Miyoshi Umeki. The Hearst Newsreels reveal Umeki wearing a kimono, beaming upon receiving her award. Then, Academy Award statuette cradled between both hands, Umeki bowed repeatedly to the crowd at the Pantages Theater while thanking them for their votes.[26] Astonished at having won the award for her supporting actress role of Katsumi in the motion picture *Sayonara*, Umeki became the first woman of Asian descent to win an Academy Award in any category. What, then, did Umeki represent so that she won this award at this particular moment?

Miyoshi Umeki was rewarded for playing a tragic war bride. Given that the 1924 Immigration Act cut off all migration from Asia, war brides such as the one portrayed by Umeki could not immigrate. Thus Asian war brides dramatized the racialized nature of American immigration law, because war brides from other areas of the world could immigrate. The 1945 War Brides Act, which had initially excluded Asian American veterans, was modified in 1947 to include them. Chinese American armed forces personnel and their Chinese brides were the biggest beneficiaries of the 1947 act.

However, the ability of Asian war brides to enter the United States was heavily circumscribed and episodic until the passage of the 1952 McCarran-Walter act. After its passage, the annual immigration of Japanese women as war brides ranged from two thousand to five thousand, which constituted 80 percent of all Japanese migrants.[27] War brides thus caused the largest influx of Asian migration since the 1924 Immigration Act effectively halted it.

Post–World War II war brides were part of the long-standing trajectory of women of Asian descent being allowed into (or prevented from) migration solely through their sexual relationship to men. The 1907 Gentlemen's Agreement allowed men of Japanese descent who could prove a minimum net worth to sponsor picture brides' migration for marriage. The 1875 Page Law forbade working-class women of Chinese descent from immigrating because they were feared to be prostitutes. Instead, under the Chinese exclusion laws, the only Chinese women who could migrate were the wives of merchants.

Miyoshi Umeki won her Academy Award for her work in a landmark film in American race relations, *Sayonara*. Created at least a decade before one of the most widely remembered movies on interracial dating, 1968's *Guess Who's Coming to Dinner*, it was the first major Academy Award–winning movie to portray a successful interracial marriage. As antimiscegenation laws still prevailed, interracial marriage could be forbidden at a state's discretion until the U.S. Supreme Court decision *Loving* v. *Virginia* (1967). As discussed in chapter 2, in the 1930s the Hollywood Hays Code censors forbade Anna May Wong from enacting interracial romances. Given the contemporary social mores, it was pathbreaking that in the film *Sayonara*, Umeki (Katsumi) played a Japanese woman who married Red Buttons (Joe Kelly), a white American air force man. Set in 1951 Kobe, Japan, during American occupation and the Korean War, the movie, released December 28, 1957, was based on the 1953 eponymous James Michener novel.[28] As a married couple, Umeki and Buttons not only provided the means for star Marlon Brando, playing Major Gruver, to meet and fall in love with Hana-Ogi, played by Miiko Taka, but demonstrated how to conduct an interracial relationship.

In *Sayonara*, the movie plot comes to a decisive moment when the army orders Buttons and other military men married to Japanese women to return to the United States. Many married couples were in a bind, for if the men wanted to obey the military orders, which were designed to break the relationship between American army men and Japanese spouses, they would have to abandon their wives in Japan with no guarantee of reunification. Since Kelly cannot bring himself to leave Katsumi in Japan, they both commit suicide.

Sayonara touched audiences and fellow Academy members to such an extent that both Red Buttons and Miyoshi Umeki won supporting-actor Academy Awards in 1958. In publicity for the Academy Awards that reminded audiences of their movie roles, Buttons and Umeki made appearances together as a couple. Their marketing paid off. *Sayonara* did exceedingly well at the box office, ranking as one of the best-attended movies of the year, and, in fact, was star Marlon Brando's greatest box office hit until the *Godfather* in 1971. *Sayonara*'s popularity, however, was not unproblematic. Although the romance between American military men and Japanese women placed the two countries on a seemingly equal footing that elided racism and imperialism, such an interracial marriage effaced the actual power hierarchies.[29] In other words, audiences might view the interracial romances as equal and reciprocal, mirroring the supposed American and Japanese equality, whereas the underlying discursive mechanisms placed the power on the American and male side.

Increasing societal acceptance of interracial marriages explains the change depicted in the motion picture *Sayonara* in 1957. Earlier movies such as *Teahouse of the August Moon, South Pacific,* and *Love Is a Many Splendored Thing* focused on the doom of interracial love. The status of war brides changed and became favorable over time.[30] And, as shown in a 1950s Los Angeles Little Tokyo Nisei Week festival booklet, most Nisei approved of interracial coupling as a sign of equality. Though most did not engage in it themselves, many believed that interracial dating and marriage were signs that antimiscegenation laws were being put to rest not only on paper but in actual practice.

However, the popularity and acceptability of the war bride was not benign. Literary scholar Caroline Chung Simpson has convincingly suggested that the focus on Japanese war brides enabled America to cope with the anxieties around race relations in a way not as immediately contentious as integrating African Americans.[31] As the Soviet Union argued that unequal race relations in America demonstrated the inequities of capitalism, American liberalism sought to prove that democratic capitalism provided harmonious race relations. The cultural focus on Japanese war brides provided a site in which racial integration and stabilized race relations could prevail.[32] Thus the wish for smoother racial integration explained one rationale for the media's attentiveness toward Umeki, Nuyen, and Kojima.

Part of Miyoshi Umeki's appeal was that she was the figure most associated with demure foreign femininity. This was manifest not only through her movie roles but through her public behavior. Though nominated for the Academy Award for her role in *Sayonara*, Umeki did not believe she would win it for her first American film role. "'I didn't think I had a chance,' she said. 'So I didn't want to invest too much. Even when they called my name, I thought they said 'Deborah Kerr.'"[33] Umeki's modest aspirations were continually reported: "Miyoshi, a Japanese singing star said, 'I didn't hope to win. I just happy to be nominated.'"[34] Her Japanese accent and ungrammatical speech reinforced the "adorable," "precious," and "foreign" aspects of her femininity.

As befits America's fascination with Japan, Miyoshi Umeki's Academy Award did not occur in a vacuum, for *Sayonara* was not the only Japan-themed movie to do well at the 1957 Academy Awards. The motion picture *The Bridge over the River Kwai*, whose story takes place in Japan and which featured another of Anna May Wong's former co-stars, Sessue Hayakawa, won the award for best picture. Though Hayakawa lost out to Red Buttons for the Best Supporting Actor award, his co-star, Alec Guinness, won the Best Actor award for his role in the film.

Despite her victory, Miyoshi Umeki's triumph did not make it into the *Life* magazine issue on the 1957 Academy Awards. Instead, photographs of Joanne Woodward, who had won the award for best actress, dominated the coverage. Perhaps the magazine found the sexually provocative image of Suzie Wong in a cheongsam, as played by France Nuyen and Nancy Kwan, to be a far better marketing device than Umeki in a kimono. Or maybe Umeki's victory paved the way for national attention to be focused on actresses of Asian descent.

In an interview with the Los Angeles newspaper *Hollywood Citizen News*, Miyoshi Umeki portrayed herself as a traditional Japanese woman, as opposed to the new, Americanized Japanese youth:

> I am a member of the last Japanese generation educated in the old tradition. Now all the books have been changed in the schools, and the customs, manners, morals and even the dress of the Japanese have been changed forever.
>
> The younger generation hasn't been exactly Americanized, but it's been somethingized.[35]

Umeki's representation of herself as part of pre–World War II Japan could have multiple meanings. According to Umeki, the hallmarks of this premodern, traditional Japan were sumo, kabuki, and gender relations in which women subsumed themselves to men. One possible meaning of her statement is that modernization brought by the post–World War II American occupation of Japan had also brought liberation to some women in Japan.[36] Umeki's response can also be interpreted as part of the new resistance that used "old traditions" to fight the neocolonial changes wrought by the American occupation of Japan. Umeki's language was couched in such a way that she did not appear to be criticizing the United States. As someone who lived through the atrocious war in Japan, including having two nuclear bombs dropped on her country, it is not surprising that she did not embrace "Western" and American culture and customs. In addition, it is entirely possible that Umeki's response played into American nostalgia for the "good old days." Umeki in a kimono could alleviate anxieties about postwar American modernity marked by changing gender roles, as well as American guilt about bombing Japan during World War II. No matter one's interpretation of Umeki's remarks, it is clear that she decried the degradation and loss of Japanese culture after American occupation. Umeki's understanding of postwar cultural politics could create the space for disrupting hegemonic interpretations of the oriental wave.

Yet, despite Miyoshi Umeki's self-affiliation with traditional Japan, her career actually put her into the "new" cultural camp. In her interview she stated: "Even though I am young myself, I remember when sumo wrestling and Kabuki theater were the main entertainments of Japan. Now it is baseball, movies and TV and rock'n'roll music."[37] Umeki was an actress and singer in Japan before she came to the United States. She had appeared in several Japanese movies and sang with the Tsunoda Sextette. Her singing had proved very popular with American GIs in Japan. In the United States, she first appeared on Arthur Godfrey's *Talent Scouts* television program in 1955.[38] When auditioning for *Sayonara*, she convinced the director Joshua Logan that she was right for the part. As one journalist asserted, "Director Joshua Logan told me that she captivated him as soon as he saw her."[39] Thus Umeki gained her livelihood by participating in those new forms of culture, including television and the movies. Umeki's subsequent television career, playing the housekeeper Mrs. Livingston in *The Courtship of Eddie's Father* (1969–1972) gave more people an opportunity to know her work.

In addition, in a real-life departure from being a "traditional" Japanese woman, Umeki crossed racial boundaries and married an American television producer in Los Angeles. Like her fellow actresses France Nuyen and Nancy Kwan, in the early 1960s, Umeki married a man of European descent. Reproducing the spirit of her role in *Sayonara*, her co-star in the film, actress Miiko Taka, served as the main attendant at her wedding.

The Tempestuous Mixed-Race "Beauty"

If Miyoshi Umeki portrayed the kimono-clad, demure war bride, France Nuyen represented the mixed-race, innocent yet sexual, long-haired, cheongsam-wearing woman. As a *Life* cover girl and film star, Nuyen, and later Nancy Kwan, hyperfeminized and hypersexualized Asian women's bodies and the cheongsam so that they became the ultimate signifier of sexual femininity.[40] Though forgotten by many of today's younger generation, Nuyen's tempestuous persona, outspoken remarks against racism, and interracial affair with Marlon Brando bestowed upon her an immense star potential that was never fulfilled.

France Nuyen's mixed-race status, including potential African blood, influenced her appeal. She was born France Nguyen Vannga in Marseille, France, of a French mother, seamstress Julie Mazaut, and a Chinese sailor father. Nuyen discussed her racial background as follows: "I was born in Marseilles. My father is Chinese. He is a sailor. I do not know what he does on the sea. My mother is French, but I think she has Moorish blood."[41] Nuyen explained how she came to the United States: "After the last war my father became an American citizen and we came here to see him a year and a half ago. My mother wanted me to become an American citizen."[42] Though France grew up believing she was half Chinese American, after her father's death she learned that she was actually half ethnic Chinese from Cambodia.[43]

France Nuyen earned her first role in a movie, in *South Pacific* (1958), when her employer showed her photograph to director Joshua Logan, the same man responsible for casting Umeki in her first American movie, *Sayonara*. Nuyen had come to New York from France to meet her father, and she had hopes of becoming a model in New York. Too short to model by American standards and unable to speak much English, she worked in a French pastry shop. Nuyen earned the newsworthy sum of $1,500 a week for *South Pacific* and that work opened the door, despite her never having acted in a play, to her being cast for the title role in the Broadway play *The World of Suzie Wong* (1958).

France Nuyen, and later Nancy Kwan, sexualized the cheongsam. Though people remember Kwan's movie portrayal of Suzie Wong, before her Nuyen earned fame and plaudits playing the prostitute with a heart of gold on Broadway. In honor of that role, Nuyen graced October 6, 1958's *Life* cover. Photographed so as to emphasize sexual availability, Nuyen reclines on a bed, head tilted slightly backward and hair flowing down her back. Her arms clasp her crossed legs. That pose accentuates the slit in her cheongsam, which reveals her legs clad in fishnet tights. She does not wear shoes and the bed is rumpled. The magazine's headline reads "Broadway's Suzie Wong—France Nuyen," and the inside feature's headline declared: "Young Star Rises as Suzie Wong."[44]

France Nuyen and Nancy Kwan established particular meanings for the cheongsam. At various points during the twentieth century, the cheongsam has stood for gender relations, modernity, nationalism, and sexuality. Introduced to China by the invading Manchu dynasty, in the twentieth century the *quipao*, or cheongsam, became regular clothing for women in urban centers and signified modernity. A symbol of gender equality, its adoption by women allowed them claim equality with men. It became a sign of decadence after the Communist revolution of 1949, while simultaneously gaining in popularity in Hong Kong because of its similarity to Western dress and its affiliation with anticommunist sensibilities. In fact, in Hong Kong the cheongsam was promoted as national dress during 1950s and 1960s beauty pageants, and it came to be adopted by Chinese American community contests. Not surprising given the garment's Western and capitalist cachet, the 1960s Cultural Revolution in communist China banned the wearing of the cheongsam.[45] It is through the character of Suzie Wong as portrayed by Nuyen and Kwan that the cheongsam became the ultimate signifier of Asian women's sexuality.

The text of *Life* spoke glowingly of France Nuyen's stardom and audience-drawing power. *Life* magazine functioned not just as a reflection of American politics and culture but as a form that intervened in and created American culture. According to the magazine article, *The World of Suzie Wong* had one of the biggest advance ticket sales for any play in U.S. theater history. Although the best-selling novel advertised the work, the real draw, according to *Life*, was Nuyen, who attracted large numbers of theater-goers. Not only did Nuyen entice one of the largest audiences to a Broadway show, but the critics considered her to be a good actress:

With masklike beauty, youthful France Nuyen portrays Suzie Wong in one of her pensive moods. By her bearing, she gives Suzie—for all her child-like exuberance—a real sense of dignity.[46]

In *Life*, Nuyen is both exoticized and praised for her acting skills. On the one hand, she will "sweeten a cup of bitter Chinese tea," her character is "childish," and her beauty is "masklike." On the other hand, giving the role of Suzie dignity and charisma was an important skill that Nuyen displayed as an actress.

The World of Suzie Wong's opening Broadway notices similarly glowed. For example, Frank Aston's review declared her success: "A new Far-Eastern star rose to eminence at the Broadhurst last evening. She was France Nuyen and her luster gleamed."[47] Like *Life* magazine, Aston waxed enthusiastic about her potential: "Miss Nuyen, presented as a girl who 'never took a lesson in acting,' is an actress of insight, compassion and sheer beauty. One senses under the surface an extraordinary power. Her small gestures, her even tones, her radiance can fill a stage and command a house. France Nuyen is a full-fledged hit and faces a lifetime of brilliance."[48] Both articles emphasized Nuyen's beauty and charisma.

Yet even when praising France Nuyen, racialized discourses continually invoked politicized viewpoints about Asians. European American male theater critics from the *Daily Mirror* and the *New York Times* particularly responded to Nuyen's "charm" and "exotic" beauty.[49] John McClain discussed her charms in terms of international relations: "This Miss Nuyen is an atomic blockbuster, a creature of such simple and natural charm as to change national boundaries."[50] In the metaphors in use during the Cold War, it was a compliment to call Nuyen an atomic blockbuster. Nuyen was considered not only beautiful but also intelligent. Walter Kerr's *New York Herald Tribune* review enthused that she was "a captivating creature with what used to be called a bee-stung upper lip, alarming black eyes, and a slippery intelligence that darts about her expressive face with a wonderful, wonderfully attractive, arrogance."[51] Kerr's labeling of Nuyen's lips as "bee-stung" was repeated in newspapers around the country. The term *slippery intelligence* refers in all likelihood to World War II prejudice about Asians being a slippery, sneaky, and untrustworthy race, reflected in popular culture and in movies such as *Little Tokyo, USA* (1942), as well as tapping into older narratives of orientalism.[52]

France Nuyen's depiction of a seemingly pliable Suzie Wong contrasted with her outspoken racial critique. After achieving fame as Liat in the motion picture *South Pacific* (1958) and as Suzie Wong on Broadway, in interviews Nuyen repeatedly commented on intense racial prejudice. Nuyen believed that although "the French are 'not so racist as in this country' (a subject on which she can become quite violent), while she was growing up she encountered discrimination because of her mixed ancestry."[53] From childhood, Nuyen was aware that she wasn't white and that not being white in post–World War II France led to ostracism. "You have no idea what it meant to be a Chinese child in a town like Marseilles. The other children laughed at me; they refused to play with me. I would run crying to my mother saying: 'Why aren't I white?' "[54] Unfortunately, the racial-purity ideology and hatreds of World War II were still present. As a colonial and postcolonial subject, Nuyen represented the feared invasion of the colonized. In addition, since Marseilles was an international seaport, people of different races inhabited the city, and thus the hierarchy of skin color was invoked on a regular basis.

In a case of real life imitating art, Nuyen made the headlines not just for her acting but for her interracial relationship with Marlon Brando, the star of *Sayonara*. Brando had a history of relationships with "dark" women, having dated actress Rita Moreno prior to Nuyen. Nuyen became even more notorious when she hit a cameraperson who was trying to take her picture when she returned with Brando from a vacation in Haiti. One newspaper headline blared "Brando's Girl Friend Swats Photographer":

> Broadway actress France Nuyen hit news photographer Doug Kennedy with her purse yesterday while the cameraman was attempting to get a shot of her and Marlon Brando returning from Haiti.
>
> The star of the New York stage show, "*The World of Suzie Wong*," socked Kennedy on the shoulder with her pocketbook when he took her picture at Miami International Airport. Then she slapped him on the head, angrily announcing, "No interviews."[55]

Thus Nuyen's notoriety was part of a larger celebrity culture that used fame as an excuse to subvert mainstream norms of appropriate behavior.[56] The coverage of her affair with Brando is a sign of her fame. Press interest in their relationship was a part of the larger interest in the lives of movie actresses, especially their scandalous love lives. In the late 1950s, married actress Ingrid Bergman shocked Hollywood and America with her affair with director Roberto Rossellini. In 1958, actress Lana Turner's daughter Cheryl had allegedly stabbed Turner's husband Johnny Stompanato. Actress Elizabeth Taylor had married and divorced a number of times. Nuyen's use of violence to express her anger at having her privacy invaded is of course inappropriate. It is possible that the incident was staged, for the photographer's body language does not express fear or dismay; instead, his face bears a smirk. In addition, there was another photographer present who could conveniently take the picture of Nuyen slapping the photographer that she was supposedly avoiding.

After starring in *The World of Suzie Wong*, France Nuyen was offered the same role in the movie version of the play. Though she worked with the same director, Nuyen's departure from the set of the movie was shrouded in secrecy and scandal. She believed there was a conspiracy to get her off the set and Nancy Kwan hired. Logan and his staff reported that Nuyen had gained a tremendous amount of weight and was depressed after her breakup with Marlon Brando, and therefore she had been fired. At least one Brando biography claims that Nuyen had a child with Brando in Mexico, rumored to be the child later adopted by Brando, named Serge and nicknamed Miko.[57] Matters on the set of *Suzie Wong* became so acrimonious that Logan vowed Nuyen would not work again in Hollywood. Shortly after Nuyen left the set and returned to Los Angeles, she was seen eating dinner with Brando at a sukiyaki restaurant in Little Tokyo, temporarily reconciled. However, soon after, they broke up for good, and Brando reportedly dated a young Filipina actress, Barbara Luna.

By replacing France Nuyen as Suzie Wong, Nancy Kwan assured her own cinematic immortality. Through her film roles as Suzie Wong, then as Linda Low in *Flower Drum Song*, Nancy Kwan has become notorious for portraying the long-haired, cheongsam-wearing woman willing to use her sexuality to get ahead. Daughter of a Hong Kong Chinese father and white British mother, Kwan represented the ultimate temptress. Perhaps in one of the most symbolic moves that exemplifies how the oriental wave operated, Kwan replaced Pat Suzuki as Linda Low in the film *Flower Drum Song*. A Japanese American born in California, Suzuki portrayed the original Linda Low in the Broadway version. In fact, the Broadway show gained such favorable publicity that Miyoshi Umeki and Suzuki graced the cover of *Time* magazine for their work in *Flower Drum Song*.[58] American audiences knew Suzuki because she sang the character Linda Low's hit song, "I Enjoy Being a Girl," on tremendously popular television shows such as Ed Sullivan's and Frank Sinatra's. Although in the film version Umeki reprised her portrayal of Mei Li, Suzuki did not have enough commercial appeal, and therefore Kwan portrayed Linda Low.

Miyoshi Umeki and Pat Suzuki on the cover of
Time magazine.

Nancy Kwan's 1961 performance of "I Enjoy Being a Girl" in *Flower Drum Song* encapsulated the mix of femininity and cultural citizenship reworked in the production of Asian America.[59] Although ostensibly portraying an American-born woman of Chinese descent, Kwan's slight accent marked her as the other. As a Rodgers and Hammerstein musical that taught the illegal immigrant (Miyoshi Umeki) how to be an American, *Flower Drum Song* stood at the juncture of the Americanized Asian American practices detailed throughout *A Feeling of Belonging* and the oriental wave. Perhaps the most lasting contribution of the movie to mainstream American culture was the image of femininity portrayed by Kwan that became the iconic look for 1960s women. By virtue of her race and her sex, Kwan stood for the uber-girl: long-haired, short-skirted, coy, and flirtatious. Combining international events and such cinematic performances, the Asian and Asian American woman represented doubly exaggerated femininity.

Racialized Standards of Beauty

What is particularly poignant and striking about Asian women's mainstream American prominence is that it came at the price of bodily manipulation, more specifically, plastic surgery and starvation slimming diets. Feminists have long decried mainstream beauty standards as harming all women and being an effect of patriarchy. Women of color in particular have argued for the impossibility of racial standards of beauty that posit the white body as the norm and all others as deviant, hence unattractive. Though Asian women triumphed over white ones in the Miss Universe pageant, the Academy Awards, and the cover of *Life* magazine, in differing ways each woman had to contend with body alterations to meet contemporary standards of appearance. Through and through, their cultural iconography was predicated upon invoking European American standards of femininity. In addition, two of the most famous "beauties" of the era, Nuyen and Kwan, were women of mixed-race heritage.

In 1959, Miss Japan, Akiko Kojima, won the Miss Universe pageant. Kojima's victory crowned hopes for a peaceful, culturally plural world. Kojima was the first woman of Asian descent as well as the first non-European-descended candidate to win a major international pageant. The Miss Universe pageant founder and sponsor, Oscar Meinhardt, declared that Kojima's victory proved the nonnationalistic and nonpartisan nature of the pageant. In all likelihood, controversy over the judging prompted Meinhardt's declaration. That same year, the Latin American sponsors had accused the judges of bias against their contestants. Though Miss Colombia had won Miss Universe the previous year, disproportionate numbers of (U.S.) American, white Australian, and white Western European candidates placed as her runner-ups. Thus Kojima's victory, and Ito's third-place finish, offset the whiteness of the successful contestants. Such condemnations both highlight racialized standards of beauty among pageant judges and underscore racial bias and stratifications throughout society.

Though Akiko Kojima as Miss Universe might have shown that Asian women were gaining acceptance as beautiful, her victory was tainted with the charges that she artificially met Western standards of beauty in order to win the title. On August 14, 1959, the *Los Angeles Times* reported that Dr. Tshizo Matsui claimed he had given Kojima injections of plastic to increase her bust.[60] Those injections allegedly would have allowed her to display a body type (reported as 37–23–38) pleasing to American judges and thus win the competition. Kojima and her family denied the allegations. Pending further proof, the pageant officials stated that they believed Kojima and remarked that there were no rules against such bodily enhancements. The latter remark implies that even if the officials did not believe Kojima, her actions remained acceptable. The *Kashu Mainichi* reported that discussion over whether or not Kojima had undergone plastic surgery was the main topic of conversation in Los Angeles' Little Tokyo.[61] In the twentieth century, actresses, models, and women in other professions that require beauty conventions are especially prey to plastic surgery, and this was doubly so for those who had to meet white standards of beauty.

Like Akiko Kojima, France Nuyen confronted pressure to conform to white standards of beauty. Bodily modification to fit beauty standards included severe diet regimens that were de rigueur for actresses. In addition to the impact of racial discrimination on her early life, as an adult star Nuyen faced intense Hollywood and Broadway pressures to be thin, which led to diet pill abuse and starvation. Nuyen reported: "When I came back from Hawaii [from filming *South Pacific*] I weighed 125 pounds. I was fat and happy. Now I am 115 pounds, but I used to be 95. I'm always hungry. They only let me eat meat and I am full of vitamin shots. Everybody's watching my weight—Mrs. Logan, my dresser, the press agent. Lots of people take me under their protection."[62] Other Hollywood actresses faced similar pressures. To remain a Hollywood and Broadway star, feminine norms of beauty required that France Nuyen weigh far less than a healthy weight for a woman 5'4", and she was policed by those around her, including *The World of Suzie Wong's* director's wife, Nedda Harrigan Logan, the actress daughter of famous vaudevillian Ned Harrigan. Like singer and actress Judy Garland, Nuyen's weight gains were forbidden, and she was kept on medication to prevent them. Apparently the wardrobe staff and the director, Joshua Logan, were unhappy that "France had gone from 95 pounds to 125 during the filming of 'South Pacific' in Hawaii." No wonder Nuyen was always hungry; her director forced her onto a starvation diet: "Logan kept her on a 700-calories-a-day regimen with assorted pills to enhance life."[63] This particular diet, though dangerously low in calories compared to the more typical two thousand daily calories required to maintain weight, was by no means unusual in Hollywood. Nuyen's battles to achieve a low body weight received much mainstream press attention.

Racialized beauty standards affected France Nuyen to such a degree as a young girl that she confessed using makeup to efface the color of her skin: "Even when I began to grow up a little and became the Chinese girl in Marseilles, I still couldn't adjust. I made up heavily all the time, and I never took my make-up off. At the time I didn't know why I was doing it, but now I know. I was trying to hide the colour of my skin. I was afraid that if they saw I was yellow they would despise me or throw stones at me."[64] Perhaps Nuyen's acting ability came from having to "perform" differing racial identities in order to avoid harassment. It is interesting how Nuyen's postcolonial subjectivity was subsumed to her Chinese ethnic heritage. Had Nuyen become an iconic American movie star, her awareness of racial attitudes could have furthered race awareness and disrupted the hegemony of the oriental wave.

Unlike many European American feminists who analyze issues of beauty solely in terms of patriarchal oppression, many feminists of color have used the issue of beauty to denaturalize the assumed female body as white and to call for the inclusion of women of color into the body female and body politic. Whereas the (white) women's movement's foundational moment occurred when they boycotted and condemned the Miss America pageant, feminists of color decried the exclusion of racial minority women in the pageant. As Natasha Barnes writes while citing Nancy Caraway, "the black female struggle for 'cultural acceptance as attractive, "respectable" beings' has been misinterpreted by white feminists who see this emphasis on 'negative imagery' as trivial and politically misguided."[65] Umeki's, Nuyen's, and Kojima's interpellation as attractive and respectable professional women is part of that racialized struggle to gain personhood and all the privileges associated with cultural citizenship.

Incorporating the Oriental Wave into Performing American Cultural Citizenship

Asian American communities saw the rewards received by those women who embodied the oriental wave and thus increasingly constituted themselves so as to incorporate Asian culture. In other words, the oriental wave shifted Asian American cultural citizenship practices from being on the American side of the equation, as shown in chapters 3 and 4, to emphasizing Asian heritage. Diasporic identification had always, to varying degrees, been present in Asian American communities. There had been hints of it even at the height of Cold War all-Americanism—remember that the Nisei Week queen's court wore kimonos when presenting the mayor of Los Angeles an invitation to the 1952 Nisei Week festival. In this era, displaying Asian heritage through dress in public events became increasingly widespread.

The hallmarks of the oriental wave, such as films like *Sayonara,* war brides, and beauty queens such as Miss Japan, circulated within Asian American communities, and their cultural importance was noted by Asian American periodicals. For example, with her favorable publicity, and given the paucity of actresses of Asian descent, France Nuyen proved to be a star to New York's Chinatown. When she paid a visit to the racial minority enclave, Chinese Americans knew who she was and idolized her. As she commented in an interview at a restaurant, "'But one thing really impresses me [pause for bite, gracefully chewed]—that was in Chinatown when all people of my race came to see me.' Her press agent added as France reached for a 10th round of melba toast, 'The children followed her and wouldn't leave her alone.'"[66] Although Nuyen was not American-born, she and her Chinatown fans identified with each other. (The aside illustrates that the reporter noticed that the calorie-restricted diet imposed by her director left Nuyen very hungry.)

Likewise, a movie such as *Sayonara* was not just viewed as a product of Japan-based race relations; Japanese Americans in Los Angeles identified with the movie. A Los Angeles clerk plucked from obscurity to make her only movie, in 1965, Miiko Taka was Los Angeles' Nisei Week parade marshal. And numerous Japanese war brides who immigrated to the United States may have been pleased to see women like themselves portrayed on screen. *Sayonara* played at the Paramount Hollywood movie theater, centrally located at Hollywood and Highland Streets in Los Angeles. Attesting to its marketing toward Japanese Americans in Southern California, for at least four weeks one Los Angeles Japanese American newspaper, the *Rafu Shimpo,* carried several different versions of *Sayonara* advertisements, many of which depicted Marlon Brando clasping Miiko Taka.[67]

Many years before the film was released, Japanese American communities learned about one of *Sayonara*'s main themes, namely, the place of Japanese war brides in America society. Interracial marriages between Japanese war brides and European American military men evoked the issue of race mixing and the fear that Asian American war brides would not be able to assimilate. *Scene* magazine worked to succor those fears. For example, on May 1950, *Scene* profiled a war-bride marriage in an article entitled "Lobby for Love":

> Pretty Mitsue Shigeno, 24-year-old Tokyo-born girl, recently arrived in the U.S. and was married to an ex-GI horticulturist, Carroll Klotzbach, 49, who had battled a bill through Congress to permit his fiancée's entry into the U.S. Introduced by Sen. S. L. Holland (D-Fla.) the private bill was passed on Valentine's Day. During the marriage ceremony in Washington D.C., the bride wears a traditional Japanese kimono at the groom's wish. The couple met 26 months ago near Tokyo where Klotzbach formerly worked.[68]

For her wedding, Shigeno wore a kimono at the request of Klotzbach, which suggests that she probably usually wore Western dress. Note that fashion marked both modernity and national affiliation. Also note that the private bill (versus a public one that would allow all war brides to enter) that allowed Shigeno to enter the United States was passed on Valentine's Day. Readers of the magazine could observe the romantic appropriateness of the day the legislation was passed.

Adaptation of American cultural practices became a hallmark of Japanese war brides.[69] Two years after *Scene* magazine profiled Shigeno, on April 1952, it published an article entitled "War Bride Becomes an American Housewife." The article focused on Mrs. William Beauchamp and showed pictures of her in her 1950s American kitchen.[70] Beauchamp's ability to manage the commodities of American consumer life showed her cultural citizenship. With the goods, the marriage, the adoption of her husband's name, and the move to the United States, Mrs. William Beauchamp proved that a Japanese woman could become an all-American housewife.

Many Japanese Americans felt that Akiko Kojima's victory as Miss Universe was an important step in restoring civil rights. Historian Lon Kurashige reported that many Japanese Americans greeted "the victory as if it marked the end of an era of anti-Japanese discrimination."[71] Japanese American presses such as the Los Angeles *Kashu Mainichi* celebrated the victory as if one from their own community had won.[72] Through her multiweek stay with Kay Matsumoto in Long Beach, Kojima got to know the Japanese American community in the greater Los Angeles area. She attended events such as the Yamaguchi-ken picnic and a Nisei Week queen contest preliminary event at the Cocoanut Grove club. Although it is unclear whether or not she judged the Nisei Week queen contest, she affected the performance of beauty and Japanese American cultural citizenship merely by her presence. After her crowning, Kojima praised the Japanese American community for being very kind to her.

Even before the advent of the Miss Universe pageant, Miss Japan toured the United States as a goodwill political act. Given the race hatred expressed so recently in World War II, Miss Japan represented Japan in non-threatening ways that (male) governmental officials could not. Throughout the 1950s, Asian beauty queens demonstrated the intersection of politics and culture that led to Kojima's 1959 victory as Miss Universe. In 1950, Miss Japan and her second and third finalists embarked on a six-week goodwill tour of the United States, visiting the cities of Chicago, Minneapolis, Washington, D.C., Philadelphia, New York, Seattle, San Francisco, and Los Angeles.

Scene used foreign-born beauty queens to explore the parameters of clothing as a means to perform modernity and cultural citizenship. What *Scene* magazine found particularly noteworthy about the Miss Japan tour was that even when the women wanted to wear modern dresses, sponsors insisted on "traditional" kimonos. Similar to the women of Chi Alpha Delta and the Nisei Week queen contestants, conflict arose over how the women wanted to appear versus how they were supposed to appear. The *Scene* article reported on "the insistence (the girls didn't like it) that everywhere they went they were to appear only in kimonos. It paid off in newspaper pictures, incidentally, and rekindled the old American notion that Japan is the land of cherry blossoms and charming people. . . . On a few occasions, however, they managed to sneak out in newly purchased western dresses."[73] As opposed to the 1941 Nisei Week festival, where kimonos signified the enemy, in this instance kimonos invoked a pre–World War II, premodern, nonthreatening, and nonwarlike Japan. Thus modernity and international politics were linked through the commodification of women's fashion.

Further underscoring the relationship between queens and international and domestic race relations, while in the United States, Miss Japan and her two attendants visited numerous symbolic figureheads, including ethnic American ones. On the goodwill tour arranged by Japanese American community groups, in Minneapolis they visited the first Jewish American Miss America, Bess Myerson, who was raising money for Israel, and Mel Bisson, president of the Minnesota American Indians. In Chicago they met with Korean War veterans as well as Marjorie Adams, Miss

Chicago. Local Japanese American groups feted the queens at Japanese and Chinese restaurants. The queen and her attendants functioned as official representatives of Japan without as much of the hostility that political or economic representatives might generate.

Chinese American communities also utilized Asian Miss Universe contestants as touchstones of modernity and cultural citizenship. In 1952, the first year the Miss Universe pageant was held, Judy Dan, Miss Hong Kong, finished fourth. Offered a Hollywood contract, Dan remained in Los Angeles and was "quickly adopted by the Chinese-American community. To the older generation, she is a symbol of China. Among their sons and daughters, she is appreciated for herself."[74] As that remark illustrates so well, the appeal of beauty queens is the ability to mean different things to different people. Miss Dan's influence was not confined to Los Angeles, for she participated in Chinese American community events up and down the Pacific Coast: "She has officiated at all kinds of Chinese-American affairs —from the opening of a recreation center in Portland, Ore., to the judging of a beauty contest in San Francisco." Public culture linked by mass media reportage enabled community to be redefined as groups connected through the figure of a beauty queen, instead of geographical proximity. As a representative to and a judge of a Chinese American beauty pageant, Dan not only represented successful femininity, but the community bestowed upon her the authority to select the "best" Asian American one and thus construct cultural citizenship.

Asian American Culture Displays the Oriental Publicly

Not only did Asian American women get to read about and meet women who represented the new foreign-born Asian beauty, but those women's representations of Asian culture permeated Asian American women's lives. Although there had always been a strand of the "oriental" in previous hybrid cultural displays (think Nisei Week kimonos and Maria Clara dresses), the oriental wave further validated the display of these costumes and cultures.

France Nuyen's and Nancy Kwan's popularization of the cheongsam changed how Chinese American queen contestants portrayed their cultural heritage. Although not a requirement in the 1950 Miss Chinatown San Francisco pageant (detailed in the previous chapter), in subsequent pageants in the late 1950s, the contestants had to wear cheongsams. Given that China had just turned communist, the Chinese Americans in 1950 had the most need to prove American allegiance. Wearing cheongsams in the later Cold War period signaled the community's desire to show both American and acceptable Chinese identities. The body-revealing cheongsam was identified with Madame Chiang Kai-shek and capitalist Taiwan, in contrast to the body-hiding Mao suit of communist China.

The late 1950s marked the cheongsam's political ascendancy. Linda Yuen rode on a float for Dwight Eisenhower's second (1957) presidential inaugural parade. Dressed in a cheongsam, with her hair in contemporary Western style, and sporting chic makeup, Yuen represented Washington, D.C.'s Chinatown and was elected to represent all Chinatowns to the Eisenhower administration. According to Yuen, she was the first Chinese American queen at a presidential inaugural parade and, as far as she could tell, the only such racial minority queen present.[75] This Miss Chinatown represented Taiwan, and given the fall of China to communism in 1949 and China's subsequent banning of the cheongsam, wearing a cheongsam highlighted Taiwan's noncommunist status as well as worthiness to be recognized as the "official" China by the Eisenhower administration.

Cheongsams rather than Western dress also marked the newly formed national Miss Chinatown USA pageant. Yet, unlike the Fourth of July all-American 1950 Chinese American Citizens League (CACA) pageant, this pageant formed in 1958 was the highlight of the Chinese New Year Festival, sponsored by the Chinatown Chamber of Commerce. In fact, despite the adoption of the cheongsam and being held on Chinese New Year, in the early years of the pageant community outsiders criticized it for being too American. Historian Judy Wu reports that in 1965 journalist Donald Canter remarked, "I wasn't quite sure whether I was viewing the Rose Parade in Pasadena or a New Year's parade of the largest Chinatown outside the Orient."[76] Canter encouraged the community to stage instead an "orientalist" spectacle, complete with sedan chairs, in order to attract tourists to San Francisco's Chinatown.

How the oriental wave shifted the performance of Asian American cultural citizenship at the local level can be seen through Chi Alpha Delta's cultural practices. Throughout the 1950s, the members of the Chi Alpha Delta sorority continually debated how to present themselves to the UCLA community. Chi Alpha Delta continually had to test the waters of acceptability and shift how they performed femininity and modernity. They used cultural markers that varied among Japanese, American, and those that, to use historian Vicki Ruiz's term, coalesced the two.[77] For a 1950 campus fundraiser, the Chis decreed that they would all wear kimonos and sell gardenias.[78] Two years later, they decided they would sell flowers again, presumably because the gardenias had sold well, but not to wear kimonos.

In 1953, the same year that Kinuko Ito wore her much-praised dress with rosebud spray, the members of Chi Alpha Delta performed the Japanese song "Gomen-nasai" for UCLA's annual Spring Sing. "Gomen-nasai" had been sung by a Japanese artist, Chiemi Eri, who was touring the United States and who had recorded it in Los Angeles for Capitol Records. Profiled in the September 1953 issue of *Scene*, Eri had performed in Western dress, and the Chi Alpha Deltas also decided to wear Western fashion —casual dress and heels—for their rendition of the song.[79] For UCLA's Mardi Gras that same year the sorors decided, as they had the previous year, to skip wearing kimonos, instead donning European peasant skirts, blouses, and organdy aprons.

By 1958, the success of the oriental wave prompted the women of Chi Alpha Delta to use the popularity of Japan-themed fashions and performances to make cultural gains at UCLA. On April 22, 1958, Chi Alpha Delta won fourth place at the University of California's Spring Sing. Involving over forty organizations, the annual singing competition was one of the largest annual campus-wide events. Chi Alpha Delta prevailed over many other groups by singing the song "Sakura" in Japanese. Based on an old Japanese folk song, "Sakura" had been popularized for the general American public by Machiko Kyo's motion picture performance in *Teahouse of the August Moon*. Thus the Chis were playing on the appeal of "oriental" exoticism.

To set the mood for the song, the kimono-clad members of Chi Alpha Delta pulled their hair back, mimicking a traditional Japanese hairstyle that had been presented in the movie. In previous competitions, such as the one in which they had performed "Gomen-nasai," when they had worn casual skirts, shoes, hairstyles, they had not placed. *Teahouse* and other movies such as *Sayonara* taught the American-born generation of young women how to act "Japanese" in ways intelligible to European American audiences. Hence the members of Chi Alpha Delta capitalized on the oriental wave and aced their competition. The spate of popular movies about Japan allowed the predominantly European American audience and judges to contextualize their performance. Won a month before Spring Sing, Miyoshi Umeki's *Sayonara* Academy Award signaled that American audiences were ready to reward similar performances. Hence deploying Japanese cultural markers paid off for the women of Chi Alpha Delta. Although Chi Alpha Delta's actions can be read as reproducing hegemonic power relations, I would argue that they could also be read as realizing an opportunity to reracialize and reconfigure power relations. The women of Chi Alpha Delta seized on current favorable attitudes toward Asia to increase their status on campus.

These cultural activities shed light on why, in an age of racial integration, Chi Alpha Delta decided to forgo university funding and privileges in order to remain an "oriental" group. The activities affirmed the desirability of remaining Asian American rather than opting to become a racially integrated group. Sorority and fraternity racial segregation had been taken up as a civil rights issue in the mainstream American media. *Look,* the same magazine that had produced the 1930s Country Club College article that valorized the UCLA European American sorority woman, in the 1950s denounced racial membership restrictions in fraternity and sorority membership. In addition, noted journalist, author, and indefatigable social commentator Carey McWilliams also examined the work being done to desegregate the Greek system. In the progressive magazine *The Nation,* McWilliams wrote: "The agitation against racial discrimination in college fraternities and sororities acquires significance as a portent of changing attitudes and ideologies when one considers the extent and influence of the fraternity and sorority system."[80] McWilliams's article placed the nationwide battles to integrate fraternities and sororities within the context of civil rights movements. According to McWilliams, such battles were welcome signs that America's racial climate was changing for the better. Such beliefs show the high hopes many had for integration in general.

As part of American national debates around civil rights, institutions of higher learning debated the efficacy of racial and religious integration of Greek organizations through acts such as UCLA's nondiscriminatory clause. For European American Christian sororities and fraternities, it meant the supposed end of excluding racial minorities and Jewish Americans. However, as a racial minority group, integration posed a very different issue for the women of Chi Alpha Delta: it called into question their ability to remain a single-race organization in a campus culture dominated by European Americans.

The women of Chi Alpha Delta debated whether to remain an Asian American organization through the issue of whether to become a national organization. If a sorority had at least six chapters on other campuses, it would be considered a national organization and would be eligible for the membership in UCLA's Panhellenic Council, which had been denied to Chi Alpha Delta for decades.[81] Becoming a national sorority would allow more chapters to be formed at universities across the country. Nationalization would also give the sorority the powerful backing and financing of a national organization. Since they needed only six chapters to qualify as a national sorority, Chi Alpha Delta members investigated joining sororities that were newly nationalizing. One of the possibilities they considered was approaching the Chinese American sorority Sigma Omicron Pi at the University of California–Berkeley.[82]

However, after exploring the possibility of joining predominantly European American fledgling sororities, the Chis decided not to nationalize and to remain a local chapter, so they could preserve their race-specific membership. As one of their members stated during the debates:

> The basic conflict to which she refers is that the National Sorority revolves around the principle of complete integration. We, as an Oriental group, would not be following this principle. Since this idea is so basic to their structure, we would probably have to completely change our structure if we want them to accept us.[83]

In 1958, Chi Alpha Delta decided not to merge with members of other racial groups and hence remained a local sorority. They believed that the benefits of banding together as a race-specific group outweighed the benefits of integration. Active agents in racial formation, the members of Chi Alpha Delta defined their own Japanese American identity and decided to remain primarily Japanese and Asian.[84]

The Reconfiguration of the Oriental Wave

The possibilities engineered by this oriental wave, such as gaining careers in Hollywood and culturally normalizing increased immigration quotas for war brides, were foreclosed by the escalation of the Vietnam War. Rather than a place filled with people who should be subjected to benevolent assimilation, Asia became a site of military aggression and control.

At the peak of the oriental wave in 1960, while cast in the all-Asian American Rodgers and Hammerstein musical *Flower Drum Song*, Anna May Wong died of a heart attack, probably due to cirrhosis of the liver, in Santa Monica, California. The oriental wave as represented by Ito, Kojima,

Nuyen, and Umeki dissipated as the sixties advanced. In the late 1960s, acting roles did not come in as quickly for any of the actresses of Asian descent, nor was East Asia the home of victorious beauty contestants. This occurred because of the escalation of the war in Vietnam as well as the difficulty for "older" women to win Hollywood acting roles, especially since the Suzie Wong type was an ingenue. Superceded by Nancy Kwan, post–*Suzie Wong* Nuyen obtained few acting roles. In the early 1960s she starred in Pearl S. Buck's *Satan Never Sleeps* and *A Girl Named Tamiko,* which also featured Miyoshi Umeki, and then co-starred with Charlton Heston in the 1964 movie *Diamond Head,* in which Philip Ahn played a cameo role as a lawyer. Afterward, Nuyen earned a master's degree in social work and psychology, working in prisons and with disadvantaged children.[85] After her work in movies such as *Sayonara* and *Flower Drum Song,* Umeki extended her repertoire to television to star in productions such as *Teahouse of the August Moon.* She gained further national recognition through her work in the television show *The Courtship of Eddie's Father* (1969–1972), playing the housekeeper, Mrs. Livingood.[86] Umeki's significance as an actress was sufficient for Mike Wallace to invite her as a main guest on his weekly interview television program.[87] After the mid-1960s, Umeki disappeared from television and films, and hence from public view. Since Akiko Kojima's 1959 victory, no Japanese woman has won the title of Miss Universe.

The Vietnam War changed how the American nation-state was racialized and gendered, which explains why Miyoshi Umeki, France Nuyen, and Japanese Miss Universe contestants disappeared from American public consciousness. The American failure to gain military mastery in Vietnam called into question the very masculine construction of the nation. As the oriental wave was predicated on seemingly reciprocal relations between Asia and the United States that nonetheless buttressed American power, the fact that Vietnam did not submit to American military might put the equation in jeopardy.[88] While America was victorious, there was room to consort with the "enemy" women as a means to win over the country. However, as the feminized Asia proved militarily unconquerable during the Vietnam War, the need to master became far more fraught with anxiety.[89] No longer patriotic women serving their country, Asian women on film mutated into foreign prostitutes who corrupted American servicemen.[90] No longer did the trope of the oriental wave act as a means to alleviate anxieties about racial integration in the United States and imperialism in Asia, and as a way to control racial difference through domesticity.

Though the poor good girl–turned–prostitute Suzie Wong has been an object of critical derision, she at least has a heart, whereas the corrupting seductresses have none. An Asian American Miss America would have been out of the question, for as in World War II, the enemy was racially defined as other and Asian, and Miss America toured the troops in Vietnam.

Yet this era also signaled the official rise of yellow power and the civil rights movement.[91] As a group, Asian Americans fought for the dismantling of racial segregation and of racialized immigration laws and for equal access to education and housing. Not only did they fight for equal rights with whites, but they also sought to affirm ethnic pride and Asian particularity through yellow power. Although the women in this book had been fighting for all these rights in intended and unintended ways, as had previous groups of Asian Americans, the civil rights era marks how mainstream society to some degree actually recognized Asian Americans as a group and granted these demands and rights.

Conclusion

This chapter explored the significance of foreign-born Asian "beauty" in the political context of liberal-democratic American race relations and Cold War American empire-without-colonies in Asia. For example, Miss Japan not only emblematized modernity and beauty but also sparked Japanese American hopes for favorable international relations in the aftermath of World War II. Wars in Asia and race relations in the United States changed racialized femininity norms that resulted in the increased prominence of Asian women in popular culture and mass media. The U.S. military occupation of Japan and the Korean War created a gendered imperial relationship between the United States and Asia and between people from those nations. A new construction of Asian womanhood emerged, captured by the femininity Umeki, Nuyen, and Kojima symbolized. The hallmarks of this new femininity included foreign birth and interracial sexual relationships framed by Asian economic dislocation and Western military and economic dominance. Asian American communities interacted with the oriental wave that changed how Asian Americans such as the women of Chi Alpha Delta performed cultural citizenship and modernity. Conjoined with the growth of ethnic and racial pride movements, the oriental wave reinforced diasporic cultural citizenship. Thus it became more politically acceptable for Asian Americans to display their Asian heritage.

However, in the mid-1960s, with the antipathy surrounding the war in Vietnam, the opportunities for women of Asian descent on the big screen decreased, and the scope of those roles narrowed. Following global politics, the Asian winners of the Miss Universe title shifted from Japanese women to Thai, Filipina, and South Asian women.[92] Finally, the aesthetics of the oriental wave were appropriated and reproduced by women of European descent.

Depending on one's vantage point, there are multiple ways of evaluating this era. If one were to look at World War II to 1959, one might say that the oriental wave was good for women of Asian descent because it brought them into the American mainstream, an Academy Award was won, and it corrected images such as that of the slab-faced Katsumi the novel *Sayonara*. Through sexuality and femininity, women of Asian descent were provisionally incorporated into the American polity. From 1959 forward, one might argue that iconic Asian American women set the stage for stereotypes that keep Asian American women in subordinate positions. To some degree, both positions simultaneously hold. Yet it would be short sighted to ignore the fact that, no matter what the image, Asian American women, from members of Chi Alpha Delta to war brides entering the United States, deployed the "oriental wave" to advance their own agendas and their own cultural citizenship. With the passing of the 1965 Immigration Act, once again the numbers of Asian-born surpassed the numbers of Asians American-born. Throughout the civil rights era and up to the present, mainstream society has continually denied acts of cultural citizenship by people of Asian descent in the United States. Thus, as race and citizenship continue to be aligned, the need to perform cultural citizenship remains differently compelling today.

Conclusion

Shortly after the demise of *Scene* magazine, in 1955 the *Saturday Evening Post* published an article on "California's Amazing Japanese" that echoed *Scene*'s main theme: negating the racial hatreds that brought about internment by demonstrating liberal-democratic ideal consumer citizenship. The *Saturday Evening Post* profiled model Japanese American citizens and used that as evidence to condemn internment. Mainstream society thus mirrored Asian American aspirations for cultural citizenship.

Changing American immigration laws had profound implications for Asian American cultural citizenship. The dominance of the American-born generations that had begun in the 1930s, which had started to change with the immigration of war brides, made a decisive shift. The Immigration Act of 1965 opened up migration from Asia that set the stage for the numbers of the immigrant-born to surpass the American-born generations. This act was a result of Cold War politics in which the Soviet Union and other countries condemned the United States' racialized immigration policies based on national origin that contradicted liberal democracy. What the 1965 law did was to introduce a new immigration preference system based on education, skills, and family reunification. In one of those glorious moments of unintended consequences, the proponents of the act predicted that immigration would mirror the current populations residing in the United States. They were wrong. People from Asia took overwhelming advantage of the 1965 act to immigrate to the United States. As a result, Asian American populations, which had shifted to American-born beginning in 1930, reconfigured to being majority foreign-born. Thus, with direct consequences for American cultural citizenship, people of Asian descent became reracialized as foreigners.

The model minority myth is an especially pernicious example of how a racial minority group cannot control the reception of the performance of cultural citizenship. Dominant society constructed the Cold War model minority myth to prove that America was not a racist country because they could show the success of a racial minority group, namely, Asian Americans. The aforementioned *Saturday Evening Post* article could be interpreted as promulgating the myth because it featured the success of the Japanese Americans despite their harrowing experience of internment. The danger of the model minority myth is that it acts as a reproach to other racial minority groups, especially to African Americans, for, as the argument goes, how can America be racist if Asian Americans are doing so well? The model minority myth is a distortion, especially given that the 1965 Immigration Act preference categories allow mainly professionals and scientists to migrate. It discounts the historical and present-day working-class migration from Asia. It also marginalizes very real issues of poverty that certain groups, especially Southeast Asian refugees, face. Thus not only does it serve to reproach other racial minority groups, but the discourse creates a situation where it is easy to underestimate government resources for Asian Americans in need.

The flip side of the model minority myth was how the war in Vietnam shifted the discourse to reracialize Asian Americans as menacing foreigners. The war also prompted gender roles to follow two tracks, namely, the specter of androgynous Vietnamese peasant women sniping at U.S. troops, on the one hand, and the Southeast Asian prostitute, on the other. During the war modernity was an issue, especially when phrases such as "Bomb Vietnam back to the Stone Age" became prevalent. Thus war in Vietnam raised the issue of how a nonmodern third world nation could defeat a first world democratic superpower such as the United States. The war also changed the nature of Asian American communities in the United States, for it paved the way for significant refugee migration from Southeast Asia.

The prevalence of the construct of race in American liberalism prompted the formation of the category "Asian American." As social scientists and government agencies increasingly used that language of race to analyze society and distribute resources, it became normalized and naturalized. Both protests against the war in Vietnam and the ongoing civil rights movement inspired Asian Americans to join together. Asian Americans have had a long-standing history of organizing for political and social change. But it is in this era that they organized politically across Asian-ethnic lines and thus both named themselves Asian American and were recognized as such. In a world determined to see race in polarized terms, activists and artists sought to show how Asian Americans were neither black nor white. Thus the movement developed the language and policies to articulate being Asian American.

Notes

NOTES TO THE PREFACE

1. Alice Walker, "Saving the Life That Is Your Own: The Importance of Models in the Artist's Life," in *In Search of Our Mother's Gardens* (New York: Harcourt, Brace, Jovanovich, 1983), p. 13.

NOTES TO THE INTRODUCTION

1. Works that interrogate this intersection of race and gender include: King-Kok Cheung, *Articulate Silences: Hisaye Yamamoto, Maxine Hong Kingston, Joy Kogawa* (Ithaca: Cornell University Press, 1993); Patricia Hill Collins, *Black Feminist Thought: Knowledge, Consciousness, and the Politics of Empowerment* (New York: Routledge, 1991); Angela Davis, *Blues Legacies and Black Feminism: Gertrude "Ma" Rainey, Bessie Smith, and Billie Holiday* (New York: Pantheon Books, 1998); Evelyn Nakano Glenn, *Issei, Nisei, Warbride: Three Generations of Japanese American Women in Domestic Service* (Philadelphia: Temple University Press, 1986); Valerie Matsumoto, "Desperately Seeking 'Deirdre': Gender Roles, Multicultural Relations, and Nisei Women Writers of the 1930s," *Frontiers: A Journal of Women's Studies* 12 (1991), pp. 19–32; Chandra Talpade Mohanty, Ann Russo, and Lourdes Torres, eds., *Third World Women and the Politics of Feminism* (Bloomington: Indiana University Press, 1991); Gail Nomura, "Tsugiki, a Grafting: A History of a Japanese Pioneer Woman in Washington State," *Women's Studies* 14.1 (1987), pp. 183–197; Peggy Pascoe, *Relations of Rescue: The Search for Female Moral Authority in the American West, 1874–1939* (New York: Oxford University Press, 1990); Barbara Posadas, "Crossed Boundaries in Interracial Chicago: Pilipino Families since 1925," in Ellen C. DuBois and Vicki Ruiz, eds., *Unequal Sisters: A Multicultural Reader in U.S. Women's History*, 2d ed. (New York: Routledge, 1994), pp. 316–329; Andrew Parker, Mary Russo, Doris Sommer, and Patricia Yeager, eds., *Nationalisms and Sexualities* (New York: Routledge, 1992); Vicki Ruiz, *From Out of the Shadows: Mexican Women in Twentieth-Century America* (New York: Oxford University Press, 1999); Virginia Sanchez Korrol, *From Colonia to Community: The History of Puerto Ricans in New York City* (Berkeley and Los Angeles: University of

California Press, 1994); Rachel Lee, *The Americas of Asian American Literature: Gendered Fictions of Nation and Transfiction* (Princeton: Princeton University Press, 1999); Judy Wu, "'Loveliest Daughter of Our Ancient Cathay!' Representations of Ethnic and Gender Identity in the Miss Chinatown U.S.A. Beauty Pageant," *Journal of Social History* 31.1 (Fall 1997), pp. 5–32; Judy Yung, *Unbound Feet: A Social History of Chinese Women in San Francisco* (Berkeley and Los Angeles: University of California Press, 1995); Catherine Ceniza Choy, *Empires of Care: Nursing and Migration in Filipino American History* (Durham: Duke University Press, 2003).

2. As Dipesh Chakrabarty, Thomas Richards, and others have argued, the legitimate historical archive has been founded to aid coercive state practices such as imperialism and legalistic control. Although all archival materials are potentially problematic, prioritizing community ones mitigates one level of control and coercion. Dipesh Chakrabarty, *Provincializing Europe: Postcolonial Thought and Historical Difference* (Princeton: Princeton University Press, 2000); Thomas Richards, *The Imperial Archive: Knowledge and Fantasy of Empire* (New York and London: Verso, 1993).

3. Angela McRobbie, *Feminism and Youth Culture: From 'Jackie' to 'Just Seventeen'* (London: Macmillan, 1991); Dick Hebdige, *Subculture: The Meaning of Style* (London: Methuen, 1979); Stuart Hall, "Notes on Deconstructing the 'Popular,'" in Samuel Raphael and Paul Kegan, eds., *People's History and Socialist Theory* (London: Routledge, 1981).

4. Sarah Banet-Weiser, *The Most Beautiful Girl in the World: Beauty Pageants and National Identity* (Berkeley and Los Angeles: University of California Press, 1999); Margaret Beetham, *A Magazine of Her Own? Domesticity and Desire in the Woman's Magazine, 1800–1914* (New York: Routledge, 1996); Jennifer Scanlon, *Inarticulate Longings: The Ladies' Home Journal, Gender, and the Promises of Consumer Culture* (New York: Routledge, 1995); Kathy Peiss, *Hope in a Jar: The Making of America's Beauty Culture* (New York: Metropolitan, 1998); Janice Radway, *Reading the Romance: Women, Patriarchy, and Popular Literature* (Chapel Hill: University of North Carolina Press, 1984); Colleen Ballerino Cohen, Richard Wilk, and Beverly Stoeltje, eds., *Beauty Queens: On the Global Stage* (New York: Routledge, 1996); Beth Bailey, *From Front Porch to Back Seat: Courtship in Twentieth-Century America* (Baltimore: Johns Hopkins University Press, 1988); Noliwe Rooks, *Ladies' Pages: African American Women's Magazines and the Cultures That Made Them* (New Brunswick: Rutgers University Press, 2004); Joan Jacobs Brumberg, *The Body Project: An Intimate History of American Girls* (New York: Vintage, 1998).

5. Nancy Armstrong, *Desire and Domestic Fiction: A Political History of the Novel* (New York: Oxford University Press, 1987), pp. 26–27.

6. Lauren Berlant, *The Queen of America Goes to Washington City: Essays on Sex and Citizenship* (Durham: Duke University Press, 1997); Rogers Brubaker, *Immigration and the Politics of Citizenship in Liberal Democratic Societies* (Lanham,

Md.: University Press of America, 1989); William Novak, "The Legal Transformation of Citizenship in Nineteenth-Century America," in Meg Jacobs, William Novak, and Julian Zelizer, eds., *The Democratic Experiment: New Directions in American Political History* (Princeton: Princeton University Press, 2003); Mae Ngai, *Impossible Subjects: Illegal Aliens and the Making of Modern America* (Princeton: Princeton University Press, 2004).

7. Sucheng Chan, *Asian Americans: An Interpretive History* (Boston: Twayne, 1991); Gary Okihiro, *Cane Fires: The Anti-Japanese Movement in Hawaii, 1865–1945,* Asian American History and Culture Series (Philadelphia: Temple University Press, 1992); Roger Daniels, *Asian America* (Seattle: University of Washington Press, 1988); Ronald Takaki, *Strangers from a Different Shore* (New York: Penguin, 1989); David Palumbo-Liu, *Asian/American: Historical Crossings of a Racial Frontier* (Palo Alto: Stanford University Press, 1999); Anthony W. Lee, *Picturing Chinatown: Art and Orientalism in San Francisco* (Berkeley and Los Angeles: University of California Press, 2001).

8. Lisa Lowe, *Immigrant Acts: On Asian American Cultural Practices* (Durham: Duke University Press, 1996).

9. Ibid., pp. 3–14; Henry Yu, *Thinking Orientals: Migration, Contact, and Exoticism in Modern America* (New York: Oxford University Press, 2001); Robert Lee, *Orientals* (Philadelphia: Temple University Press, 1998); Jack Tchen, *New York before Chinatown: Orientalism and the Shaping of American Culture, 1776–1882* (Baltimore: Johns Hopkins University Press, 1999); Alexander Saxton, *The Indispensable Enemy: Labor and the Anti-Chinese Movement in California* (Berkeley and Los Angeles: University of California Press, 1971); Carl Gutierrez-Jones, *Rethinking the Borderlands: Between Chicano Culture and Legal Discourse* (Berkeley and Los Angeles: University of California Press, 1995); David G. Gutierrez, *Walls and Mirrors: Mexican Americans, Mexican Immigrants, and the Politics of Ethnicity* (Berkeley and Los Angeles: University of California Press, 1995); Karen Shimakawa, *National Abjection: The Asian American Body Onstage* (Durham: Duke University Press), p. 5.

10. Erika Lee, "Exclusion Acts: Chinese Women during the Chinese Exclusion Era, 1882–1943," in Shirley Hune and Gail Nomura, eds., *Asian Pacific American Women: A Historical Anthology* (New York: New York University Press, 2003) and *At America's Gates: Chinese Immigration during the Exclusion Era, 1882–1943* (Chapel Hill: University of North Carolina Press, 2003); George A. Peffer, *If They Don't Bring Their Women Here: Chinese Female Immigration before Exclusion* (Urbana and Chicago: University of Illinois Press, 1999); Sucheng Chan, "The Exclusion of Chinese Women, 1870–1943," in Sucheng Chan, ed., *Entry Denied: Exclusion and the Chinese Community in America* (Philadelphia: Temple University Press, 1991); Lucie Cheng Hirata, "Free, Indentured, Enslaved: Chinese Prostitutes in Nineteenth-Century America," *Signs: Journal of Women in Culture and Society* 5.1 (Autumn 1979), pp. 3–29.

11. Lee, "Exclusion Acts," p. 82; Him Mark Lai, Genny Lim, and Judy Yung, *Island: Poetry and History of Chinese Immigration on Angel Island, 1910–1940*, reprint (Seattle: University of Washington Press, 1999).

12. David Yoo, *Growing Up Nisei: Race, Generation, and Culture among Japanese Americans of California, 1924–1949* (Urbana: University of Illinois Press, 2000); Valerie Matsumoto, "Japanese American Women during World War II," in DuBois and Ruiz, eds., *Unequal Sisters,* pp. 436–449, originally published in *Frontiers* 8.1 (1984) pp. 6–14; K. Scott Wong and Sucheng Chan, eds., *Claiming America: Constructing Chinese American Identities during the Exclusion Era* (Philadelphia: Temple University Press, 1998); Madeline Y. Hsu, *Dreaming of Gold, Dreaming of Home: Transnationalism and Migration between the United States and South China, 1882–1943* (Palo Alto: Stanford University Press, 2002).

13. Carole Pateman, *The Sexual Contract* (Stanford: Stanford University Press, 1988); Joan Scott, *Gender and the Politics of History* (New York: Columbia University Press, 1988); Kathleen Wilson, *The Island Race: Englishness, Empire, and Gender in the Eighteenth Century* (New York: Routledge, 2002); Linda Kerber, *No Constitutional Right to Be Ladies: Women and the Obligations of Citizenship* (New York: Hill and Wang 1999); Mary Beth Norton, *Founding Mothers and Fathers: Gendered Power and the Forming of American Society* (New York: Vintage, 1997); Karin Hausen, "Mother's Day in the Weimar Republic," in Renate Bridenthal, Atina Grossman, and Marion Kaplan, eds., *When Biology Became Destiny: Women in the Weimar and Nazi Germany* (New York: Monthly Review Press, 1984), pp. 131–151; Geoff Eley and Ronald Grigor, eds., *Becoming National: A Reader* (New York: Oxford University Press, 1996).

14. Paul Gilroy, *Ain't No Black in the Union Jack: The Cultural Politics of Race and Nation* (London: Hutchinson, 1987); Jacqueline Nassy Brown, "Black Liverpool, Black America, and the Gendering of Diasporic Space," *Cultural Anthropology* 13.3 (1998), pp. 291–325.

15. Robyn Wiegman, *American Anatomies: Theorizing Race and Gender* (Durham: Duke University Press, 1995), p. 6.

16. Rajeswari Sunder Rajan ed., *Signposts: Gender Issues in Post-Independence India* (New Brunswick: Rutgers University Press, 2001), p. 7.

17. Renato Rosaldo, "Cultural Citizenship, Inequality, and Multiculturalism," in William V. Flores and Rina Benmayor, eds., *Latino Cultural Citizenship: Claiming Identity, Space, and Rights* (Boston: Beacon Press, 1997); Aiwha Ong, "Cultural Citizenship as Subject Making: Immigrants Negotiate Racial and Cultural Boundaries in the United States," in Rodolfo Torres, Louis Miron, and Jonathan Inda, eds., *Race, Identity, and Citizenship: A Reader* (New York: Blackwell, 1999); May Joseph, *Nomadic Identities: The Performance of Citizenship* (Minneapolis: University of Minnesota Press, 1999); Lok Siu, "Diasporic Cultural Citizenship: Chineseness and Belonging in Panama and Central America," *Social Text* 69.19 (Winter 2001), pp. 7–28.

18. Harry Stecopoulos and Michael Ubel, eds., *Race and the Subject of Masculinities* (Durham: Duke University Press, 1997), pp. 10; Juan Flores, *From Bomba to Hip Hop, 2000* (New York: Columbia University Press, 2000).

19. Fatimah Tobing Rony, *The Third Eye: Race, Cinema, and Ethnographic Spectacle* (Durham: Duke University Press, 1996).

20. "How to Tell Your Friends from the Japs," *Time*, December 22, 1941, p. 33.

21. Caren Kaplan, Norma Alarcon, and Minoo Moallem, eds., *Between Woman and Nation: Nationalisms, Transnational Feminisms, and the State* (Durham: Duke University Press, 1999), pp. 1–16.

22. Lowe, *Immigrant Acts*, p. 97; Kaplan, Alarcon, and Moallem, eds., *Between Woman and Nation*; Brown, "Black Liverpool, Black America, and the Gendering of Diasporic Space," pp. 291–325.

NOTES TO CHAPTER 1

1. "Pledge" is the term for women and men who have agreed to join a particular sorority or fraternity but have not fulfilled the training for membership.

2. Roger Daniels, *Prisoners without a Trial: Japanese Americans in World War II* (New York: Hill and Wang, 1993).

3. Valerie Matsumoto, "Japanese American Girls' Clubs in Los Angeles during the 1920s and 1930s," in Shirley Hune and Gail M. Nomura, *Asian/Pacific Islander American Women: A Historical Anthology* (New York: New York University Press, 2003), pp. 172–187; Lon Kurashige, *Japanese American Celebration and Conflict: A History of Ethnic Identity and Festival in Los Angeles, 1934–1990* (Berkeley and Los Angeles: University of California Press, 2002); David Yoo, *Growing Up Nisei: Race, Generation, and Culture among Japanese Americans of California, 1924–1949* (Urbana and Chicago: University of Illinois Press, 2000). Under Jim Crow segregation, African Americans had to face horrific racial segregation in every aspect of daily life as well as in the political-economic structures but did not face the same anti-immigrant issues.

4. William V. Flores, with Rina Benmayor, *Latino Cultural Citizenship: Claiming Identity, Space, and Rights* (Boston: Beacon Press, 1997), p. 15.

5. Other items include alumnae minutes, constitutions, correspondence, newsletters, newspaper clippings. "Active" is the term used to refer to women currently in school who are sorority members, whereas the alumnae are members who are no longer in school but who are still active in sorority events, often in their own alumnae organization.

6. Since Japanese Americans could take only a few possessions to the internment camps, most club and institutional records were lost or destroyed. The European American advisers stored the Chi Alpha Delta prewar records.

7. There are no published scholarly historical monographs on European American sororities. Hence women's club networks are the most relevant historio-

graphical tradition for this chapter. Having had to piece together the meaning of sororities from two 1950s sociological surveys, popular literature, and UCLA campus publications, I would welcome in-depth scholarship assessing European American sororities as well as African American, Jewish American, and any Latina/Chicana and Native American women's collegiate activities.

8. Paula Giddings, *In Search of Sisterhood: Delta Sigma Theta and the Challenge of the Black Sorority Movement* (New York: William Morrow, 1988); Nora Stark Rogers, "A Study of Certain Personality Characteristics of Sorority and Non-Sorority Women at the University of California, Los Angeles" (Ed.D. diss., Department of Education, UCLA, 1952); Marianne Sanua, "Going Greek: A Social History of Jewish College Fraternities" (Ph.D. diss., Department of History, Columbia University, 1994); Bonnie Galloway, "Evolving Sisterhood: An Organizational Analysis of Three Sororities" (Ph.D. diss., Western Michigan University, 1994), Stuart Howe Collection, National Panhellenic Conference Archives, University of Illinois at Urbana. Galloway focuses on national sororities, not local ones, and Sanua concentrates on Jewish American fraternities, not sororities. See also Edith Chen, "Continuing Significance of Race: A Case Study of Asian American Women in White, Asian American, and African American Sororities" (Ph.D. diss., Department of Sociology, UCLA, 1998).

9. As Lisa Lowe eloquently argues, Asian American cultural productions are countersites to U.S. national memory and national culture (*Immigrant Acts: On Asian American Cultural Politics* [Durham: Duke University Press, 1996], p. 29).

10. Minutes of the Meetings, April 19, 1929, Chi Alpha Delta Active Files, Chi Alpha Delta Archives, Department of Special Collections–University Archives, Powell Library, University of California, Los Angeles (UCLA).

11. Shizue Morey Yoshina, Oral History Interview, Chi Alpha Delta Active Files, Chi Alpha Delta Archives, Department of Special Collections–University Archives, Powell Library, UCLA, 1992–1994.

12. Mae Ngai, "The Architecture of Race in American Immigration Law: A Reexamination of the Immigration Act of 1924," *Journal of American History* 86 (June 1999), pp. 67–92.

13. For more on race, ethnicity, and pre–World War II Los Angeles, see George Sanchez, *Becoming Mexican American: Ethnicity, Culture, and Identity in Chicano Los Angeles, 1900–1945*, reprint (New York and London: Oxford University Press, 1995).

14. Yoshina, Oral History Interview.

15. Paula Fass, *The Damned and the Beautiful: American Youth in the 1920s* (New York: Oxford University Press, 1977).

16. Fraternities and Sororities Files, May 8, 1987, Department of Special Collections–University Archives, Powell Library, UCLA, for *Bruin Life* yearbook.

17. "UCLA Greeks Face a Challenging Future," Fraternity Monthly, October 1945, p. 6; Katherine Hewitt, "The UCLA Greater Panhellenic Plan," November 14,

1946, p. 3, in Chancellor's Office/Sorority and Fraternity Files, University Archives, UCLA. Ms. Hewitt was then the current Panhellenic administrator.

18. UCLA yearbook, 1941, Chi Alpha Delta, p. 305.

19. Galloway, "Evolving Sisterhood," p. 3.

20. *The Claw*, 1918.

21. *The Claw*, October 1940.

22. The terms *Greek letter* and *Greek organization* can refer to fraternities and sororities in general and at times specifically to European American organizations.

23. *The Claw*, September 25, 1931, p. 26

24. Patricia Hill Collins, *Black Feminist Thought: Knowledge, Consciousness, and the Politics of Empowerment* (New York: Routledge, 1991); Herman Gray, *Watching Race: Television and the Struggle for the Sign of Blackness* (Minneapolis: University of Minnesota Press, 1997); Donald Bogle, *Toms, Coons, Mulattoes, Mammies, and Bucks: An Interpretive History of Blacks in American Films* (New York: Continuum, 1994).

25. *Look*, December 19, 1939, pp. 52–55.

26. *Daily Bruin*, March 10, 1966, UCLA, discusses the lawsuit against Acacia and Pi Beta Phi.

27. Yoshina, Oral History Interview.

28. Survey of Race Relations Collection, Hoover Institute, Stanford University, June 5, 1924, Box 28, Folder 225.

29. Though the women themselves infrequently recognized their alliances with other racial and religious minority women, I am deploying this term strategically and politically. First, though with different historical experiences, racial and religious minority women faced the double social-structure oppressions of race and sex. Second, by deploying the organizing tactic of "strategic essentialism," to borrow the phrase from Gayatri Spivak, I would like to use the phrases "women of color" and "racial/religious minority women" as a critical, not biological, perspective that builds academic as well as political coalitions.

30. *Pacific Ties*, May/June 1982, p. 15.

31. Jere Takahashi, *Nisei/Sansei: Shifting Japanese American Identities and Politics* (Philadelphia: Temple University Press, 1997), p. 122; Eileen Tamura, *Americanization, Acculturation, and Ethnic Identity: The Nisei Generation in Hawaii* (Urbana and Chicago: University of Illinois Press, 1994), p. 217.

32. *Pacific Ties*, May/June 1982, p. 15.

33. Fraternities and Sororities Files, University Archives, May 8, 1987, UCLA, for *Bruin Life* yearbook, p. 6.

34. Gamma Phi Beta bought the first plot of land, while Delta Gamma opened the first chapter house on sorority row. Chi Alpha Delta adviser and dean of women Helen Laughlin championed the idea of separating fraternity and sorority houses, and so the Janss Investment Company offered fraternities lots on Gayley Avenue, which formed the opposite, western campus boundary. For a case study

on the role of the dean of women at the University of California (Berkeley), see Joyce Antler, *Lucy Sprague Mitchell: The Making of a Modern Woman* (New Haven: Yale University Press, 1987).

35. Galloway, "Evolving Sisterhood," p. 85. Galloway's study focuses on three powerful national sororities: Kappa Alpha Theta, Pi Beta Phi, and Chi Omega.

36. Alumnae board meeting minutes, Nov. 30, 1938, Chi Alpha Delta Archives, Department of Special Collections–University Archives, UCLA.

37. Minutes, Nov. 30, 1938, Chi Alpha Delta Archives.

38. Sucheng Chan, *Asian Americans: An Interpretive History* (Boston: Twayne, 1991); Eiichiro Azuma, "Japanese Immigrant Farmers and California Alien Land Laws: A Study of the Walnut Grove Japanese Community," *California History* (Spring 1994), pp. 14–29.

39. Kenneth T. Jackson, *Crabgrass Frontiers: The Suburbanization of the United States* (New York: Oxford University Press, 1985).

40. Today, a conservative estimate of the price of one of the sorority houses on Hilgard Avenue would be $2 million. Chi Alpha Delta never solved their housing crisis, for today they still do not own a house.

41. Flora Adams, "Chinese Student Life at the University of Southern California" (M.S. thesis, Department of Education, University of Southern California, 1935), pp. 39–40.

42. Judy Yung, *Unbound Feet* (Berkeley and Los Angeles: University of California Press, 1995), p. 128. Unfortunately, Yung does not provide any details about this provocative incident. She tells us that "Chinese students at Stanford University, expelled from the dormitory by white students, had to establish their own residential Chinese Club House." So we don't know the year, nor the reasons why they were expelled.

43. Takahashi, *Nisei/Sansei*, p. 43.

44. As Flores and Benmayor explain, "the motivation [behind cultural citizenship] is simply to create a space where people feel 'safe' and 'at home,' where they feel a sense of belonging and membership" (*Latino Cultural Citizenship*, p. 15); Mabel Ota, Oral History Interview, Chi Alpha Delta Active Files, Chi Alpha Delta Archives.

45. Giddings, *In Search of Sisterhood*, pp. 43–45.

46. Ibid., p. 15.

47. Ibid., pp. 15–17.

48. Homi Bhabha, "Of Mimicry and Man: The Ambivalence of Colonial Discourse," in *The Location of Culture* (New York and London: Routledge, 1994), pp. 85–92.

49. Lilly Fujioka Tsukahira, Oral History Interview, Chi Alpha Delta Archives, Special Collections, UCLA, 1992–1994.

50. Dean Laughlin was proud that this was an organization in which members could put Greek versus non-Greek hostilities aside. "UCLA Greeks," p. 7.

51. Letter from the files of the chancellor's office, Robert G. Sproul, to the dean of women, Helen Laughlin, and the Dean of Men, Earl Miller, December 21, 1936.

52. Flora Belle Jan, Survey of Race Relations Collection, Hoover Institute, Stanford University, June 5, 1924, Box 28, Folder 225.

53. *The Claw,* September 25, 1931, p. 29.

54. Beth Bailey, *From Front Porch to Back Seat: Courtship in Twentieth-Century America* (Baltimore: Johns Hopkins University Press, 1988), pp. 25–56.

55. Frances Wakamatsu Kitagawa, Oral History Interview, conducted by Edith Chen, July 22, 1997, Chi Alpha Delta Archives.

56. National Panhellenic started in 1890. The first Inter-Sorority Conference met in Chicago on May 24, 1902. See Galloway, "Evolving Sisterhood," p. 92. In 1913, the National Panhellenic conference adopted a uniform scholarship card and uniform house rules. The Panhellenic Council opened the Panhellenic House in New York City in 1928, the same year as its nineteenth Congress. See ibid., p. 78.

57. Constitution of Women's Inter-Fraternity Council, University of California, Southern Branch, University Archives, UCLA.

58. Yoo, *Growing Up Nisei*; Yung, *Unbound Feet*; Joe Austin and Michael Nevin Willard, eds., *Generations of Youth: Youth Cultures and History in Twentieth-Century America* (New York: New York University Press, 1998); Valerie Matsumoto, "Japanese American Women during World War II," in Ellen C. DuBois and Vicki Ruiz, eds., Unequal Sisters: A Multicultural Reader in U.S. Women's History, 2d ed.(New York: Routledge, 1994), originally published in *Frontiers* 8.1 (1984).

59. Rose Hum Lee, *The Chinese in the United States of America* (Hon Kong: Hong Kong University Press; New York and Oxford: Oxford University Press, 1960), p. 92. In the pre–World War II era, there were far fewer second-generation Chinese Americans than Japanese Americans. The communities developed at different rates in large part due to the sex-ratio imbalance in the Chinese American population, which resulted in lower birth rates.

60. Matsumoto, "Japanese American Women," p. 174.

61. Yoshina, Oral History Interview.

62. Sanua, "Going Greek," p. 324.

63. Judy Yung, *Unbound Voices: A Documentary History of Chinese Women in San Francisco* (Berkeley and Los Angeles: University of California Press, 1999), p. 378.

64. *Chinese Digest* (March 1937), p. 10.

65. Alumnae board minutes, Constitution, May 2, 1933.

66. *Beta* is the second letter of the Greek alphabet and thus marks the second chapter. *Alpha,* the first letter of the Greek alphabet, designates the first.

67. Edna Bonacich and John Modell, *The Economic Basis of Ethnic Solidarity: Small Business in the Japanese American Community* (Berkeley: University of California Press, 1980), pp. 57–58; Roger Daniels, "Japanese America, 1930–1941: An

Ethnic Community in the Great Depression," *Journal of the West* 24.4 (October 1985), pp. 35–49.

68. Yoshina, Oral History Interview.

69. Many last names in membership rosters were not strictly Japanese. It is possible that these women were half Japanese and had Japanese mothers. It is also possible that those members were not Japanese but were nonetheless acceptable because they were of Asian descent. Constitution files, Chi Alpha Delta Archives.

70. Fujioka Tsukahira, Oral History Interview.

71. Yuji Ichioka, *The Issei: The World of First Generation Japanese Immigrants, 1885–1924* (New York: Free Press, 1988).

72. The two aforementioned black sororities, Alpha Kappa Alpha and Delta Sigma Theta, were the first to form UCLA chapters. There are discrepancies in the historical record as to when they were established at UCLA. The 1926 "Frosh Bible," the nickname of the incoming students' handbook, listed both organizations.

73. It is possible that during the Great Depression, they did not have the money to buy a yearbook page. It is also entirely possible that the chapters consisted mainly of alumnae from other campuses, not current UCLA active members, for Giddings reported that Delta Sigma Theta formed a chapter of graduates (alumnae) in 1928 in Los Angeles (*In Search of Sisterhood*, pp. 114–115). In the prewar period, judging from the addresses of the houses listed in the Frosh Bible, both African American sororities remained near the old university location and did not move to Westwood, probably due to restrictive housing covenants. And if they were primarily graduate alumnae, then it would not be as critical for them to move closer to UCLA.

74. Yoshina, Oral History Interview.

75. UCLA Yearbook, 1956.

76. In the famous follow-up study *Middletown in Transition*, Robert and Helen Lynd discovered that in the 1930s, higher percentages of women attended college than did men. In 1934, fourteen men and twenty-one women per hundred went to college compared to thirty-five men and thirty women in 1931. The Lynds speculated that whereas men had a greater choice of occupations, women needed college in order to enter the few fields open to them. See Robert S. Lynd and Helen Merrell Lynd, *Middletown in Transition: A Study in Cultural Conflicts* (New York: Harcourt, Brace, and World, 1937), pp. 211–212.

77. 1925 UCLA Yearbook. Five years later, in 1930, a second yearbook page, *sans* picture, stated that they were waiting out their one-year mandatory probationary period in order to become a recognized club at the university. However, after that, they dropped out of historical sight. In 1926 and 1927, the Filipino Bruin Club did not have a yearbook page but was mentioned in the Frosh Bible.

78. Unfortunately, records for Sigma Omicron Pi are almost nonexistent. Judy Yung mentions them in one sentence in *Unbound Feet* on p. 128, stating that they

were founded at San Francisco State. However, the UC–Berkeley yearbook claims that they were founded there, not at San Francisco State. Regardless of where they were founded, Sigma Omicron Pi appeared in the UC–Berkeley yearbook, but did not leave their papers or scrapbooks to the university. As with the Chi Alpha Deltas, the official university records all but ignore the Sigma Omicron Pis.

79. Neil Gabler, *An Empire of Their Own: How the Jews Invented Hollywood* (New York: Crown Books, 1988); George Lipsitz, *Time Passages: Collective Memory and American Popular Culture* (Minneapolis: University of Minnesota Press, 1990); Kathy Peiss, *Hope in a Jar: The Making of America's Beauty Culture* (New York: Metropolitan, 1998); Jennifer Scanlon, *Inarticulate Longings: The Ladies' Home Journal, Gender, and the Promises of Consumer Culture* (New York: Routledge, 1995); Jackson Lears, *Fables of Abundance: A Cultural History of Advertising in America* (New York: Basic Books, 1994); Roy Rosenzweig, *Eight Hours for What We Will: Workers and Leisure in an Industrial City, 1870–1920* (New York and Cambridge: Cambridge University Press, 1983).

80. Elaine S. Abelson, *When Ladies Go a-Thieving: Middle-Class Shoplifters in the Victorian Department Store* (New York and Oxford: Oxford University Press, 1992); Lewis A. Erenberg, *Steppin' Out: New York Nightlife and the Transformation of American Culture, 1890–1930*, reprint (Chicago: University of Chicago Press, 1984); Bill Lancaster, *The Department Store: A Social History* (Leicester: Leicester University Press, 1995).

81. Vicki L. Ruiz, *From Out of the Shadows: Mexican Women in Twentieth-Century America* (New York and Oxford: Oxford University Press, 1998).

82. Linda Maram, "Brown 'Hordes' in McIntosh Suits: Filipinos, Taxi Dance Halls, and Performing the Immigrant Body in Los Angeles, 1930s–1940s," in Austin and Willard, eds., *Generations of Youth*, p. 119.

83. Donna Gabaccia, *From Sicily to Elizabeth Street: Housing and Social Change among Italian Immigrants, 1880–1930*, SUNY Series in American Social History (Albany: SUNY Press, 1984); Janet Billson, *Keepers of the Culture: The Power of Tradition in Women's Lives* (Latham, Md.: Lexington Books, 1995); Micaela di Leonardo, *The Varieties of Ethnic Experience: Kinship, Class, and Gender among California Italian Americans* (Ithaca: Cornell University Press, 1984); Robert Orsi, *Madonna on 115th Street: Faith and Community in Italian Harlem, 1880–1950* (New Haven: Yale University Press, 1985); Vicki Ruiz, *From Out of the Shadows*; Elizabeth Ewen, *Immigrant Women in the Land of Dollars: Life and Culture on the Lower East Side, 1890–1925* (New York: Monthly Review Press, 1985).

84. Kurashige, *Japanese American Celebration and Conflict*, p. 25.

85. *Daily Bruin*, UCLA Yearbook, 1941, p. 305.

86. *Kashu Mainichi*, September 11, 1938.

87. UCLA clipping files, Chi Alpha Delta, "Chi Girls Rewarded with Big Crowd at Chi Whoopee," September 19, 1930.

88. Tamura, *Americanization, Acculturation, and Ethnic Identity*, p. 178.

89. Kurashige, *Japanese American Celebration and Conflict.*

90. *Rafu Shimpo,* August 10, 1941, p. 5.

91. *Rafu Shimpo,* August 16, 1934, front page.

92. Sanua, "Going Greek," p. 386. Given that sorority colors range from purple to orange to green, creating appetizing refreshments in sorority colors would not be an easy task.

93. Chi Alpha Deltas were not unusual in their expenditures on clothing; UCLA women in general spent much money on clothes, which enabled them to show membership in the educated upper classes. A group of economics students at UCLA surveyed female students in 1931 and discovered that the average woman student spent $392.76 a year on clothes. Press release, February 25, 1931—category student budget, University Archives, UCLA.

94. There has been considerable interest in dress and the constitution of the 1920s New Woman. See, for example, Valerie Steele, *Fashion and Eroticism: Ideals of Feminine Beauty from the Victorian Era to the Jazz Age* (New York and Oxford: Oxford University Press, 1985). There have also been numerous recent studies on the significance of women's dress. See Jane Gaines and Charlotte Herzog, eds., *Fabrications: Costume and the Female Body* (New York: Routledge, 1990).

95. Chi Alpha Delta Rush Photographs, 1931.

96. Ibid.

97. Minutes from meetings, yearbook photographs, scrapbooks 1930s, 1940s, 1950s, Chi Alpha Delta Archives.

98. Adrienne Rich, "Compulsory Heterosexuality and Lesbian Existence," *Signs: Journal of Women in Culture and Society* 5 (Summer 1980), pp. 631–660.

99. John Finley Scott, "Sororities and Marriage," *Daily Bruin Spectra,* November 30, 1965.

100. Ibid., p. 5.

101. Peggy Pascoe, "Miscegenation Law, Court Cases, and Ideologies of 'Race' in Twentieth-Century America," *Journal of American History* 83 (June 1996), pp. 44–69. For a popular account, see John Steinbeck's short story "Johnny Bear."

102. Edward W. Soja, *Postmodern Geographies: The Reassertion of Space in Critical Social Theory* (London and New York: Verso, 1989), p. 195.

103. Valerie Matsumoto, "Japanese American Women and the Creation of Urban Nisei Culture" (paper presented and discussed at UCLA's Center for Study of Women Feminist Research Seminar, May 13, 1997), p. 11.

104. Kitagawa, Oral History Interview.

105. Evelyn Brooks Higginbotham, *Righteous Discontent: The Women's Movement in the Black Baptist Church, 1880–1920* (New York and Cambridge: Cambridge University Press, 1993), pp. 95–96. However, as Deborah Gray White has found, gender and race did not always overcome class differences among African American women. Deborah Gray White, "The Cost of Club Work, the Price of

Black Feminism," in Nancy Hewitt, ed., *Visible Women: New Essays on American Activism* (Urbana: University of Illinois Press, 1993).

106. Michael Rogin, *Blackface, White Noise* (Berkeley and Los Angeles: University of California Press, 1996), pp. 150–155.

107. Gary Okihiro, *Cane Fires: The Anti-Japanese Movement in Hawaii, 1865–1945* (Philadelphia: Temple University Press, 1991); Ronald Takaki, *Pau Hana: Plantation Life and Labor in Hawaii, 1835–1920* (Honolulu: University of Hawaii Press, 1983).

108. As Jewish American sorority experiences indicate, almost all the mainstream sororities' rituals not only uphold Hellenic (Greek) culture but are inflected with Christianity. See Sanua, "Going Greek."

109. David Yoo's dissertation "Growing Up Nisei" points out that second-generation Japanese Americans were far more Christian than the first. His work shows that in the 1930s, 78 percent of the Issei (first generation) identified as Buddhist and 18 percent affiliated as Christian, whereas in 1942, the Nisei self-identified as 39 percent Buddhist and 51.5 percent Christian, a dramatic increase in Christian affiliation that speaks to the influence of growing up in a predominantly Christian nation such as the United States. Yoo, "Growing Up Nisei: Second Generation Japanese-Americans of California, 1924–1945" (Ph.D. diss., Department of History, Yale University, 1994), p. 113. Another study by the War Relocation Authority reported that in 1942, 48.5 percent of the American-born were Buddhist and 34.8 percent were Christian, as compared to 68.5 percent Buddhist and 23 percent Christian for the Japanese born (Yoo, "Growing Up Nisei," p. 300). No matter which percentage is the closest to correct, increasing numbers of the second generation identified as Christian.

110. Sorority minutes show fundraisers being held in locations such as the Venice and West Los Angeles Buddhist Temple recreation rooms.

111. At the beginning of the Second Sino-Japanese War in 1937, Chiang Kai-shek's Chinese Nationalist Army was allied with their previous enemies, the Chinese Communists, to fend off Japanese imperial aggression. However, Chiang's alliance with the Communists broke down.

112. Yoo, *Growing Up Nisei*.

113. Beth Bailey, *From Front Porch to Back Seat: Courtship in Twentieth-Century America* (Baltimore: Johns Hopkins University Press, 1988).

114. Yung, *Unbound Feet*, p. 167.

115. Micaela di Leonardo's work corroborates that women bear the burden of adapting ethnic culture; see her *Varieties of Ethnic Experience*.

116. *Rafu Shimpo*, August 10, 1941, p. 5.

117. Ibid.

118. Ibid.

119. Ibid.

120. Ibid.

121. Kurashige, *Japanese American Celebration and Conflict*, p. 97.

122. As Greg Robinson has shown, political pressure, public outcry, and military expediency, combined with President Franklin Delano Roosevelt's view that Japanese Americans were incapable of being "true Americans" resulted in the signing of Executive Order 9066 and the internment of West Coast Japanese Americans. Greg Robinson, *By Order of the President: FDR and the Internment of Japanese Americans* (Cambridge: Harvard University Press, 2001), p. 121.

123. Stuart Hall, "Notes on Deconstructing the 'Popular,'" in Samuel Raphael and Paul Kegan, eds., *People's History and Socialist Theory* (London: Routledge, 1981), p. 52.

NOTES TO CHAPTER 2

1. *King of Chinatown*, directed by Nick Grinde (Paramount, 1939).

2. For more on Dr. Margaret Chung, see Judy Tzu-Chun Wu, "Was Mom Chung a 'Sister Lesbian'? Asian American Gender Experimentation and Interracial Homoeroticism," *Journal of Women's History* 13.1 (Spring 2001), pp. 58–82.

3. Although Wong did not play a Chinese American professional in the film *Dangerous to Know*, Paramount Studios heavily promoted this starring vehicle.

4. *Life*, October 6, 1958, cover.

5. For an excellent discussion of previous scholarship on Wong that focused on (negative) stereotypes, see Cynthia Liu, "When Dragon Ladies Die, Do They Come Back as Butterflies? Re-imagining Anna May Wong," in Darrell Hamamoto and Sandra Liu, eds., *Countervisions: Asian American Film Criticism* (Philadelphia: Temple University Press, 2000), pp. 23–39; and Shirley Jennifer Lim, "Girls Just Wanna Have Fun: The Politics of Asian American Women's Public Culture, 1930–1960" (Ph.D. diss., UCLA, 1998), chap. 2. For the most substantial biographical work to date, see Karen Leong, "China Mystique" (Ph.D. diss., UC–Berkeley, 1999). Graham Hodges's *Anna May Wong* (New York: Palgrave, 2004) has borrowed heavily from Leong's painstaking research. See also Philip Leibfried and Chei Mi Lane, *Anna May Wong: A Complete Guide to Her Film, Stage, Radio, and Television Work* (New York: McFarland and Company, 2003); Anthony C. Chan, *Perpetually Cool: The Many Lives of Anna May Wong, 1905–1961* (New York: Rowman and Littlefield, 2003).

6. Vasant Kaiwar and Sucheta Mazumdar, *The Antimonies of Modernity: Essays on Race, Orient, Nation* (Durham: Duke University Press, 2003); Edward Said, *Orientalism* (New York: Pantheon, 1978); Nancy Leys Stephan and Sander L. Gilman, "Appropriating the Idioms of Science: The Rejection of Scientific Racism," in Dominick LaCapra, ed., *The Bounds of Race: Perspectives on Hegemony and Resistance* (Ithaca: Cornell University Press, 1991).

7. Viet Than Nguyen, *Race and Resistance: Literature and Politics in Asian America* (New York and London: Oxford University Press, 2002).

8. Laura Mulvey, "Visual Pleasure and Narrative Cinema," in Constance Penley, ed., *Feminism and Film Theory* (New York: Routledge, 1988), originally published in *Screen* 16.3 (Autumn 1975); Andrew Parker, Mary Russo, Doris Sommer, and Patricia Yeager, eds., *Nationalisms and Sexualities* (New York: Routledge, 1992).

9. Robert Lee, *Orientals: Asian Americans in Popular Culture* (Philadelphia: Temple University Press, 1999).

10. Jack Tchen, *New York before Chinatown: Orientalism and the Shaping of American Culture, 1776–1882* (Baltimore: Johns Hopkins University Press, 1999).

11. Erika Lee, "Exclusion Acts: Chinese Women during the Chinese Exclusion Era, 1882–1943," in Shirley Hune and Gail Nomura, eds., *Asian Pacific American Women: A Historical Anthology* (New York: New York University Press, 2003) and *At America's Gates: Chinese Immigration during the Exclusion Era, 1882–1943* (Chapel Hill: University of North Carolina Press, 2003); George A. Peffer, *If They Don't Bring Their Women Here: Chinese Female Immigration before Exclusion* (Urbana and Chicago: University of Illinois Press, 1999); Sucheng Chan, "The Exclusion of Chinese Women, 1870–1943," in Sucheng Chan, ed., *Entry Denied: Exclusion and the Chinese Community in America* (Philadelphia: Temple University Press, 1991); Lucie Cheng Hirata, "Free, Indentured, Enslaved: Chinese Prostitutes in Nineteenth-Century America," *Signs: Journal of Women in Culture and Society* 5.1 (Autumn 1979), pp. 3–29; Andrew Gyory, *Closing the Gate: Race, Politics, and the Chinese Exclusion Act* (Chapel Hill: University of North Carolina Press, 1998).

12. For an excellent discussion of race, gender, and postmodernity, see Inderpal Grewal and Caren Kaplan, *Scattered Hegemonies: Postmodernity and Transnational Feminist Practice* (Minneapolis: University of Minnesota Press, 1994), pp. 4–9. For modernity in twentieth-century China, see Valerie Steele and John S. Major, eds., *China Chic: East Meets West* (New Haven: Yale University Press, 1999); Leo Ou-Fan Lee, *Shanghai Modern: The Flowering of a New Urban Culture in China, 1930–1942* (Cambridge: Harvard University Press, 1999); Shu-mei Shih, *The Lure of the Modern: Writing Modernism in Semicolonial China, 1917–1937* (Berkeley and Los Angeles: University of California Press, 2001).

13. Useful frameworks for conceptualizing primitivism include Mariana Torgovnick, *Gone Primitive: Savage Intellects, Modern Lives* (Chicago: University of Chicago Press, 1990); and Fatimah Tobing Rony, *The Third Eye: Race, Cinema, and the Ethnographic Spectacle* (Durham: Duke University Press, 1996).

14. Johannes Fabian, *Time and the Other: How Anthropology Makes Its Object* (New York: Columbia University Press, 1983).

15. Lisa Lowe, *Immigrant Acts: On Asian American Cultural Politics* (Durham: Duke University Press, 1996).

16. For theorizing of performativity, see Judith Butler, *Gender Trouble: Femi-*

nism and the Subversion of Identity (New York: Routledge, 1990); Dorinne Kondo, *About Face: Performing Race in Fashion and Theater* (New York: Routledge, 1997).

17. As a historian, I did not have access to two of the sources scholars most value, namely, Anna May Wong's personal papers or extensive Chinese American ethnic newspaper coverage. The first Chinese American all-English newspaper, *Chinese Digest*, was founded in 1935 in San Francisco, but the circulation never exceeded five hundred and it stopped publishing in 1940. (See Xiaojian Zhao, *Remaking Chinese America: Immigration, Family and Community, 1940–1965* [New Brunswick: Rutgers University Press, 2002], p. 105; and Karl Lo and Him Mark Lai, *Chinese Newspapers Published in North America, 1854–1975* [Washington, D.C.: Center for Chinese Research Materials, Association for Research Libraries, 1975].) Believing in the role of Anna May Wong as an emblem of racialized femininity that deserved the fullest and most careful consideration, I turned to her movies. I am inspired by Mary Lowenthal Felstiner, whose work to uncover the life of Charlotte Salomon was prodigious, as shown in her book *To Paint Her Life: Charlotte Salomon in the Nazi Era* (New York: HarperCollins, 1994). I thank Valerie Matsumoto for first alerting me to her work through a lecture at the Simon Wiesenthal Museum of Tolerance in Los Angeles. Felstiner's lecture showed the audience that any historical topic, no matter how difficult, could be researched.

18. Judy Chu, "Anna May Wong," in Emma Gee, ed., *Counterpoint: Perspectives on Asian America* (Los Angeles: UCLA Asian American Studies Center, 1976), pp. 284–288.

19. Garland Kyle, "The Legend of Anna May Wong," *Gum Saam Journal* (October 1988).

20. Michael Rogin, *Blackface, White Noise: Jewish Immigrants in the Hollywood Melting Pot* (Berkeley and Los Angeles: University of California Press, 1996); Daniel Bernardi, ed., *The Birth of Whiteness: Race and the Emergence of U.S. Cinema* (New Brunswick: Rutgers University Press, 1996); Neil Gabler, *An Empire of Their Own: How the Jews Invented Hollywood* (New York: Crown Books, 1988); Lary May, *Screening Out the Past: The Birth of Mass Culture and the Motion Picture Industry* (Chicago: University of Chicago Press, 1980).

21. As film scholar Gina Marchetti's study's opening line states, "Hollywood has long been fascinated by Asia, Asians, and Asian themes" (*Romance and the "Yellow Peril": Rage, Sex, and Discursive Strategies in Hollywood Fiction* [Berkeley and Los Angeles: University of California Press, 1993], p. 1).

22. Gervasio Luis Garcia, "I Am the Other: Puerto Rico in the Eyes of North America, 1898," *Journal of American History* 87.1 (June 2000), pp. 39–64, paragraph 12.

23. Frederick Jackson Turner, "The Significance of the Frontier in American History," State Historical Society of Wisconsin, Proceedings, 1893; Kerwin Klein, *Frontiers of Historical Imagination* (Berkeley and Los Angeles: University of California Press, 1997); Harold Isaacs, *Scratches on Our Minds: American Views of*

China and India (New York: John Day, 1958); Malini Johar Schueller, *U.S. Orientalisms: Race, Nation, and Gender in Literature, 1790–1890* (Ann Arbor: University of Michigan Press, 1998); Amy Kaplan and Donald E. Pease, eds., *Cultures of United States Imperialism* (Durham: Duke University Press, 1993).

24. *Toll of the Sea*, directed by Chester M. Franklin, Technicolor, (Motion Picture Corporation, 1922); Cari Beauchamp, *Without Lying Down: Frances Marion and the Powerful Women of Early Hollywood* (New York: Scribner's, 1997); Nick Browne, "The Undoing of the Other Woman: Madame Butterfly in the Discourse of American Orientalism," in Bernardi, ed., *Birth of Whiteness*, pp. 227–256.

25. Mari Yoshihara, *Embracing the East: White Women and American Orientalism* (New York and London: Oxford University Press, 2002).

26. James Moy, *Marginal Sights: Staging the Chinese in America* (Iowa City: University of Iowa Press, 1993), p. 89.

27. Rogin, *Blackface, White Noise*; Lee, *Orientals*.

28. Rogin, *Blackface, White Noise*, p. 129.

29. For more on Anna May Wong in Europe, see Shirley Jennifer Lim, *Subversive Sirens: Anna May Wong and Josephine Baker* (forthcoming). For a thoughtful overview of Anna May Wong's reception in Europe, see Tim Bergfelder, "Negotiating Exoticism: Hollywood, Film Europe and the Cultural Reception of Anna May Wong," in Andrew Higson and Richard Maltby, eds., *"Film Europe" and "Film America": Cinema, Commerce and Cultural Exchange, 1920–1939* (Exeter: University of Exeter Press, 1999).

30. Phyllis Rose, *Jazz Cleopatra: Josephine Baker in Her Time* (New York: Doubleday, 1989); Olga Barrios, "The Afro-American Performer between 1920 and 1945: Paul Robeson and Josephine Baker and Their Artistic Fight for Freedom" (M.A. thesis, African American Studies, UCLA, 1987).

31. Robert Young, *Colonial Desire: Hybridity in Theory, Culture, and Race* (New York: Routledge, 1995).

32. Nancy Nenno, Tim Berfelder, Erica Carter, and Deniz Goturk, eds., *The German Cinema Book* (London: British Film Institute, 2003).

33. Since she changed her citizenship to French and remained in Europe, Baker, unlike Wong, continued her European career into the post–World War II period. For more on Josephine Baker's 1950s politics, see the fascinating article by Mary L. Dudziak, "Josephine Baker, Racial Protest, and the Cold War," *Journal of American History* (September 1994), pp. 543–570.

34. *Los Angeles Times* clipping file, Margaret Herrick Library, UCLA Academy of Motion Pictures, Arts and Sciences (AMPAS), Los Angeles.

35. Anna May Wong file, AMPAS.

36. Anna May Wong clipping file, AMPAS, October 26, 1932.

37. Anna May Wong clipping file, AMPAS.

38. *Tatler*, March 20, 1929; *Sketch*, August 22, 1928.

39. Keye Luke, followed by Bessie Loo, Southern California Chinese Historical

Association (SCCHA) Oral History Interview #25, 1978–1982, UCLA Special Collections.

40. "Anna May Wong," in James Robert Parish and William T. Leonard, eds., *Hollywood Players: The Thirties* (New Rochelle, N.Y.: Arlington House, 1976), p. 534.

41. Instead of searching for more nuanced interpretations, scholars have used Anna May Wong's characters' death at the end of plays and films to underscore how she was manipulated by cultural producers.

42. Sumiko Higashi, "DeMille's *The Cheat*," in Lester Friedman, ed., *Unspeakable Images: Ethnicity and the American Cinema* (Urbana: University of Illinois Press, 1991), pp. 112–139.

43. Betty Willis, "Famous Oriental Stars Return to the Screen," *Motion Picture*, October 1931, pp. 44–45.

44. For an insightful analysis of Sessue Hayakawa's creation and use of stereotypes in his silent-movie roles, see Donald Kirihara, "The Accepted Idea Displaced: Stereotype and Sessue Hayakawa," in Bernardi, ed., *Birth of Whiteness*, pp. 81–99.

45. In *Bridge*, like the foreign-born actors Umeki, Nuyen, and Kwan, he found an opportunity to display his acting talents and non-American-accented English voice and was rewarded with an Academy Award nomination for best supporting actor.

46. Doris Mackie, "I Protest, by Anna May Wong," in *Film Weekly* 10.53, August 18, 1933, p. 11.

47. Judy Yung, *Unbound Voices: A Documentary History of Chinese Women in San Francisco* (Berkeley and Los Angeles: University of California Press, 1999), p. 274.

48. Southern California Chinese Historical Society Oral History Collection, *Forbidden City USA*, Arthur Dong; Gloria H. Chun, *Of Orphans and Warriors: Inventing Chinese-American Culture and Identity* (New Brunswick: Rutgers University Press, 2000), p. 67.

49. Hodges, *Anna May Wong*, photographic insert between pp. 120 and 121.

50. Anna May Wong clipping file, AMPAS, 1932: "Anna May Wong Denied Admittance to Canada," March 29, 1932.

51. Though the movie character Chang rapes Wong, she ends up with a $20,000 reward and being proclaimed a hero to China. For more on *Shanghai Express*, see Marchetti, *Romance and the "Yellow Peril"*; and Lim, "Girls Just Wanna Have Fun," chap. 2.

52. Richard Oehling, "Hollywood and the Image of the Oriental," *Film and History* (May 1978), pp. 33–67.

53. Anna May Wong clipping file, AMPAS.

54. *New York Times*, April 14, 1930.

55. Gloria H. Chun, "Go West to China," in K. Scott Wong and Sucheng Chan,

eds., *Claiming America: Constructing Chinese Identities during the Exclusion Era* (Philadelphia: Temple University Press, 1998), p. 168.

56. Thomas Cripps, *Slow Fade to Black: The Negro in American Film, 1900–1942* (New York: Oxford University Press, 1976), p. 306.

57. Section 5 of the Hays code cautioned against the use of ethnic slurs: "[T]he Production Code Administration may take cognizance of the fact that the following words and phrases are obviously offensive to patrons of the motion pictures in the United States and more particularly to the patrons of motion pictures in foreign countries: Chink, Dago, Frog, Greaser, Hunkie, Kike, Nigger, Spic, Wop, Yid." Thus the code encouraged movies more palatable to ethnic Americans and international audiences, such as a film featuring a Chinese American female doctor.

58. Keye Luke, SCCHA Oral History Interview, #25, 1978–1982.

59. *The Good Earth,* directed by Victor Fleming (MGM, 1937.

60. Isaacs, *Scratches on Our Minds,* p. 157.

61. Robert McElwaine, "Third Beginning," *Modern Screen,* (no date), pp. 41, 80; United Artists 11D Research Data, P85–958, Reel 20, Micro 1054, Division of Archives and Manuscripts, State Historical Society of Wisconsin. I thank Karen Leong for this citation.

62. Liu, "When Dragon Ladies Die," p. 29.

63. Karen Shimikawa, *National Abjection: The Asian American Body Onstage* (Durham: Duke University Press, 2002), p. 3.

64. Chu, "Anna May Wong," p. 286, describes them as "routine and easily forgettable"; Kyle, "Legend of Anna May Wong," pp. 7–11; and Philip Leibfried, "Anna May Wong," *Films in Review* (March 1987), pp. 147–152, ignores them.

65. B movies were often shown before main features. I am still trying to locate information about which movies showed with Anna May Wong's.

66. *Click,* December 1938, pp. 8–9.

67. Roger Moley, *The Hays Office* (Indianapolis: Bobbs-Merrill, 1945); James Combs, ed., *Movies and Politics, the Dynamic Relationship* (New York: Garland, 1993).

68. The 1934 movie *Limehouse Blues* provides an interesting contrast with *King of Chinatown* and *Daughter of Shanghai. Limehouse Blues* is like a less-developed, less-focused-on-Wong version of *Dangerous to Know.* In *Limehouse,* she is dressed in Chinese clothing and plays a nightclub dancer. In the movie she doesn't smile and exhibits great jealousy of the European American female lead. At this point in her career, she was listed third in the credits.

69. One can see this disruption of the Madame Butterfly theme in movies of the late 1950s such as *South Pacific, Love Is a Many Splendored Thing,* and *The World of Suzie Wong.*

70. Judy Tzu-Chun Wu, *Doctor Mom Chung of the Fair-Haired Bastards: The Life of a Wartime Celebrity* (Berkeley and Los Angeles: University of California Press, 2005).

71. Yung, *Unbound Voices,* p. 439.

72. Chinese Historical Society of Southern California, *Linking Our Lives: Chinese American Women of Los Angeles* (Los Angeles: Westland, 1984), p. 98.

73. Isaacs, *Scratches on Our Minds.*

74. *Island of Lost Men* is the third in the Paramount movie quartet. Though Wong is given credit as the lead, given the movie's ending and given little screen time, one might assume that she played supporting role instead of a leading role. In *Island* she plays a Chinese, not Chinese American, role as the daughter of a leading Chinese general whose mission is to recover her father's honor. She is still portrays the role with the trappings of upper-class costume and speaks with an upper-class accent.

75. Paramount Studio files, *Daughter of Shanghai,* Paramount script files, University of Southern California. I thank Cynthia Liu for calling my attention to this point.

76. *Chinese Digest,* May 1937, p. 12. For more information on the history of Chinese community newspapers in the United States, see Lo and Lai, *Chinese Newspapers;* Him Mark Lai, "The Chinese Vernacular Press in North America, 1900–1950: Their Role in Social Cohesion," *Annals of the Chinese Historical Society of the Pacific Northwest* (1984), pp. 170–178.

77. *Chinese Digest,* July 1937, p. 8.

78. I thank Scott Sandage for this insight.

79. The absence of female heroines' mothers was common in this era. For instance, 1930s child actress Shirley Temple's movies lacked mothers and placed Temple as a lone female in a world of men. Both Angela Davis and Ann DuCille have commented that this is a pattern they have found in their own research. Angela Davis, *Blues Legacies and Black Feminism: Gertrude "Ma" Rainey, Bessie Smith, and Billie Holiday* (New York: Pantheon Books, 1998); Ann DuCille, "Shirley Temple" (paper presented at UCLA, 1997).

80. Ella Shohat, "Ethnicities-in-Relation: Toward a Multicultural Reading of the American Cinema," in Lester Friedman, ed., *Unspeakable Images: Ethnicity and the American Cinema* (Urbana and Chicago: University of Illinois Press, 1991), p. 233. For a study on Hollywood and Asian–European/American sexual relationships, see Marchetti, *Romance and the "Yellow Peril."*

81. Andrea Walsh, *The Women's Film and Female Experience, 1940–1950* (Westport, Conn.: Praeger, 1984), p. 33.

82. Peggy Pascoe, "Race, Gender, and Intercultural Relations: The Case of Interracial Marriage," *Frontiers: A Journal of Women Studies* 12.1 (1991), pp. 5–18.

83. *Loving* v. *Virginia,* 388 U.S. 1, 18 L. ed 2d 1010, 87 S.Ct. 1817 (U.S. Supreme Court 1967).

84. Mulvey, "Visual Pleasure and Narrative Cinema," p. 62. Originally published in 1975, Mulvey's provocative article has generated over two decades of feminist film studies on female identity, pleasure, and psychoanalysis.

85. Scholars working after Mulvey published "Visual Pleasure" have argued that women have had more power as actresses and as spectators. See works such as Jackie Byars, *All That Hollywood Allows: Re-reading Gender in 1950s Melodrama* (Chapel Hill: University of North Carolina Press, 1991); Jacqueline Bobo, *Black Women as Cultural Readers* (New York: Columbia University Press, 1995); Jackie Stacey, *Star Gazing: Hollywood Cinema and Female Spectatorship* (London: Routledge, 1994); Jeanine Basinger, *A Woman's View: How Hollywood Spoke to Women, 1930–1960* (New York: Alfred Knopf, 1993); Walsh, *Women's Film and Female Experience*. As film scholar Jackie Stacey has found, the relationship between stars and spectators involves a complex interplay of multiple feminine identities (*Star Grazing*, p. 227). Thus female audiences could rework potentially exploitative roles to highlight the star's attributes.

86. Judy Yung, *Unbound Feet* (Berkeley and Los Angeles: University of California Press, 1995).

87. Cripps, *Slow Fade to Black*, p. 5.

88. Ibid.

89. Arthur Knight, *Disintegrating the Musical: Black Performance and American Musical Film* (Durham: Duke University Press, 2002).

90. Pearl Bowser and Louise Spence, "Identity and Betrayal: *The Symbol of the Unconquered* and Oscar Micheaux's 'Biographical Legend,'" in Bernardi, ed., *Birth of Whiteness*, pp. 56–80.

91. Ed Guerrero, *Framing Blackness: The African American Image in Film* (Philadelphia: Temple University Press, 1993); Anna Everett, *Returning the Gaze: A Genealogy of Black Film Criticism, 1909–1949* (Durham: Duke University Press, 2001); Valerie Smith, *Representing Blackness: Issues in Film and Video* (New Brunswick: Rutgers University Press, 1997).

92. Ana Lopez, "Are All Latins from Manhattan? Hollywood, Ethnography, and Cultural Colonialism," in Friedman, ed., *Unspeakable Images*, pp. 406–424.

93. Gabler, *Empire of Their Own*; Patricia Erens, *The Jew in American Cinema* (Bloomington: Indiana University Press, 1984); Lester Friedman, *The Image of the Jew in Hollywood* (New York: Frederick Ungar, 1982).

94. For more on early cinema and Chinese Americans in Los Angeles, see Lim, "Girls Just Wanna Have Fun," chap. 2.

95. Chinese Historical Society of Southern California, *Linking Our Lives*.

96. Eddie Lee, SCCHA Oral History Interview, 1978–1982.

97. Louise Leung, "Night Call—In Chinatown," *Los Angeles Times*, July 26, 1936, p. 3.

98. Lulu Kwan (younger sister of Anna May Wong), telephone interview, 1993.

99. Swan Yee, SCCHA Oral History Interview #163, 1978–1982.

100. Louise Leung Larson, *Sweet Bamboo: A Memoir of a Chinese American Family* (Berkeley and Los Angeles: University of California Press, 1989), p. 189.

101. Lisa See, *On Gold Mountain: The One-Hundred-Year Odyssey of My Chinese American Family* (New York: Vintage, 1995), p. 215.

102. Chinese Historical Society of Southern California, *Linking Our Lives.*

103. For more on San Francisco Chinatown and metaphors of disease, see Nayan Shah, *Contagious Divides: Epidemics and Race in San Francisco's Chinatown* (Berkeley and Los Angeles: University of California Press, 2001); Yong Chen, *Chinese San Francisco, 1850–1943: A Trans-Pacific Community* (Palo Alto: Stanford University Press, 2000).

104. Michael Omi and Howard Winant, *Racial Formation in the United States: From the 1960s to the 1980s* (New York: Routledge, 1986).

105. Ronald Takaki, *Pau Hana: Plantation Life and Labor in Hawaii, 1835–1920* (Honolulu: University of Hawaii Press, 1983); Gary Okihiro, *Cane Fires: The Anti-Japanese Movement in Hawaii, 1865–1945* (Philadelphia: Temple University Press, 1991).

106. Paramount press release, Paramount Studio Production Files, AMPAS, December 28, 1937.

107. *Chinese Digest,* April 1938, p. 15.

108. Patricia Hill Collins, *Black Feminist Thought: Knowledge, Consciousness, and the Politics of Empowerment* (New York: Routledge, 1991).

109. Yu, "Thinking Orientals," p. 25.

110. "Little" clearly refers to an affectionate diminutive, for in the *Look* photographs Wong is the same height as Lowell Thomas, Dietrich and Riefenstahl, and her brother Roger. There have been rumors, but no confirmations, of a sexual affair between Dietrich and Wong (conversation between the author and poet and writer John Yau, Santa Monica, Calif.) Letters from Wong to Dietrich are held in the soon-to-be-opened Marlene Dietrich Museum but have not been made available for scholarly research.

111. Anna May Wong clipping file, AMPAS.

112. Lopez, "Are All Latins from Manhattan?" p. 410.

113. The leading work on Dolores del Rio' sexual and racial imaging is Joanne Hershfield's *The Invention of Dolores del Rio* (Minneapolis: University of Minnesota Press, 2000).

114. Alicia Rodriquez, "Dolores del Rio and Lupe Velez," in Sue Armitage and Elizabeth Jameson, eds., *Writing the Range: Race, Class and Culture in the Women's West* (Norman: University of Oklahoma Press, 1997). I eagerly await Rodriquez's dissertation, which focuses not only del Rio and Velez but on other racial/ethnic minority movie stars such as Lena Horne, Rita Hayworth, Freddy Washington, and Dorothea Dandridge.

115. For more on gendered pleasure in looking, see Ien Ang, *Watching Dallas: Soap Opera and the Melodramatic Imagination* (London: Methuen, 1985). Laura Mulvey argues that pleasure should be destroyed ("Visual Pleasure and Narrative Cinema," p. 62).

116. Renee Tajima, "Lotus Blossoms Don't Bleed: Images of Asian Women," in Diane Wong and Emilya Cachapero, eds., *Making Waves: An Anthology of Writings by and about Asian American Women* (Boston: Beacon Press, 1989), p. 309.

117. Two other movies of 1934, *Java Head* and *Chu Chin Chow,* might more properly be placed in an earlier genre of roles played by Wong, for both movies were based on 1920s silent movies and plays whose original leading actresses were European American.

118. Though *Dangerous to Know* is part of Wong's Paramount contract to play Chinese American roles, since this movie is based on a late 1920s play, the plot line does not fit in with her later movies. However, the costuming of Wong as an elite woman, the focus on Wong as the star, and the centrality of her character to the plot do fit in with the Chinese American movies *King of Chinatown* and *Daughter of Shanghai.* Hence I have placed it here in an intermediary position.

119. *Dangerous to Know,* directed by Robert Florey (Paramount, 1938).

120. *Dangerous to Know* press release, Anna May Wong/Paramount Studio Clipping Files, AMPAS, January 11, 1938.

121. Steele and Major, eds., *China Chic*; Lee, *Shanghai Modern*; Shih, *The Lure of the Modern.*

122. I thank Scott Sandage for pointing this out. I eagerly await Karen Leong's forthcoming excellent work on Madame Chiang Kai-shek, *The China Mystique: Pearl S. Buck, Anna May Wong, Mayling Soong, and the Transformation of American Orientalism* (Berkeley and Los Angeles: University of California Press, 2005).

123. Yung, *Unbound Feet,* pp. 246–247, 251.

124. *Chinese Digest,* March 1937, pp. 10–11. For more on Chinese American female newspaper columnists, see Zhao, *Remaking Chinese America.*

125. *Chinese Digest,* March 1937, pp. 10–11.

126. Paramount press release, Anna May Wong/Paramount Studio Files, AMPAS, February 7, 1938.

127. One does have to pause and consider what it means that the information about Anna May Wong's refusal to bob her hair came from studio sources. Why was the studio invested in publicizing the defiance of one of its stars to studio dictates? Did Anna May Wong's Asian American identity enable her to be defiant because there weren't other women who could play the roles left on her Paramount contract?

128. Yung, *Unbound Voices,* p. 424.

129. Paramount Studios publicity release, Anna May Wong/Paramount Studio Files, AMPAS, January 13, 1938.

130. Program cover, *The Willow Tree,* August 2, 1943, from AMPAS.

131. Anna May Wong Biographical File, AMPAS, *Los Angeles Times,* July 7, 1944.

NOTES TO CHAPTER 3

1. Rogers M. Smith, *Civic Ideals: Conflicting Visions of Citizenship in U.S. History* (New Haven and London: Yale University Press, 1997); James Kloppenberg, *The Virtues of Liberalism* (New York and Oxford: Oxford University Press, 1998); Louis Hartz, *The Liberal Tradition in America* (New York: Harcourt, Brace, Jovanovich, 1955).

2. Mary Dudziak, *Cold War Civil Rights* (Princeton: Princeton University Press: 2000); Lary May, ed., *Recasting America: Culture and Politics in the Age of Cold War* (Chicago: University of Chicago Press, 1989); Elaine Tyler May, *Homeward Bound: American Families in the Cold War Era* (New York: Basic Books, 1988).

3. Steve Fraser and Gary Gerstle, eds., *The Rise and Fall of the New Deal Order, 1930–1980* (Princeton: Princeton University Press, 1989); Robert S. McElvaine, *The Great Depression: America, 1929–1941* (New York: Times Books, 1984, 1993); William E. Leuchtenberg, *Franklin D. Roosevelt and the New Deal* (New York: Harper and Row, 1963); Robin D. G. Kelley, *Hammer and Hoe: Alabama Communists during the Great Depression* (Chapel Hill: University of North Carolina Press, 1990).

4. Lizabeth Cohen, *A Consumer's Republic: The Politics of Mass Consumption in Postwar America* (New York: Alfred A. Knopf, 2003).

5. Gunnar Myrdal, *An American Dilemma: The Negro Problem and Modern Democracy* (New York: Harper and Row, 1944; reprint, 1962); Henry Yu, *Thinking Orientals: Migration, Contact, and Exoticism in Modern America* (New York and London: Oxford University Press, 2001).

6. Taylor Branch, *Parting the Waters: Martin Luther King and the Civil Rights Movement, 1954–1963* (New York: Pan Macmillan, 1990); Clayborne Carson, *In Struggle: SNCC and the Black Awakening of the 1960s* (Cambridge: Harvard University Press, 1981); Howard Sitcoff, *The Struggle for Black Equality, 1954–1992* (New York: Hill and Wang, 1993).

7. Waldo Martin, *Brown v. Board of Education: A Brief History with Documents* (New York: Bedford/St. Martin's, 1998), pp. 28–29.

8. George L. Mosse, *Nationalism and Sexuality: Middle-Class Morality and Sexual Norms in Modern Europe* (Madison: University of Wisconsin Press, 1985), chap. 6: "War Youth and Beauty."

9. For more on diasporic citizenship, see Lok Siu, "Diasporic Cultural Citizenship: Chineseness and Belonging in Panama and Central America," *Social Text* 69.19 (Winter 2001), pp. 7–28; Aiwa Ong and Donald Nonini, eds., *Ungrounded Empires: The Cultural Politics of Modern Transnationalism* (New York: Routledge, 1997).

10. Judy Yung, *Unbound Feet* (Berkeley and Los Angeles: University of California Press, 1995), p. 227. See also Judy Tzu-Chun Wu, *Doctor Mom Chung of the*

Fair-Haired Bastards: The Life of a Wartime Celebrity (Berkeley and Los Angeles: University of California Press, 2005).

11. Meg Jacobs, "Pocketbook Politics: Democracy and the Market in Twentieth-Century America," in *The Democratic Experiment* (Princeton: Princeton University Press, 2003).

12. Cohen, *Consumer's Republic,* p. 43.

13. Yung, *Unbound Feet,* pp. 293, 304.

14. For example, in Stockton, California, by the 1940s there were about five hundred American-born Filipinos; see Ronald Takaki, *Strangers from a Different Shore* (New York: Penguin, 1989), p. 343. In addition, as Fred Cordova has written, thousands of Filipino "nationals" became citizens, sometimes in mass induction ceremonies, in order to fight in the armed services.

15. *Philippines Star Press,* April 28, 1945, part 1, page 3.

16. Chinese Historical Society of Southern California, *Linking Our Lives* (Los Angeles: Westland, 1984), p. 97.

17. Soo-Young Chin, *Doing What Had to Be Done: The Life Narrative of Dora Yum Kim* (Philadelphia: Temple University Press, 1999).

18. Karen Anderson, *Wartime Women: Sex Roles, Family Relationships, and the Status of Women during World War II* (Westport, Conn.: Greenwood Press, 1981); William Chafe, *The American Woman: Her Changing Social, Economic, and Political Roles* (London: Oxford University Press, 1972); Susan Hartmann, *The Home Front and Beyond: American Women in the 1940s* (Boston: Twayne, 1982).

19. Yung, *Unbound Feet,* pp. 249–277; see also Xiaojian Zhao, *Remaking Chinese America: Immigration, Family, and Community, 1940–1965* (New Brunswick: Rutgers University Press, 2002).

20. Sucheng Chan, ed., *Entry Denied: Exclusion and the Chinese Community in America, 1882–1943* (Philadelphia: Temple University Press, 1992).

21. Toshi Miyamoto, Oral History Interview, Chi Alpha Delta Archives, Department of Special Collections–University Archives, Powell Library, University of California, Los Angeles, 1992–1994.

22. Jeanne Houston, *Farewell to Manzanar: A True Story of Japanese American Experiences during and after the World War II Internment* (Toronto and New York: Bantam Books, 1973); Michi Weglyn, *Years of Infamy: The Untold Story of America's Concentration Camps* (New York: Morrow, 1976); Roger Daniels, *Concentration Camp USA: Japanese Americans and World War II* (New York: Holt, Rinehart, and Winston, 1972); Gordon Chang, "'Superman Is about to Visit the Relocation Camps' and the Limits of Wartime Liberalism," *Amerasia* 19.1 (Winter 1993), pp. 37–59.

23. *Daily Bruin,* UCLA University Archives, December 1941–May 1942.

24. Chi Alpha Delta, Actives Minutes from Meetings, Chi Alpha Delta Archives, December 8, 1941; also canceled December 12, 1941.

25. Chi Alpha Delta, Actives Minutes from Meetings, Chi Alpha Delta Archives, February 1, 1942.

26. Chi Alpha Delta, Actives Minutes from Meetings, Chi Alpha Delta Archives, March 13, 1942.

27. Gary Okihiro and Leslie Ito, *Storied Lives: Japanese American Students and World War II* (Seattle: University of Washington Press, 1999); Jenness Hall, "Japanese American College Students during the Second World War: The Politics of Relocation" (Ph.D. diss., Indiana University, August 1993), p. 52.

28. Hall, "Japanese American College Students," p. 52.

29. Ibid.

30. Ibid., p. 48.

31. Ibid., p. 206.

32. Ibid., p. 211.

33. Ibid., p. 219.

34. Jere Takahashi, *Nisei/Sansei: Shifting Japanese American Identities and Politics* (Philadelphia: Temple University Press, 1997).

35. Ibid., pp. 106–108.

36. Valerie Matsumoto, "Japanese American Women during World War II," in Ellen C. DuBois and Vicki Ruiz, eds., *Unequal Sisters: A Multicultural Reader in U.S. Women's History,* 2d ed. (New York: Routledge, 1994), pp. 436–449, originally published in *Frontiers* 8.1 (1984), pp. 6–14.

37. Deborah Gray White, *Ar'n't I a Woman? Female Slaves in the Plantation South* (New York: Norton, 1981).

38. Mary Paik, *Quiet Odyssey: A Pioneer Korean Woman in America* (Seattle: University of Washington Press, 1990), p. 95.

39. Yung, *Unbound Feet,* p. 250.

40. "How to Tell Your Friends form the Japs," *Time,* December 22, 1941, p. 33.

41. *Life,* December 22, 1941, pp. 81–82.

42. Margaret Beetham, *A Magazine of Her Own? Domesticity and Desire in the Woman's Magazine, 1800–1914* (New York: Routledge, 1996); Jennifer Scanlon, *Inarticulate Longings: The Ladies' Home Journal, Gender, and the Promises of Consumer Culture* (New York: Routledge, 1995).

43. Benedict Anderson, *Imagined Communities: Reflections on the Origin and Spread of Nationalism* (London: Verso, 1983); Scanlon, *Inarticulate Longings.*

44. In fact, Japanese American youth magazines were published as early as the 1930s.

45. Leonard Broom and Ruth Reimer, *Removal and Return: The Socio-Economic Effects of the War on Japanese Americans* (Berkeley and Los Angeles: University of California Press, 1949), p. 41.

46. David Yoo, *Growing Up Nisei: Race, Generation and Culture among Japanese Americans of California, 1924–1949* (Urbana: University of Illinois Press, 2000), chaps. 3, 4, 5, p. 127.

47. *Scene,* July 1952, p. 7.

48. John Dower, *War without Mercy: Race and Power in the Pacific War* (New York: Pantheon, 1986).

49. *Scene,* April 1952, p. 16. Dillon Myer, who had headed the war relocation authority, was subsequently appointed the U.S. Commissioner of Indian Affairs.

50. *Scene,* September 1950, p. 37.

51. *Scene,* September 1950, p. 5.

52. Jade Snow Wong, *Fifth Chinese Daughter* (Seattle: University of Washington Press, 1945). For exciting work on Jade Snow Wong and American liberalism, please see Cynthia Tolentino's forthcoming work.

53. Cohen, *Consumer's Republic,* p. 127.

54. For more on the LaChoy food company, see Anne Soon Choi, "Embracing the Oriental: Korean Immigrant Entrepreneurship before World War II" (paper presented at the American Studies Association Annual Meeting, October 16, 2003).

55. *Scene,* April 1953, p. 45; *Scene,* August 1951, p. 5.

56. *Scene,* September 1953, p. 21.

57. *Scene,* April 1953, p. 45.

58. *Scene,* August 1953, p. 20.

59. *Scene* deliberately used its pages to promote better understanding between the United States and Japan and Japanese Americans. See Togo Tanaka, Oral History Interview by James Gatewood, in "Regenerations Oral History Project: Rebuilding Japanese America," December 13, 1997, Japanese American National Museum, Los Angeles.

60. *Scene,* August 1953, p. 25.

61. For more information on European American youth of the 1950s, see Wini Breines, *Young, White, and Miserable: Growing Up Female in the Fifties* (Boston: Beacon Press, 1992).

62. For more on Asian American youth culture, see Jennifer Lee and Min Zhou, eds., *Asian American Youth: Culture, Identity, and Ethnicity* (New York: Routledge 2004); Sunaina Marr Maira, *Desis in the House: Indian American Youth Culture in New York City* (Philadelphia: Temple University Press 2002).

63. Hall, "Japanese American College Students," p. 280; Robert O'Brien and Roger Daniels, *The College Nisei,* reprint (New Stratford, N.H.: Ayer, 1979), p. 116.

64. Paula Fass, "Creating New Identities: Youth and Ethnicity in New York City High Schools in the 1930s and 1940s," and Beth Bailey, "From Panty Raids to Revolution: Youth and Authority, 1950–1970," both in Joe Austin and Michael Nevin Willard, eds., *Generations of Youth: Youth Cultures and History in Twentieth-Century America* (New York: New York University Press, 1998).

65. Rafu Shimpo, September 8, 1947. For more on Mary Oyama, see Valerie Matsumoto, "Desperately Seeking 'Deirdre': Gender Roles, Multicultural Relations, and Nisei Women Writers of the 1930s," *Frontiers: A Journal of Women's Studies* 12 (1991), pp. 19–32.

66. Chi Alpha Delta, Active Minutes of the Meeting, September 1946–June 19, 1948.

67. *Scene,* April 1953, p. 3.

68. *Scene,* June 1953, p. 37.

69. The "Feminine Scene" was a column written by women, for women. It did not appear consistently in all issues of the magazine. This column was one of the few times women appeared as writers in the magazine.

70. *Scene,* September 1949, p. 28.

71. Grace Palladino, *Teenagers: An American History* (New York: Basic Books, 1996), p. 107.

72. Donna Gabaccia, *We Are What We Eat: Ethnic Food and the Making of Americans* (Cambridge: Harvard University Press, 2000); Linda Keller Brown and Kay Mussell, eds., *Ethnic and Regional Foodways in the United States: The Performance of Group Identity* (Knoxville: University of Tennessee Press, 1984).

73. Angela McRobbie, *Feminism and Youth Culture: From 'Jackie' to 'Just Seventeen'* (London: Macmillan, 1991).

74. Ibid.; Dick Hebdige, *Subculture: The Meaning of Style* (London: Methuen, 1979); Stuart Hall, "Notes on Deconstructing the 'Popular,'" in Samuel Raphael and Paul Kegan, eds., *People's History and Socialist Theory* (London: Routledge, 1981).

75. *Nisei Vue,* Summer 1949, p. 31.

76. Erica Rand, *Barbie's Queer Accessories* (Durham: Duke University Press, 1995).

77. Vicki L. Ruiz, *From Out of the Shadows: Mexican Women in Twentieth Century America* (New York: Oxford University Press, 1998); Noliwe Rooks, *Ladies' Pages: African American Women's Magazines and the Cultures That Made Them* (New Brunswick: Rutgers University Press, 2004).

78. 1959 Fashion Show Report, Active Folders, Chi Alpha Delta, University Archives, UCLA.

79. *Scene,* July 1950, p. 44.

80. *Scene,* May 1950, p. 8.

81. Beetham, *A of Her Own?* p. 2.

82. *Scene,* May 1950, p. 8.

83. Ibid.

84. Anderson, *Imagined Communities.*

85. For more on the Japanese American press, see Yoo, *Growing Up Nisei.*

86. Kenneth Jackson, *Crabgrass Frontiers: The Suburbanization of the United States* (New York: Oxford University Press, 1985); Robert O. Self, *American Babylon* (Princeton: Princeton University Press, 2003).

87. Elaine Tyler May, *Homeward Bound: American Families in the Cold War Era* (New York: Basic Books, 1988).

88. Joanne Meyerowitz, ed., *Not June Cleaver: Women and Gender in Postwar America, 1945–1960* (Philadelphia: Temple University Press, 1994).

89. Yen Le Espiritu, *Asian American Panethnicity: Bridging Institutions and Identities* (Philadelphia, Temple University Press, 1992); William Wei, *The Asian American Movement* (Philadelphia: Temple University Press, 1993).

90. See Espiritu, *Asian American Panethnicity.*

91. *Scene,* January 1953, p. 13.

92. *Scene,* July 1953, p. 3.

93. *Scene,* November 1953, p. 5.

94. Ibid., pp. 30–31; *Scene,* February 1954, p. 31.

95. *Scene,* July 1953, pp. 31–34.

96. Ruthanne Lum McCunn, *Thousand Pieces of Gold* (San Francisco: Design Enterprises of San Francisco, 1981).

97. *Scene,* September 1953, p. 21.

98. Sherrie Tucker, *Swing Shift* (Durham: Duke University Press), p. 164.

99. *Scene,* August 1953, p. 19.

100. Ibid.

101. Ibid., p. 21.

102. Ibid.

103. *Scene,* April 1953, p. 31.

104. Espiritu, *Asian American Panethnicity.*

105. Pledge lists—lists of women who have agreed to join the sorority but have not been initiated into membership—show more non-Japanese Asian-descent last names than the membership rosters, which may indicate that the heavily Japanese focus of the philanthropic activities, the membership, and social life made the sorority less appealing for women of other Asian origins. Membership rosters and pledge lists in Minutes of Meetings, Active Files, Chi Alpha Delta Archives.

106. President's List, Active Files, Chi Alpha Delta Archives.

107. *Philippines Star Press,* April 9, 1948, p. 5.

108. Chin, *Doing What Had to Be Done,* pp. 48–51.

NOTES TO CHAPTER 4

1. Colleen Ballerino Cohen, Richard Wilk, and Beverly Stoeltje, eds., *Beauty Queens: On the Global Stage* (New York: Routledge, 1996).

2. Ruth Rosen, *The World Split Open: How the Modern Women's Movement Changed America* (New York: Penguin Putnam, 2001); Gloria Steinem, *Outrageous Acts and Everyday Rebellions* (New York: Owl Books, 1983).

3. Judy Wu, "'Loveliest Daughter of Our Ancient Cathay!' Representations of Ethnic and Gender Identity in the Miss Chinatown U.S.A. Beauty Pageant," *Journal of Social History* 31.1 (Fall 1997), pp. 5–31; Nhi T. Lieu, "Remembering 'the Na-

tion' through Pageantry: Femininity and the Politics of Vietnamese Womanhood in the Hoa Hau Ao Dai Contest," *Frontiers* 21.1/2 (2000); Rick A. Lopez, "The India Bonita Contest of 1921 and the Ethnicization of Mexican National Culture," *Hispanic American Historical Review* 82.2 (2002), pp. 291–328.

4. Richard Wilk, "Connections and Contradictions: From the Crooked Tree Cashew Queen to Miss World Belize," in Cohen, Wilk, and Stoeltje, eds., *Beauty Queens*, pp. 217–232; Lopez, "India Bonita Contest of 1921," pp. 291–328; Natasha Barnes, "Face of the Nation: Race, Nationalisms and Identity in Jamaican Beauty Pageants," in Jennifer Scanlon, ed., *The Gender and Consumer Culture Reader* (New York: New York University Press, 2000), pp. 355–371; Lieu, "Remembering 'the Nation' through Pageantry," 127–151.

5. Carole McGranahan, "Miss Tibet, or Tibet Misrepresented? The Trope of Woman-as-Nation in the Struggle for Tibet," in Cohen, Wilk, and Stoeltje, eds., *Beauty Queens*, p. 171.

6. Lary May, ed., *Recasting America: Culture and Politics in the Age of Cold War* (Chicago: University of Chicago Press, 1989); Peter J. Kuznick and James Gilbert, eds., *Rethinking Cold War Culture* (Washington, D.C.: Smithsonian Institution Press, 2001); Gordon H. Chang, *Friends and Enemies: The United States, China, and the Soviet Union, 1948–1972* (Palo Alto: Stanford University Press, 1989; reprint, 1991).

7. Mary Dudziak, *Cold War Civil Rights: Race and the Image of American Democracy* (Princeton: Princeton University Press, 2000); Thomas Borstelmann, *The Cold War and the Color Line: Race Relations and American Foreign Policy since 1945* (Cambridge: Harvard University Press, 2001); Martha Biondi, *To Stand and Fight: The Struggle for Civil Rights in Postwar New York City* (Cambridge: Harvard University Press, 2003).

8. Rajeswari Sunder Rajan ed., *Signposts: Gender Issues in Post-Independence India* (New Brunswick: Rutgers University Press, 2001), p. 7.

9. Lena Moskalenko, "Beauty, Women, and Competition: 'Moscow Beauty 1989,'" in Cohen, Wilk, and Stoeltje, eds., *Beauty Queens*, pp. 64–65.

10. Ibid.

11. Elaine Tyler May, *Homeward Bound: American Families in the Cold War Era* (New York: Basic Books, 1988).

12. Barbara Ehrenreich, *The Hearts of Men: American Dreams and the Flight from Commitment* (New York: Anchor Books, 1983); Erica Rand, *Barbie's Queer Accessories* (Durham: Duke University Press, 1995).

13. May, *Homeward Bound.*

14. Ibid., p. 19.

15. For more on the "red scare," see Richard Fried, *Nightmare in Red: The McCarthy Era in Perspective* (New York and London: Oxford University Press, 1990); Ellen Schrecker, *Many Are the Crimes: McCarthyism in America* (Princeton: Princeton University Press, 1998).

16. For more on the McCarran Walter Act, also known as the Immigration and Nationality Act of 1952, see Robert A. Divine, *American Immigration Policy, 1924–1952* (New York: Da Capo Press, 1972), pp. 167, 179; Mae Ngai, *Impossible Subjects: Illegal Aliens and the Making of Modern America* (Princeton: Princeton University Press, 2004).

17. Sarah Banet-Weiser, *The Most Beautiful Girl in the World: Beauty Pageants and National Identity* (Berkeley and Los Angeles: University of California Press, 1999), p. 9.

18. Ibid., p. 127.

19. Barnes, "Face of the Nation," pp. 355–371.

20. *Los Angeles Times,* Obituaries, March 2, 2002.

21. Shirley Jennifer Lim, "Girls Just Wanna Have Fun: The Politics of Asian American Women's Public Culture, 1930–1960" (Ph.D. diss., UCLA, 1998).

22. Benedict Anderson, *Imagined Communities: Reflections on the Origins and Spread of Nationalism* (New York: Verso, 1983).

23. Barbara M. Posadas, *The Filipino Americans* (Westport, CT: Greenwood Press, 1999); Rick Bonus, *Locating Filipino Americans: Ethnicity and the Cultural Politics of Space* (Philadelphia: Temple University Press, 2000).

24. K. Sue Jewell, *From Mammy to Miss America and Beyond: Cultural Images and the Shaping of U.S. Social Policy* (New York: Routledge, 1993).

25. Cohen, Wilk, and Stoeltje, eds., *Beauty Queens,* p. 5.

26. Sue Fawn Chung, "Fighting for Their American Rights: A History of the Chinese American Citizens Alliance," in *Claiming America: Constructing Chinese American Identities during the Exclusion Era* (Philadelphia: Temple University Press, 1998), p. 106.

27. Y. C. Hong, "55 Years of CACA's History," *Chinese Press,* June 30, 1950, pp. 7–8. Hong was the Chinese American Citizens Alliance Grand Lodge's president.

28. Chung, "Fighting for Their American Rights," p. 104.

29. Ibid., p. 111.

30. *Chinese Press,* May 26, 1950, p. 1.

31. *Philippines Star Press,* May 7, 1948, front page.

32. Bonus, *Locating Filipino Americans*; Vicente Rafael, *Discrepant Histories: Translocal Essays on Filipino Cultures* (Philadelphia: Temple University Press, 1995).

33. Arleen G. de Vera, "Rizal Day Queen Contests, Filipino Nationalism, and Femininity," in Jennifer Lee and Min Zhou, eds., *Asian American Youth: Culture, Identity, and Ethnicity* (New York: Routledge, 2004), and "Constituting Community: A Study of Nationalism, Colonialism, Gender, and Identity among Filipinos in California, 1919–1946" (Ph.D. diss., Department of History, UCLA, 2002).

34. Posadas, *Filipino Americans,* p. 64.

35. Lon Kurashige, *Japanese American Celebration and Conflict: A History of Ethnic Identity and Festival, 1934–1990* (Berkeley and Los Angeles: University of California Press, 2002). For more on Japanese American communities, see Valerie

Matsumoto, "Japanese American Girls' Clubs in Los Angeles during the 1920s and 1930s," in Shirley Hune and Gail M. Nomura, eds., *Asian/Pacific Islander American Women: A Historical Anthology* (New York: New York University Press, 2003), pp. 172–187; David Yoo, *Growing Up Nisei: Race, Generation, and Culture among Japanese Americans of California, 1924–1949* (Urbana and Chicago: University of Illinois Press, 2000).

36. Kurashige, *Japanese American Celebration and Conflict*, p. 30.

37. For more on African American women and respectability, see Victoria W. Wolcott, *Remaking Respectability: African American Women in Interwar Detroit* (Chapel Hill: University of North Carolina Press, 2001).

38. *Philippines Star Press*, July 28, 1945, front page, p. 3 (not numbered, torn corner, on microfilm roll as if p. 3).

39. Robert Lavenda, "'It's Not a Beauty Pageant': Hybrid Ideology in Minnesota Community Queen Pageants," in Cohen, Wilk, and Stoeltje, eds., *Beauty Queens*, p. 33.

40. *Chinese Press*, April 28, 1950, front page.

41. May, *Homeward Bound*, pp. 110–111.

42. *Chinese Press*, May 12, 1950, front page.

43. Ibid.

44. George Lipsitz, *The Possessive Investment in Whiteness: How White People Benefit from Identity Politics* (Philadelphia: Temple University Press, 1998); Karen Brodkin Sacks, *How Jews Became White Folks, and What That Says about Race in America* (New Brunswick: Rutgers University Press, 1998); and Matthew Jacobson, *Whiteness of a Different Color: European Immigrants and the Alchemy of Race* (Cambridge: Harvard University Press, 1998).

45. *Rafu Shimpo*, August 4, 1952, p. 1.

46. Lim, "Girls Just Wanna Have Fun," chaps. 1 and 3.

47. *Rafu Shimpo*, August 11, 1952, p. 1.

48. Ibid.

49. *Scene*, September 1951, p. 40.

50. *Scene*, May 1950, p. 60.

51. Perhaps the flexible or part-time hours of beauty-product distribution would appeal to married women. For the four Japanese American beauty counselors, the race- and gender-segregated labor market ensured that beauty culture would also appeal to them. Given the demand for aestheticians, the typically low equipment start-up costs, and low barriers to entry, working in the beauty trade provided opportunities for economic advancement.

52. Kathy Peiss, *Hope in a Jar: The Making of America's Beauty Culture* (New York: Metropolitan, 1998) pp. 91–92.

53. "NFJ–Lecture by Anna May Wong. Chinese Beauty Customs," G23, Columbia University Project on Contemporary Cultures, Research Materials–China,

Documents VI, Margaret Mead Collection, Library of Congress; cited in Karen Leong, "China Mystique" (Ph.D. diss., UC–Berkeley, 1999), p. 405.

54. *Chinese Press*, December 21, 1948, p. 3.

55. Vicente Rafael, "Nationalism, Imagery, and the Filipino Intelligentsia," in *Discrepant Histories*, pp. 133–158. For an insightful discussion of the significance of fashion in an earlier era, see Nan Enstad, *Ladies of Labor, Girls of Adventure: Working Women, Popular Culture, and Labor Politics at the Turn of the Twentieth Century* (New York: Columbia University Press, 1999).

56. *Philippines Star Press*, April 9, 1948, p. 5.

57. *Chinese Press*, September 29, 1950, front page.

58. *Rafu Shimpo*, August 4, 1952, p. 1.

59. Anthropologist Robert Lavenda has observed that Czech American women who entered a Minnesota community queen contest tended to appeal to members of the small-business community; see his "It's Not a Beauty Pageant," p. 33.

60. Since tickets were frequently a measure of community clout or family wealth, judging by people outside the community instead of according to ticket sales could lead to discrepancies with community values. *Rafu Shimpo*, July 28, 1952, p. 1.

61. The editors obligingly printed clip-out entry forms.

62. *Rafu Shimpo*, August 11, 1952, p. 1.

63. *Rafu Shimpo*, August 20, 1952, p. 5.

64. *Chinese Press*, July 16, 1948, p. 1.

65. Ibid.

66. Although patriotism is one manifestation of cultural citizenship, not all forms of cultural citizenship are overtly patriotic. By patriotism, I am referring to allegiance to hegemonic notions of nationalism, whereas cultural citizenship can have counterhegemonic meanings and at times seeks to shift what is dominant.

67. Lim, "Girls Just Wanna Have Fun," chap. 5.

68. *Scene* denied Schweer's request, stating that they did not send photographs to readers. *Scene*, June 1953, p. 3.

69. Joanne Meyerowitz, "Beyond the Feminine Mystique: A Reassessment of Postwar Mass Culture, 1946–1958," *Journal of American History* 79.4 (March 1993), pp. 1455–1482.

70. Margaret Beetham, *A Magazine of Her Own? Domesticity and Desire in the Woman's Magazine, 1800–1914* (London: Routledge, 1996), p. 2.

71. *Scene*, June 1952, p. 8.

72. *Scene*, July 1950, pp. 18–20.

73. I am indebted to Valerie Matsumoto for this insight. On Hawaii's labor-immigration history, see Ronald Takaki, *Pau Hana: Plantation Life and Labor in Hawaii, 1835–1920* (Honolulu: University of Hawaii Press, 1983); Gary Okihiro, *Cane Fires: The Anti-Japanese Movement in Hawaii, 1865–1945* (Philadelphia: Temple University Press, 1991).

74. *Scene,* July 1950, pp. 18–20.

75. *Chinese Press,* July 20, 1951, p. 3.

76. Ibid.

77. *Chinese Press,* August 3, 1951, p. 3.

78. Lim, "Girls Just Wanna Have Fun," chap. 5.

79. The judges were supposed to derive 80 percent of the points from a contestant's face and figure.

80. *Chinese Press,* July 7, 1950, p. 7.

81. Ibid.

82. Ibid.

83. *Rafu Shimpo,* August 4, 1952, p. 1.

84. I thank Dawn Mabalon for calling my attention to this incident. I eagerly anticipate her forthcoming dissertation (Department of History, Stanford University).

85. *Chinese Press,* August 10, 1951, p. 4.

86. *Chinese Press,* September 28, 1951, p. 2.

87. Bonus, *Locating Filipino Americans,* p. 116.

88. Banet-Weiser, *Most Beautiful Girl in the World,* p. 9.

89. *Chinese Press,* June 9, 1950, p. 1.

90. Vicki Ruiz has found that for Chicana women, popular culture offered a legitimate alternative to parental expectations and church authority. See her *From Out of the Shadows: Mexican Women in Twentieth-Century America* (New York: Oxford University Press, 1998), p. 67.

91. Banet-Weiser, *The Most Beautiful Girl in the World*; Lavenda, "'It's Not a Beauty Pageant,'" pp. 31–46; Dorinne Kondo, *About Face: Performing Race in Fashion and Theater* (New York: Routledge, 1997), p. 13.

92. Emily Lawsin, e-mail to the author, May 2000. Although Lawsin's family pressured her to participate in the Seattle queen pageant, she adamantly refused.

93. *Rafu Shimpo,* August 16, 1952, front page.

94. Homi Bhabha, "Of Mimicry and Man: The Ambivalence of Colonial Discourse," in *The Location of Culture* (New York and London: Routledge, 1994), pp. 85–92.

95. *Rafu Shimpo,* August 19, 1952, p. 1.

96. Ibid.

97. Lavenda, "'It's Not a Beauty Pageant,'" p. 37.

98. *Rafu Shimpo,* August 19, 1952, front page; Judy Yung, *Unbound Feet: A Social History of Chinese Women in San Francisco* (Berkeley: University of California Press, 1995), p. 97.

99. No matter how effective the mimicry, unavoidably the subaltern peoples are "not quite, not white" a fact that implicitly threatens the colonizers' hegemony. See Bhabha, "Of Mimicry and Man," pp. 85–92.

100. "Three Queens'-Eye View of U.S.," *Scene,* August 1951, pp. 10–13.

101. "Girls in Kimono," *Scene*, May 1951, pp. 18–19.

102. *Philippines Star Press*, July 3, 1948, front page.

103. Steffi San Buenaventura, "Filipino Folk Spirituality and Immigration: From Mutual Aid to Religion," *Amerasia* 22.1 (Spring 1996), p. 27.

104. Michael Salman, *The Embarrassment of Slavery: Controversies over Bondage and Nationalism in the American Colonial Philippines* (Berkeley and Los Angeles: University of California Press, 2001), pp. 133–134.

105. Lopez, "India Bonita Contest of 1921," pp. 291–328.

106. *Philippines Star Press*, May 7, 1948, p. 1.

107. *Philippines Star Press*, January 22, 1951, p. 1.

108. Posadas, *Filipino Americans*, pp. 56–58.

109. Ngai, *Impossible Subjects*, pp. 202–224.

110. *Chinese Press*, July 7, 1950, p. 2.

111. Bonus, *Locating Filipino Americans*, p. 116.

NOTES TO CHAPTER 5

1. *Kashu Mainichi*, July 25, 1959, front page.

2. Numerous scholars have focused on the films *Sayonara, Teahouse of the August Moon*, and *Flower Drum Song*, including Anne Cheng, "Beauty and Ideal Citizenship" in *Melancholy of Race* (New York: Oxford University Press, 2000); Gina Marchetti, "Tragic and Transcendent Love," in *Romance and the "Yellow Peril"* (Berkeley and Los Angeles: University of California Press, 1993); Robert Lee, "The Cold War Origins of the Model Minority Myth," in *Orientals: Asian Americans in Popular Culture* (Philadelphia: Temple University Press, 1999); Traise Yamamoto, "The Feminization of Japan," in *Masking Selves, Making Subjects: Japanese American Women, Identity, and the Body* (Berkeley and Los Angeles: University of California Press, 1999); Caroline Chung Simpson, "'Out of an Obscure Place': Japanese War Brides and Cultural Pluralism of the 1950s," *Differences* 10.3 (1998); and Eugene Wong, *On Visual Media Racism: Asians in the American Motion Pictures* (New York: Arno, 1978).

3. For more on Tokyo Rose, see Caroline Chung Simpson, *An Absent Presence: Japanese Americans in Postwar American Culture, 1945–1960* (Durham: Duke University Press, 2001); Masayo Duus, *Tokyo Rose, Orphan of the Pacific* (New York: Kodansha International, 1979).

4. Edward Said, *Orientalism* (New York: Pantheon, 1978); Jack Tchen, *New York before Chinatown: Orientalism and the Shaping of American Culture, 1776–1882*. (Baltimore: Johns Hopkins University Press, 1999); Lee, *Orientals*; Mari Yoshihara, *Embracing the East: White Women and American Orientalism* (New York and Oxford: Oxford University Press, 2002).

5. Katherine Kinney, "Foreign Affairs: Women, War, and the Pacific," in John Carlos Rowe, ed., *Post-Nationalist American Studies* (Berkeley and Los Angeles:

University of California Press, 2000); Melani McAlister, *Epic Encounters: Culture, Media, and U.S. Interests in the Middle East, 1945–2000* (Berkeley and Los Angeles: University of California Press, 2001).

6. Christina Klein, *Cold War Orientalism: Asia in the Middlebrow Imagination, 1945–1961* (Berkeley and Los Angeles: University of California Press, 2003), p. 15; Yamamoto, "Feminization of Japan."

7. Klein, *Cold War Orientalism,* p. 9–61.

8. *Scene,* September 1953, p. 12.

9. As discussed in chapter 3, *Scene* deliberately used its pages to promote better understanding between the United States and Japan and Japanese Americans. See Togo Tanaka, Oral History Interview by James Gatewood, in "Regenerations Oral History Project: Rebuilding Japanese America," December 13, 1997, Japanese American National Museum, Los Angeles.

10. On diasporic cultural citizenship, see Lok Siu, "Diasporic Cultural Citizenship: Chineseness and Belonging in Panama and Central America," *Social Text* 69.19 (Winter 2001), pp. 7–28; Aiwa Ong and Donald Nonini, eds., *Ungrounded Empires: The Cultural Politics of Modern Transnationalism* (New York: Routledge, 1997).

11. *Scene,* September 1952, p. 23 caption.

12. Ito was paired with Miss Colorado, whose husband had been stationed in Japan.

13. *Scene,* September 1953, p. 22.

14. Ibid.

15. Colleen Ballerino Cohen, Richard Wilk, and Beverly Stoeltje, eds., *Beauty Queens: On the Global Stage* (New York: Routledge, 1996), p. 8.

16. *Scene,* September 1953, p. 12.

17. Ibid.

18. Cynthia Enloe, *Bananas, Beaches, and Bases: Making Feminist Sense of International Politics* (Berkeley and Los Angeles: University of California Press, 1990).

19. *Los Angeles Times,* July 18, 1953, front page.

20. *Los Angeles Times,* July 19, 1953, section 1, p. 3; *Los Angeles Times,* July 18, 1958, front page.

21. *Los Angeles Times,* July 19, 1953, section 1, p. 3.

22. Robert Rydell, *All the World's a Fair: Visions of Empire at American International Expositions, 1876–1916* (Chicago: University of Chicago Press, 1984); Adira L. Imada, "Hawaiians on Tour: Hula Circuits through the American Empire," *American Quarterly* 56.1 (2004), pp. 111–149.

23. Yamamoto, "Feminization of Japan," p. 35.

24. James Michener, *Tales of the South Pacific* (Binghamton, N.Y.: Vail-Ballou Press, 1946), p. 158.

25. Anna May Wong clipping File, UCLA Academy of Motion Pictures, Arts and Sciences (AMPAS), Los Angeles.

26. Hearst Newsreel footage, 1957 Oscars, AMPAS. Unfortunately, this footage does not include Miyoshi Umeki's acceptance speech.

27. Sucheng Chan, *Asian Americans: An Interpretive History* (Boston: Twayne, 1991), p. 140.

28. James Michener, *Sayonara* (New York: Random House, 1953).

29. Yamamoto, "Feminization of Japan," p. 52.

30. Caroline Chung Simpson, "American Orientalisms: The Cultural and Gender Politics of America's Postwar Relationship with Japan" (Ph.D. diss., University of Texas, Austin, 1994), p. 307.

31. Simpson, *Absent Presence*.

32. Simpson, "Out of an Obscure Place," p. 49.

33. James Bacon, Hollywood AP wire, printed in the *Rafu Shimpo*, March 27, 1958, front page.

34. *Rafu Shimpo*, March 27, 1958, front page.

35. Vernan Scott, interview with Miyoshi Umeki, *Hollywood Citizen News*, August 6, 1960, Miyoshi Umeki biographical file, AMPAS, Margaret Herrick Library.

36. Scholarship by Miriam Silverberg and others contradicts the notion that all women in Japan were traditional and oppressed by gender norms before World War II. See Miriam Silverberg, "The Modern Girl as Militant," in Gail Bernstein, ed., *Recreating Japanese Women, 1600–1945* (Berkeley and Los Angeles: University of California Press, 1991), pp. 239–266.

37. Scott interview, *Hollywood Citizen News*, August 6, 1960.

38. Darrell Y. Hamamoto, *Monitored Peril: Asian Americans and the Politics of TV Representation* (Minneapolis: University of Minnesota Press, 1994), p. 11.

39. James Bacon, Hollywood AP wire, printed in the *Rafu Shimpo*, March 27, 1958, front page. Presumably the *Rafu Shimpo* couldn't afford to have their own correspondent cover the Academy Awards. However, they were able to use the AP story in ways which emphasized the victories of Umeki and Buttons.

40. For a revised look at the meaning of Nancy Kwan's iconography, see Peter X. Feng, "Recuperating Suzie Wong: A Fan's Nancy Kwan-dry," in Darrell Y. Hamamoto and Sandra Liu, eds., *Countervisions: Asian American Film Criticism* (Philadelphia: Temple University Press, 2000).

41. It would be interesting to find out why Nuyen's name changed from Nguyen. *Life*, October 6, 1958, p. 98.

42. Ibid.

43. Ibid.

44. *Life*, October 6, 1958, cover.

45. Hazel Clark, "The Cheung Sam: Issues of Fashion and Cultural Identity," in Valerie Steele and John S. Major, eds., *China Chic: East Meets West* (New Haven: Yale University Press, 1999), pp. 155–166.

46. *Life*, October 6, 1958, p. 95, caption.

47. Frank Aston, "'World of Suzie Wong' Bows at the Broadhurst," *New York World-Telegram and Sun,* October 15, 1958.

48. Ibid.

49. Brooks Atkinson, "Theater: 'Suzie Wong,'" *New York Times,* October 15, 1958; Robert Coleman, "'Suzie Wong' Do All Right," *Daily Mirror,* Theater column, October 15, 1958, France Nuyen biographical file, AMPAS.

50. John McClain, "A Tender Drama That Can Survive," *New York Journal American,* October 15, 1958.

51. Walter Kerr, "First Night Report; 'The World of Suzie Wong,'" *New York Herald Tribune,* October 15, 1958, France Nuyen biographical file, AMPAS.

52. See John Dower, *War without Mercy: Race and Power in the Pacific War* (New York: Pantheon, 1986); Clayton R. Koppes and Gregory D. Black, *Hollywood Goes to War* (Berkeley and Los Angeles: University of California Press, 1990).

53. *New York Post,* October 26, 1958, p. M2.

54. *Sunday Express* (London), July 23, France Nuyen biographical file, AMPAS.

55. "Brando's Girl Friend Swats Photographer," UPI, September 28, 1959, France Nuyen biographical file, AMPAS.

56. Charles L. Ponce de Leon, *Self-Exposure: Human-Interest Journalism and the Emergence of Celebrity in America, 1890–1940* (Chapel Hill: University of North Carolina Press, 2002).

57. Peter Manso, *Brando: The Biography* (New York: Hyperion, 1994), p. 521.

58. *Time,* December 22, 1958.

59. Anne Cheng, *Melancholy of Race* (New York and Oxford: Oxford University Press, 2001), pp. 31–63.

60. *Los Angeles Times,* August 14, 1959, section 1, p. 2.

61. *Kashu Mainichi,* August 15, 1959, front page.

62. *Life,* October 6, 1958, p. 98.

63. *New York Post,* October 26, 1958, p. M2.

64. *Sunday Express* (London), July 23, France Nuyen biographical file, AMPAS.

65. Natasha Barnes, "Face of the Nation: Race, Nationalisms and Identity in Jamaican Beauty Pageants," in Jennifer Scanlon, ed., *The Gender and Consumer Culture Reader* (New York: New York University Press, 2000), p. 370 n. 12.

66. *New York Post,* October 26, 1958, p. M2.

67. *Rafu Shimpo,* advertisement, January 16, 1958, front page.

68. *Scene,* May 1950, p. 11.

69. Evelyn Nakano Glenn, *Issei, Nisei, Warbride: Three Generations of Japanese American Women in Domestic Service* (Philadelphia: Temple University Press, 1986), pp. 60–61; Ji-Yeon Yuh, *Beyond the Shadow of Camptown: Korean Military Brides in America* (New York: New York University Press, 2002).

70. *Scene,* April 1952, pp. 17–21.

71. Lon Kurashige, *Japanese American Celebration and Conflict: A History of*

Ethnic Identity and Festival, 1934–1990 (Berkeley and Los Angeles: University of California Press, 2002), p. 146.

72. *Kashu Mainichi,* July 25, 1959, front page.

73. *Scene,* 1950 (probably August/September), p. 11.

74. *Scene,* November 1953, p. 31.

75. Thank you to Lisa Yuen and Linda Yuen for providing this information.

76. Judy Wu, "'Loveliest Daughter of our Ancient Cathay!' Representations of Ethnic and Gender Identity in the Miss Chinatown U.S.A. Beauty Pageant," *Journal of Social History* 31.1 (Fall 1997), pp. 5–31.

77. See Vicki Ruiz, *From Out of the Shadows: Mexican Women in Twentieth Century America* (New York and London: Oxford University Press, 1998), p. xvi, for a discussion of cultural coalescence for Mexican American women during the twentieth century.

78. Chi Alpha Delta, Active Minutes, March 19, 1950, Chi Alpha Delta Archives, Department of Special Collections–University Archives, UCLA.

79. Chi Alpha Delta, Active Minutes, March 28, 1953, Chi Alpha Delta Archives; *Scene,* September 1953. See chapter 3 for a discussion of Chiemi Eri and her song "Gomen-nasai" as portrayed in *Scene* magazine.

80. Carey McWilliams, "Fraternity Comes to the Frat House," *Negro Digest,* January 1951, p. 92; originally printed in *The Nation.*

81. Chi Alpha Delta, Minutes of the Active Meetings, November 2, 1958, Chi Alpha Delta Archives.

82. Ibid. The only archived historical source information on Sigma Omicron Pi is the University of California–Berkeley yearbooks. Hence there is very little information on the actions of the sorority. Judy Yung's *Unbound Feet* (Berkeley and Los Angeles: University of California Press, 1995) contains only one sentence on Sigma Omicron Pi, stating they were founded at San Francisco State University (p. 128). Their yearbook page at UC–Berkeley states that they had only one chapter and that it had been founded at UC–Berkeley.

83. Chi Alpha Delta, Active Minutes, November 22, 1961.

84. Though it would be helpful to know how African American sororities handled issues of integration, the only book-length scholarly study on African American Greek organizations, Paula Giddings's *In Search of Sisterhood* (New York: William Morrow, 1988) does not discuss Delta Sigma Theta's handling of integration debates. Since Giddings uses national records, not local records, perhaps the local chapters' struggles with integration were not recorded in the national organization's papers.

85. In the late 1980s, Nuyen acted in the television series *St. Elsewhere.* Most recently she played Ying Ying St. Clare in Amy Tan's novel-turned-movie *Joy Luck Club,* directed by Wayne Wang.

86. See L. S. Kim, "Maid in Color: The Figure of the Racialized Domestic in

American Television" (Ph.D. diss., Department of Film and Television, UCLA, 1997).

87. This interview is currently unavailable for viewing. While UCLA's Film and Television Archive owns a copy of Mike Wallace's interview of Miyoshi Umeki, it was recorded on a format for which there are no screening facilities.

88. Susan Jeffords, *The Remasculinization of America: Gender and the Vietnam War* (Bloomington: Indiana University Press, 1989), p. xi.

89. For example, the description of the film *The Virgin Soldier* reads as follows: "Pvt. Brigg is one of the soldiers who succumbs to the local prostitute, Juicy Lucy" (Maryann Oshana, *Women of Color: A Filmography of Minority and Third World Women* [New York: Garland, 1984], p. 265).

90. For example, seventy thousand American soldiers are estimated to have been entertained in Bangkok between 1968 and 1969. See Penny Van Esterik, "The Politics of Beauty in Thailand," in Cohen, Wilk, and Stoeltje, eds., *Beauty Queens*, and her *Materializing Thailand* (New York: Berg, 2000), p. 175; Katharine H. S. Moon, *Sex Among Allies* (New York: Columbia University Press, 1997); Yuh, *Beyond the Shadow of Camptown*. Although in 1957 there were twenty thousand prostitutes in Thailand, seven years later, after the United States had established seven bases in that country, the number reached four hundred thousand. During the Vietnam War, South Vietnam housed around four hundred thousand prostitutes. In South Korea and the Philippines, other sites of American military bases, prostitution correspondingly increased as the wars and U.S. military occupation economically devastated the regions and local women had to turn to one of the only viable means of economic survival. Thus movies about Asian women changed from depictions of smiling, loving Japanese war brides to images of barely human prostitutes.

91. William Wei, *The Asian American Movement* (Philadelphia: Temple University Press, 1993); Helen Zia, *Asian American Dreams: The Emergence of an American People* (New York: Farrar, Straus and Giroux, 2000); Timothy Fong, *The Contemporary Asian American Experience: Beyond the Model Minority* (Upper Saddle River, N.J.: Prentice Hall, 1998); Eric K. Yamamoto, *Interracial Justice: Conflict and Reconciliation in Post–Civil Rights America* (New York: New York University Press, 1999).

92. Women of Asian descent who have won the Miss Universe title are Akiko Kojima, Japan, 1959; Apasra Hongsakula, Thailand, 1965; Gloria Diaz, Philippines, 1969; Margarita Moran, Philippines, 1973; Porntip Nakhirunkanok, Thailand, 1988; Sushmita Sen, India, 1994; Lara Dutta, India, 2000.

Index

Patriotism, 91–93; and cultural citizen-
ship, 94
Pavement Butterfly (film), 56
Performance: as analytical tool, 8; per-
forming the Cold War civil rights
body, 130–37
Philippine national identity, 129
Philippines: decolonization, 92; indepen-
dence, 129
"Pocketbook politics," 91
"Portrait of Spring" contest, 142–43
Prejudice, 89
"Pretty party sandwiches," 108
Public culture, 13

Queen: contest manners of, 133–34; first
Chinese American, 4; pageants,
bathing suits in, 129
"Queen of the Seventh Annual Spring Informal," 131–33

Race: and performance, 8; and the visual,
9; hatreds, U.S. toward Japan, 100
Race relations anxieties, 167
Racial anxiety cinema, 51
Racial discrimination, 14; film and, 52;
and housing, 20; and France Nuyen,
172; and segregation, 14; sorority, 19;
and the teaching profession, 19; UCLA
campus publication, 17–18; women's
clubs and, 28; and sororities, 27
Racial integration, 167; integration anxiety, 155
Racial minority: clubs, 31–32; sororities,
23
Racial non-discrimination in fraternity
and sorority membership, 184
Racial segregation, 125; Nisei, 12
Racial stereotypes, 17–18
Racialized standards of beauty, 110, 114,
124, 141–42, 145, 158–59, 175–78; and
diet, 176; and plastic surgery, 176

Rafu Shimpo (community newspaper),
35, 44, 106, 110, 140
Real estate costs, Los Angeles, 20
Religious hybridity, 41
Riefenstahl, Leni, 48
Rizal, Jose, 150

"Sakura" (song), 8, 183
"Salinas Tid-Bits" (newspaper column),
9, 136–37
San Francisco: American Day Parade, 93;
Japanese American clubs, 106
Sayonara, 166–67
Scene, 89, 98, 183; advertisements in, 103–
4; beauty ads, 135; as arbiter of taste
and style, 109; Kathleen Asano cover,
141; for the Asian American consumer,
102–5; Asian American focus of, 117;
on beauty pageant as democracy, 159;
and Chi Alpha Delta, 106; Chinese
Americans and, 117–18; and cross-cul-
tural performers, 118; and dance performance, 118; editors, 99; "Feminine
Scene" column, 108; hairstyle controversy, 111–14; interethnic relations, 116;
international circulation, 101; Japanese
diaspora, 101; Korean Americans, 116;
letter to the editor (1953), 106; mainstream reactions to, 100; Miss Japan,
157; Miss Japan kimono, 180; monthly
format, 102; overview, 99; patriotic
act, 101; "pretty party sandwiches," 108;
readership, 106, 111–14; subscription
cost, 101; subtitle change, 102; war
brides, 179; "War Bride Becomes an
American Housewife," 179
Scientific racism, 48
Second generation: demographics, 26;
Korean Americans, 117
"Second wave" of feminism, 123
Shanghai Express, 60
"Short-Cut to Glamor," 89, 111–14

About the Author

Shirley Jennifer Lim is Assistant Professor of History at the State University of New York at Stony Brook.